THIS BOOK BELONGS
TO:

SCHIZOPHRENIA AND MANIC-DEPRESSIVE DISORDER

OTHER BOOKS BY E. FULLER TORREY

Ethical Issues in Medicine (ed.)
The Death of Psychiatry
Why Did You Do That?
Schizophrenia and Civilization
Witchdoctors and Psychiatrists
The Roots of Treason: Ezra Pound and the Secret of St. Elizabeths
Care of the Seriously Mentally Ill: A Rating of State Programs
Surviving Schizophrenia: A Family Manual
Nowhere to Go: The Tragic Odyssey of the Homeless Mentally Ill
Frontier Justice: The Rise and Fall of the Loomis Gang
*Freudian Fraud: The Malignant Effect of Freud's Theory on
American Thought and Culture*

OTHER BOOKS BY IRVING I. GOTTESMAN

*Man, Mind, and Heredity: The Selected Papers of Eliot Slater on Psychiatry and
Genetics* (with J. Shields)
Schizophrenia and Genetics: A Twin Study Vantage Point (with J. Shields)
Schizophrenia: The Epigenetic Puzzle (with J. Shields and the assistance of
D. R. Hanson)
Vital Statistics, Demography, and Schizophrenia (ed.)
Schizophrenia Genesis: The Origins of Madness
*Schizophrenia and Genetic Risks: A Guide to Genetic Counseling for Patients,
Their Families, and Mental Health Workers* (with S. O. Moldin)
Psychiatric Genetics (with P. McGuffin, M. Owen, M. O'Donovan,
and A. Thapar)

Schizophrenia and Manic-Depressive Disorder

*The Biological Roots of Mental Illness as
Revealed by the Landmark Study of Identical Twins*

E. FULLER TORREY, M.D.

IN COLLABORATION WITH
ANN E. BOWLER, M.S.,
EDWARD H. TAYLOR, PH.D.,
AND
IRVING I. GOTTESMAN, PH.D.

BasicBooks
A Division of HarperCollins*Publishers*

For permission to reproduce Figure 2.2, the authors thank Dr. John G. Rogers, Royal Children's Hospital, Parkville, Australia; the *American Journal of Medical Genetics*; and Wiley-Liss, a division of John Wiley and Sons, Inc. Figure copyright © 1982.

Designed by Ellen Levine

Library of Congress Cataloging-in-Publication Data

Schizophrenia and manic-depressive disorder: the biological roots of
    mental illness as revealed by the landmark study of identical twins / E.
    Fuller Torrey in collaboration with Ann E. Bowler, Edward H. Taylor,
    and Irving I. Gottesman.
        p.   cm
    Includes bibliographical references and index.
    ISBN 0-465-01746-0
    1. Schizophrenia.   2. Schizophrenia—Genetic aspects.   3. Manic-
    depressive psychoses.   4. Manic-depressive psychoses—Genetic
    aspects.   5. Diseases in twins.   I. Torrey, E. Fuller (Edwin Fuller),
    1937–
RC514.S33457   1994
616.89'82—dc20   93-32458
                                                                                          CIP

---

94 95 96 97 ♦/HC 9 8 7 6 5 4 3

This book is dedicated to the twins and triplets
who took part in the study. They unselfishly participated in
extensive and sometimes uncomfortable testing so that
research on schizophrenia and bipolar disorder could move
forward. Without such individuals research is not possible,
and we are all indebted to them.

All authors' royalties from this book have been assigned to
the National Alliance for the Mentally Ill.

Contents

About the Authors

E. Fuller Torrey, M.D.: Dr. Torrey is a clinical and research psychiatrist in Washington, D.C., who specializes in schizophrenia and other serious mental illnesses. He has worked for the National Institute of Mental Health and St. Elizabeths Hospital in Washington, D.C., and has carried out field research on schizophrenia in Ireland and in Papua New Guinea. He has authored more than 200 professional publications, including 14 books. Among these are *Schizophrenia and Civilization, Surviving Schizophrenia: A Family Manual, The Roots of Treason, Nowhere to Go: The Tragic Odyssey of the Homeless Mentally Ill,* and most recently *Freudian Fraud: The Malignant Effect of Freud's Theory on American Thought and Culture.* Dr. Torrey directed the twin study.

Ann E. Bowler, M.S.: Ms. Bowler is a biostatistician presently employed as a clinical trial coordinator at the National Institute of Child Health and Development, the National Institutes of Health. She received her degree in biostatistics from Georgetown University in 1982 and has been a contributing author to more than 25 published papers. Ms. Bowler coordinated all the data collection and data analysis for the twin study.

Edward H. Taylor, Ph.D., A.C.S.W.: Dr. Taylor is currently on the faculty of the School of Social Work and the School of Medicine at the University of North Carolina at Chapel Hill. He has been recognized nationally for his writing and lecturing on the interaction between the biological, psychological, and social aspects of psychiatric illness. His interests center on child and family studies, with an emphasis on the biological development of serious mental illness in children. Dr. Taylor was responsible for designing, administering, and interpreting data on the bio-psycho-social assessment of the twins, from the mothers' pregnancy to onset of illness.

Irving I. Gottesman, Ph.D., F.R.C. Psych. (Hon.): Dr. Gottesman is Commonwealth Professor of Psychology at the University of Virginia. Widely known for his work on genetics and schizophrenia, he is an Honorary Fellow of the Royal College of Psychiatrists and winner of the 1988 Stanley R. Dean Award for schizophrenia research and the 1990 Dobzhansky Award for lifelong contributions to behavioral genetics. He is the author of *Schizophrenia: The Epigenetic Puzzle* and *Schizophrenia Genesis: The Origins of Madness,* among other books. Dr. Gottesman was the senior consultant for the planning of the present research, participated in all diagnoses, and coordinated the analyses of personality tests to assess the effects of schizophrenia on personality.

Contributing Researchers

The following individuals contributed directly to the planning, testing, and data analysis for the project. However, the interpretation of the data in the following chapters is the responsibility of the authors alone and does not necessarily reflect the views of the contributing researchers.

I. Lead Researchers

Karen F. Berman, M.D.: Dr. Berman is Chief of the Unit on Positron Emission Tomography, NIMH Neuroscience Center at St. Elizabeths Hospital. She has specialized in neuroimaging studies and has authored over 100 professional publications. In 1986 she received the A. E. Bennett Foundation Award for Neuropsychiatric Research from the Society of Biological Psychiatry and in 1992 was awarded a U.S. Public Health Service Commendation Medal. Dr. Berman planned and carried out the PET scan and cerebral blood flow studies on the twins.

Llewellyn B. Bigelow, M.D.: Dr. Bigelow is a senior scientist in the Clinical Brain Disorder Branch, NIMH Neuroscience Center at St. Elizabeths Hospital. He has 25 years experience as a researcher on serious mental illnesses and is the author of more than 80 professional papers. In 1985 he received a Meritorious Service Award from the U.S. Public Health Service. Dr. Bigelow shared responsibility for all clinical measures and diagnoses of the twins.

H. Stefan Bracha, M.D.: Dr. Bracha, a child and adolescent psychiatrist and neuropsychiatrist, is Associate Professor of Psychiatry and Neurology at the University of Arkansas for Medical Sciences, Little Rock. He is an expert on prenatal brain development and dermatoglyphics and has written more than 50 articles about neurobiological brain disorders. He received clinical and research training at the Bronx VA Hospital, NIMH, and the University of California, San Diego. In 1989 he was awarded the Young Scientist Award by the National Alliance for the Mentally Ill. Dr. Bracha was responsible for research planning and data analysis of finger ridge counts and other dermatoglyphic measures in the twin study.

Richard Coppola, D.Sc.: Dr. Coppola is Chief of the Neuro-Imaging Unit, NIMH Neuroscience Center at St. Elizabeths Hospital. He has specialized in imaging techniques and the processing of neurophysiological data for studying brain activity. He has authored over 100 professional publications and been awarded a Commendation Medal and Outstanding Service Medal by the U.S. Public Health Service. Dr. Coppola was responsible for the collection of MRI and EEG data on the twins.

Terry E. Goldberg, Ph.D.: Dr. Goldberg, Chief of the Neuropsychology Unit, NIMH Neuroscience Center at St. Elizabeths Hospital, is one of the leading researchers in neuropsychology, especially in individuals with serious mental illnesses. He has published more than 100 professional papers and abstracts, including reviews of this research area. Dr. Goldberg was responsible for planning, coordinating, and analyzing the 3-hour battery of neuropsychological tests administered to the twins.

Thomas F. McNeil, Ph.D.: Dr. McNeil is Professor and Chairman of the Department of Psychiatry at the University of Lund, Sweden, where he has been associated since 1970. He has published many professional papers and book chapters on the relationship of obstetrical complications to serious mental illnesses and is a world authority on this subject. Prior to going to the University of Lund, Dr. McNeil was associated with the Lafayette Clinic in Detroit. Dr. McNeil was responsible for the data analysis on obstetrical complications in this study.

Patricia O. Quinn, M.D.: Dr. Quinn, Clinical Assistant Professor of Pediatrics and Child Psychiatry at Georgetown University School of Medicine, is in the private practice of developmental pediatrics. She has conducted research and published professional papers on minor physical anomalies for 20 years. She is also coauthor of *Putting on the Brakes: A Young People's Guide to*

Understanding Attention Hyperactivity Disorder, published in 1991. Dr. Quinn planned and carried out all examinations for minor physical anomalies.

Robert R. Rawlings, M.S.: Mr. Rawlings is a mathematical statistician with the Laboratory of Clinical Studies, National Institute of Alcohol Abuse and Alcoholism. He was trained in astrophysics and mathematics and is used as a consultant expert on statistical methodology and data analysis. He has been a contributor to more than 60 professional publications. Mr. Rawlings was the principal consultant for research design and statistical methodology for the twin study.

Kenneth C. Rickler, M.D.: Dr. Rickler, who is a neurologist with the Forensic Division at St. Elizabeths Hospital and a senior consultant to the NIMH Neuroscience Center, is also Clinical Associate Professor of Neurology and Clinical Assistant Professor of Psychiatry at the George Washington University School of Medicine. He has published many articles on neurological dysfunction in individuals with psychiatric illnesses and is an acknowledged authority in this field. Dr. Rickler planned the neurological examination and personally evaluated most of the twins in the study.

Daniel R. Weinberger, M.D.: Dr. Weinberger is Chief of the Clinical Brain Disorders Branch, NIMH Neuroscience Center at St. Elizabeths Hospital. Trained in both psychiatry and neurology, he is a leading researcher on neurobiological studies of serious mental illnesses and has been a major contributor to the recent explosion of knowledge in this area. He has authored more than 200 professional papers and coedited *The Neurology of Schizophrenia.* He was the recipient of the Judith B. Silver Award from the National Alliance for the Mentally Ill in 1985, the Foundations Fund Prize for Research from the American Psychiatric Association in 1991, and a Distinguished Service Medal from the U.S. Public Health Service in 1992. Dr. Weinberger planned and coordinated the MRI and cerebral metabolism studies of the twins.

Robert H. Yolken, M.D.: Dr. Yolken, Professor of Pediatrics and Director of the Division of Pediatric Infectious Diseases, Johns Hopkins University School of Medicine, is the author of close to 200 professional publications on viruses and viral diseases. In 1986 he received the Abbott Award from the American Society of Microbiology and in 1989 the E. Mead Johnson Award for Research in Pediatrics. Dr. Yolken coordinated the viral and immunological studies done on serum, lymphocytes, and cerebrospinal fluid from the twins.

II. Participating Researchers

Anisa Abi-Dargham, M.D., currently with the Department of Psychiatry, Yale University Medical Center, assisted with cerebral blood flow studies.

Alycia J. Bartley, B.A., currently a medical student, assisted with MRI analysis.

Elizabeth Cantor-Graae, M.S., Department of Psychiatry, University of Lund, Sweden, assisted with analysis of obstetrical complications.

Nicholas W. Carosella, M.D., is with the Allegheny Neuropsychiatric Institute in Pittsburgh and assisted with MRI analysis.

Constance Carpenter, Ph.D., NIMH Neuroscience Center, assisted with neuropsychological testing.

Manuel F. Casanova, M.D., Professor of Psychiatry and Neurology at the Medical College of Georgia, assisted with MRI analysis.

George W. Christison, M.D., currently with the Department of Psychiatry, Loma Linda University, assisted with MRI analysis.

David G. Daniel, M.D., who is with Dominion Hospital in Falls Church, Virginia, assisted with cerebral blood flow studies.

David L. DiLalla, Ph.D., Department of Psychology, Southern Illinois University, assisted with analysis of the psychological data pertaining to personality traits of the twins.

Paula Domenici, B.A., who will be starting a graduate program in psychology, assisted with data analysis of the neuropsychological tests.

Darlene R. Doshen, NIMH Neuroscience Center, assisted with the collection of dermatoglyphics.

James M. Gold, Ph.D., NIMH Neuroscience Center, assisted with neuropsychological testing and analysis.

Julie G. Gorey, M.A., NIMH Neuroscience Center, assisted with the cerebral blood flow studies.

Monica Gourovitch, Ph.D., NIMH Neuroscience Center, assisted with neuropsychological testing and analysis.

Ronald L. Green, M.D., Department of Psychiatry, Dartmouth Medical Center, assisted with MRI analysis.

Edmund S. Higgins, M.D., currently with the Department of Psychiatry, Medical University of South Carolina, assisted with the analysis of obstetrical data.

Thomas M. Hyde, M.D., Ph.D., NIMH Neuroscience Center, assisted with neurological and EEG testing.

Douglas W. Jones, Ph.D., NIMH Neuroscience Center, assisted with the MRI, SPECT, and PET testing.

Henrietta Kulaga, Ph.D., NIMH Neuroscience Center, assisted with immunological and virological studies.

Jennifer J. Kulynych, M.A., a doctoral candidate in psychology at American University, assisted with MRI analysis.

Robert E. Litman, M.D., Section on Clinical Studies, NIMH Intramural Research Program, conducted the studies of eye tracking.

Laura Marsh, M.D., currently with the Department of Psychiatry and Behavioral Sciences, Stanford University School of Medicine, assisted with MRI analysis.

Henry McFarland, M.D., National Institute of Neurological Diseases and Stroke, coordinated the collection and testing of lymphocytes.

Michael S. Myslobodsky, M.D., D.Sc., Department of Psychology, Tel Aviv University, Israel, assisted with MRI analysis.

J. Thomas Noga, M.D., NIMH Neuroscience Center, assisted with MRI analysis.

Jill L. Ostrem, B.A., NIMH Neuroscience Center, assisted with cerebral blood flow studies.

Mihael H. Polymeropoulos, M.D., NIMH Neuroscience Center, coordinated genetic DNA studies of the twins using minisatellite probes.

J. Daniel Ragland, Ph.D., currently an assistant professor in the Department of Psychiatry, University of Pennsylvania, assisted with neuropsychological testing and analysis.

Mark H. Rapaport, M.D., Department of Psychiatry, University of California at San Diego School of Medicine, assisted with the immunologic studies.

Susan M. Resnick, Ph.D., Gerontology Research Center, National Institute on Aging, carried out some of the cerebral blood flow studies.

Angelo Sambunaris, M.D., NIMH Neuroscience Center, assisted with immunologic studies.

Roy H. Sexton, B.S., NIMH Neuroscience Center, assisted with cerebral blood flow studies.

Karin Sjostrom, M.D., Department of Psychiatry, University of Lund, Sweden, assisted with analysis of the obstetrical data.

Hans H. Stassen, Ph.D., Psychiatric University Hospital, Zurich, Switzerland, is analyzing the EEG data.

Richard L. Suddath, M.D., currently with Centennial Peaks Hospital, Louisville, Colorado, assisted with MRI analysis.

Alejandro Terrazas, B.S., President of Terrazas Analytical Systems in Washington, D.C., assisted with data analysis.

Katalin Vladar, M.D., a National Fogarty Fellow at NIMH, assisted with MRI analysis.

Ivan N. Waldman, M.S., NIMH Neuroscience Center, assisted with data analysis and computer programming.

Jeffrey R. Zigun, M.D., currently with the Department of Psychiatry, Medical College of Wisconsin, assisted with MRI analysis.

Mark Zito, M.S., NIMH Neuroscience Center, assisted with MRI analysis.

Preface

THIS BOOK reports the findings of a 6-year study of schizophrenia and bipolar disorder in 66 pairs of identical twins. The study was funded primarily by the National Institute of Mental Health and cost in total just over $1 million for the 6 years.

Although data from the study are still being analyzed, the vast majority of preliminary analyses have been completed. We therefore decided to publish the findings to date, since neuroscience research is moving so rapidly ahead in this decade of the brain. The largest data sets unanalyzed are the electroencephalographs (EEGs). Data analyses are also continuing on MRI, PET, and eye-tracking findings. In addition, genetic, immunological, and virological studies are continuing on the serum, lymphocytes, and cerebrospinal fluid collected from the twins. It is likely, in fact, that these analyses will continue for several more years because identical twins provide such a unique opportunity for understanding these diseases.

The twins are not identified by name in the book. Personal facts have been slightly altered in a few narratives to ensure anonymity.

It may be questioned whether the results of this study of identical twins with schizophrenia and bipolar disorder are applicable to non-twins with these diseases. Most researchers have assumed that they are, and recently this fact was confirmed. Twins with schizophrenia and bipolar disorder in the Maudsley twin register in London were compared with non-twins with the same diagnoses. No clinical differences were found between the twins and the non-twins, or between identical and fraternal twins (Marshall et al., 1993). It is reasonable to assume, therefore, that the results of the present study are applicable to non-twins with these diseases.

Acknowledgments

THE LOGISTICS involved in bringing 66 twin pairs to Washington, D.C., for evaluation and testing are fearsome. The research was accomplished with the exceptional cooperation and help from many people. Camille DiRienzo-Callahan coordinated the logistics for 5 years with unsurpassed enthusiasm, and Theresa Kordestani capably managed the office for the final year. Iva Chambers, Helen Ball, and Joseph Navarro selflessly served as driver-escorts for the twins for the entire length of the project. Richard H. Meacham, Patrick Bogan, Eleanor Bruns, and Wanda Cross of Friends Medical Science Research Center in Baltimore administered the funds for the project, minimizing administrative headaches for the researchers and providing exemplary support. David Shore at the NIMH Schizophrenia Research Branch provided crucial guidance and encouragement as we tried to decipher federal grant regulations, and Lou Ellen Rice of NIMH was most helpful in administering our NIMH contract.

The NIMH Neuroscience Center at St. Elizabeths Hospital generously provided us with space and support, and for this we are indebted to Rex Cowdry, Richard J. Wyatt, Daniel R. Weinberger, and Joel E. Kleinman. Richard Staub, Mollie Strotkamp, Theresa Tolbert, Delores Freeman, Joyce Williams, Leroy Sundberg, Kyle Christiansen, Laverne Corum, and Dera Tompkins were all graciously responsive to our needs. Diane Venable and Thomas Bryant assisted us with laboratory work, and Barry Sydnor provided computer assistance. Mary Herman kindly reviewed portions of the manuscript.

For assistance in testing the twins, we are grateful to Stanley Perl and the staff at MRI Associates, Clinton, Maryland; Jeanette Black and Susie Inscoe at the NIH MRI unit; Paul Andreasen at the NIH PET unit; and Regina Dowling and the staff of the NIH Aphoresis Center. Chris C. Plato, Terrence Reid, and Beverly B. Linington provided support for the dermatoglyphic research. Delores Mallory at the National Reference Laboratory of the American Red Cross coordinated the zygosity testing. Recruitment of the twins was facilitated by Laurie M. Flynn and the staff at the National Alliance for the Mentally Ill and by its state chapters. David Carroll at Patton State Hospital, Los Angeles, and the staff of the Vietnam Era Twin Registry were also helpful. The staff of the Executive Club in Arlington was most hospitable to the twins.

We also acknowledge the kind cooperation of the following businesses for giving employees leave time to participate in the study: Cognos Inc., Ottawa, Ontario; Commonsense Housing, Brewer, Maine; Chambers Hair Institute, Virginia Beach; Great Rivers Mental Health Services, St. Louis; G. H. Buss and Co., Wilton, Maine; Honeywell Inc., Irvine; Lincoln General Hospital, Ruston, Louisiana; Middle States Tennis Association, Wayne, Pennsylvania; Ohio Youth Services Network, Columbus; Ruston Vo-Tech School, Ruston; Telematics International, Ft. Lauderdale; Temple University School of Business and Management, Philadelphia; Tokheim Corporation, Ft. Wayne; 8th Transportation Brigade, Ft. Eustis, Virginia; the United States Probation Office, New York; Herb White, Richmond; R. C. Baker, Virginia Beach; and Ray T. Culpepper, Chesapeake, Virginia.

In addition to the grant and contract funds from NIMH, which supported most of the costs of this project, we received a timely grant from the Theodore and Vada Stanley Foundation. We are also grateful for gifts received from Mr. and Mrs. Brian Jacobs; the Alliance for the Mentally Ill (AMI) of Alabama and its Birmingham, Shoals, and Coffee County chapters; AMI of Massachusetts and its North Central chapter; Ft. Wayne AMI; memorial funds for Stephen C. McKinnon, Charles M. Holloway, George DuBose, and Neil B. Murphy; and from Gordon Jensen and Evelyn Smith.

The typing of the manuscript was done by Judy Miller with great skill and good humor. Jo Ann Miller, Melanie Kirschner, and Matthew Shine at Basic Books provided excellent technical support.

List of Tables

List of Illustrations and Figures

Monozygotic twins are "experiments" which nature has con-ducted for us, starting in each case with identical sets of genes and varying environmental factors.
  —Bronson Price, *Primary Biases in Twin Studies*, 1950

Psychiatry and neuropathology are not merely two closely related fields; they are but one field in which only one language is spoken and the same laws rule.
  —Wilhelm Griesinger, M.D., 1866

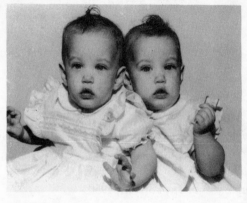

Identical twins, now age 30, in which the twin on the left has remained well and the one on the right developed manic-depressive disorder at age 24.

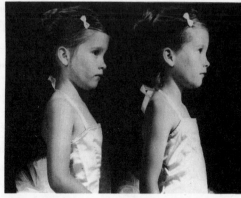

Identical twins, now age 24, in which the twin on the left has remained well and the one on the right developed manic-depressive disorder at age 17.

Identical twins, now age 31, in which the twin on the right has remained well and the one on the left developed schizophrenia at age 20.

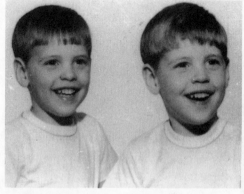

Identical twins, now age 29, in which the twin on the left has remained well and the one on the right developed schizophrenia at age 22.

SCHIZOPHRENIA AND
MANIC-DEPRESSIVE DISORDER

CHAPTER 1

The Politics and Science of Twin Studies

HUMAN TWINS have been objects of fascination throughout human history. To have two—and sometimes more—babies emerge sequentially from a mother's birth canal seems to contravene the laws of human procreation. Historically, the impact of this event was rendered even greater because, until the recent availability of X rays and other diagnostic equipment, multiple births were usually unexpected.

In mythology and history, twins have provoked reactions ranging from awe to aversion and from deification to death. Mesopotamia, Babylonia, and Persia all worshipped twin gods. In the mythology of India, the Asvin twins were said to be "beautiful and strong. . . . Compassionate toward the weak and the oppressed, these god-doctors worked miracles for all who suffered" (Gedda, 1961, p. 3); they are memorialized by 50 hymns in the Rig-Veda, the oldest and most important of the Hindu sacred books. In the biblical book of Genesis, Jacob and Esau were fraternal twins.

Ancient Greece and Rome also had twin gods, the most famous of whom were Castor and Pollux. Conceived by Leda and Zeus when he posed as a swan, the twins became famous for the rescue of their sister, Helen (who would later cause the Trojan War), and by their saving of the Argonaut expedition from a storm. Zeus rewarded them by transforming them into a constellation of stars, the Gemini (Latin for twins), which is the third sign of the zodiac. In ancient Rome a common expletive was "by Pollux! by Castor!," an expression that has come down to us as "by jiminy!," a modified form of "by Gemini."

Romulus and Remus are also well-known Roman twins and reflect the darker side of such mythology. Sons of Mars and one of the vestal virgins, they were cast into the Tiber River and left to die. Rescued and suckled by a she-wolf, the twins were raised by a shepherd before being restored to their proper status; Romulus became the first king of Rome, and the twins remain the emblem of the city to this day (although Romulus later murdered Remus).

The reaction of different cultures to twins has varied widely. Among the Yoruba in Nigeria, where twins are very common (see Chapter 2), twin births were considered to be a propitious sign from the gods. The twins were believed to bring good fortune and to have unusual powers; a curse issued by them was considered to be lethal. Among some other African tribes, however, twins were considered to bring bad luck, and one or both of them were sometimes killed. Among American Indians some tribes venerated twins; for example, among the Akwaala "it was customary for all twins of that tribe to wear magnificent garb as a mark of distinction for their privileged status" (ibid., p. 6). Other tribes considered twins to be part gods and to have clairvoyant abilities. On the other hand, the Alsea Indians routinely killed the second-born twin, whom they considered not to be a real person; the North Pomo Indians killed both twins; and among the Northwest Maidus, the mother was also sometimes put to death.

In medieval European cultures some people believed that twins were caused by the mother being impregnated by two different men, implying infidelity. In Wales twins were thought to portend future fertility, whereas in England and Scotland twins augured infertility. Twins were guaranteed to women who drank a glass of water from the Scottish well of Saint Mungo, but women not wishing for twins could negate the guarantee by drinking only half the glass (MacGillivray et al., 1988, p. 2).

Twins have also figured prominently in European and American literature. Shakespeare, himself the father of twins, used them prominently in *The Comedy of Errors* as well as in *Twelfth Night*. In literature identical twins have been used to entertain, as Tweedledum and Tweedledee in Lewis Carroll's *Through the Looking Glass*, and to further plots in such books as George Sand's *La Petite Fadette*, Alexander Dumas's *The Man in the Iron Mask*, Thornton Wilder's *The Bridge of San Luis Rey*, and Margaret Mitchell's *Gone with the Wind*, in which identical twin brothers both fall in love with Scarlett O'Hara. Aldous Huxley in *Brave New World* carried the twin idea further by artificially producing identical twins in incubators.

*   *   *

From Galton to Mengele

At the end of the nineteenth century, twins emerged from mythology, history, and literature and entered the realm of science. Sir Francis Galton, the cousin of Charles Darwin, is usually credited with being the first to promote twins vigorously for research purposes. In an 1875 publication entitled "The History of Twins as a Criterion of the Relative Powers of Nature and Nurture," Galton claimed that twins "afford means of distinguishing between the effects of tendencies received at birth, and of those that were imposed by the circumstances of their after lives; in other words, between the effects of nature and of nurture" (Galton, 1875). He thus used twins to coin the terms of the nature-nurture debate, which has continued unabated ever since.

Although Galton did not fully recognize that there are two distinct types of twins—today called identical (monozygotic) and fraternal (dizygotic)—he focused his research attention on the former group by collecting case histories of those who were most clearly alike. He proposed research projects such as the following: "It would be an interesting experiment for twins who were closely alike to try [sic] how far dogs could distinguish between them by scent" (ibid.). Galton himself claimed to understand the relative importance of inherited versus environmental influences: "Nature is far stronger than nurture within the limited range that I have been careful to assign to the latter. . . . There is no escape from the conclusion that nature prevails enormously over nurture" (ibid.).

In addition to being the father of twin research, however, Galton was also the father of the eugenics movement. Eugenics is the belief that human beings can be improved through selective breeding, and it was a subject of immense controversy in the United States in the early years of the 20th century. On one side were the followers of Galton, who advocated compulsory sterilization for individuals deemed unfit and the restriction of immigration, especially for Italians and Jews, who were said to be polluting the American gene pool. On the other side were those who argued that selective breeding would accomplish nothing because environmental circumstances such as poverty and slums, not genes, were the causes of most undesirable behavior. Galton's 1869 book, *Hereditary Genius*, was considered to be the bible of the eugenics movement. Because of Galton's close association with eugenics as well as with twin research, the latter became associated in people's minds with the eugenicists' views.

With the rise of Mussolini and Hitler in Europe, eugenics became considerably less respectable. In 1933 Germany passed a Law for the Prevention of Genetically Diseased Offspring, which mandated compulsory sterilization for conditions thought to be genetic in origin, including alcoholism, epilepsy, mental retardation, and schizophrenia; what is often forgotten is that the architects of the German law drew heavily from existing American statutes on compulsory sterilization, especially a model law formulated by the Eugenics Record Office in New York.

Twin research flourished in Nazi Germany. Such studies offered the most convincing means for proving that a given condition was "genetic" in origin and therefore a candidate for compulsory sterilization. The most common form of the twin research was to compare the concordance rate of a disease in identical (monozygotic) twins with the concordance rate in fraternal (dizygotic) twins—in other words, to answer the question of how often when one twin is affected with the disease is the other twin also affected. If 100% of second twins in identical pairs but only 10% of second twins in fraternal pairs get the disease, that would constitute strong evidence for a genetic origin. Establishing the relative concordance rates for various physical and mental diseases in identical and fraternal twins became a high priority in 1930s Germany.

In order to accomplish this, twin research was lavishly funded by the German Research Council and other groups. Some twin researchers cooperated with these government efforts, but many did not. In 1936 two summer camps were established exclusively for young twins so that they could be studied. By 1939 twin studies had become so important that the German interior minister ordered the registration of all twins born in Germany so that they could be identified for research purposes. The leading German twin researcher was Otmar von Verschuer, who held prestigious academic positions in Berlin and Frankfurt; he called twin research the "sovereign method for genetic research in humans" (Proctor, 1988, p. 43). Eugen Fischer, one of von Verschuer's colleagues, said that research in twins was "*the* single most important research tool in the field of racial hygiene" (ibid.).

One of von Verschuer's research assistants at the University of Frankfurt was the infamous Josef Mengele, who had earned a Ph.D. in genetics as well as a medical degree and had done research on twins. He was an enthusiastic supporter of Hitler and in 1938 joined the elite Waffen SS. Following the outbreak of war he served in the Race and Resettlement Office on the eastern front, then in 1943 was transferred to Auschwitz as the chief physician in the women's section. According to Robert Jay Lifton's *The Nazi Doctors*, Mengele was probably transferred to Auschwitz specifically to do twin research (Lifton, 1986, p. 347).

Mengele recruited twins for study from the incoming trainloads of Jewish and Gypsy prisoners by standing on the platform as they were being unloaded and shouting "*Zwillinge, Zwillinge*," the German word for twins. According to one observer, when he found identical twins, "Mengele beamed—he was happy" (ibid., p. 355). He identified approximately 1,500 twin pairs, many of whom were given special status and housing as research subjects and marked with a "ZW" on their identification tattoo. He then subjected the twins to experiments, including many that were painful or fatal, and Mengele himself murdered some twins so that he could do autopsies on them. He was said to be "fiercely enthusiastic" because of his "passionate involvement in twin research" (ibid., p. 354), a prototypical mad scientist whose image has been perpetuated by books and movies such as *The Boys from Brazil*. Mengele, however, was not working in isolation; his research was done in direct collaboration with high-ranking German academics, including von Verschuer, to whom he regularly sent research specimens, and Mengele hoped to use his twin research at Auschwitz to obtain a university appointment following the war (ibid., p. 358).

For half a century the shadow of Josef Mengele has hung heavily over twin research. In Germany it is said that "Germans have an abiding and understandable fear of anything to do with genetic research" (Specter, 1990). Thomas Bouchard, a psychologist who has helped direct the study at the University of Minnesota of identical twins who were raised apart, recently commented that "there are colleagues who think I'm a racist, sexist, fascist pig" (Aldous, 1992). In 1988 the senior author of the present study was publicly called "a new Mengele" by a psychiatrist at a national conference (Breggin, 1988). For a few people it seems that anybody who studies twins is automatically assumed to be a fascist or worse.

Such a belief betrays ignorance. Twin research is inherently value-free, useful for proving that diseases or traits are *not* genetic in origin or that they *are* genetic in origin. Twin studies are like an ax, which can be used either as a weapon to harm or as a tool to clear land for growing food and building houses. Such research continues to be invaluable in helping to unravel the complex causation of many diseases including diabetes, heart disease, and cancers, and to sort out the tangled skeins that interweave nature and nurture in human behavior (Hrubec & Robinette, 1984). As noted in the epigraph for this book, twins are experiments of nature—indeed they are among the most valuable experiments that nature has carried out. Not to use such experiments to improve our understanding of human diseases would be foolish indeed.

Previous Twin Studies of Schizophrenia

Benjamin Rush, the father of American psychiatry, was among the first to recognize the psychiatric research potential of twins. Commenting in 1812 on a pair of identical twins both of whom had suicided, Rush observed the "hereditary sameness of organization of the nerves, brain and blood vessels on which . . . the predisposition to madness dwells" (Price, 1978). During the remainder of the 19th century, other observations were made on twins in which one or both had developed "lunacy." One of the most complete such reports was that of Jean Moreau, a French physician, who in 1859 wrote about "two young men who are so nearly alike that one is easily mistaken for the other." The twins had been confined to an asylum because of their remarkably similar illness: "They both consider themselves subject to imaginary persecutions; the same enemies have sworn their destruction and employ the same means to effect it. Both have hallucinations of hearing. They are both of them melancholy and morose; they never address a word to anybody . . . " (ibid.).

Systematic studies of schizophrenia in twins began in the 1920s in Germany in an effort to prove that the disease had a genetic origin. Hans Luxenburger collected a sample of such twins from the Munich Psychiatric Clinic and other mental hospitals in Bavaria, and reported a much higher concordance rate of schizophrenia for identical twins (58%) than for fraternal twins (0%) (Gottesman & Shields, 1982, p. 44). Luxenburger was also impressed by the clinical dissimilarities in twin pairs in which both had developed the disease.

Franz Kallmann's research on the genetics of schizophrenia also began in Germany with the records of a large Berlin mental hospital, but because his father had been Jewish, Kallmann lost his university position in Berlin in 1935 and emigrated to New York. There he carried out an extensive twin research project, utilizing the records of New York State mental hospitals. In many of the pairs in which only one twin had developed schizophrenia, Kallmann noted that the twins were young and so there was still time for the second twin to develop the disease. He therefore corrected for this age factor and reported concordance rates of 86% for identical twins and only 15% for fraternal twins. According to Kallmann, such figures proved that schizophrenia is caused by a recessive gene. Since no other twin researcher has reported concordance rates close to those of Kallmann's, the methodology of his research has been the subject of spirited debate among both detractors (Lewontin et al., 1984, pp. 207–213) and defenders (Shields et al., 1967).

Kallmann's studies highlight several methodological problems that have complicated twin research on schizophrenia. Foremost among these was his reliance on state hospital records both to identify twins and to verify their diagnoses. Twins more severely affected with schizophrenia would have been more likely to have been hospitalized. Furthermore, since it is believed by some researchers that twins with more severe forms of schizophrenia are more likely to be concordant for the disease, then Kallmann was sampling from a population skewed toward being concordant. It may also be questioned whether Kallmann was able to make accurate diagnoses without personally examining the twins, as was true for most of his sample. The diagnostic criteria used for schizophrenia has not, until recent years, been standardized. Still another problem is that of establishing zygosity and verifying that identical twins are truly identical. Kallmann said that he established zygosity on the basis of physical similarity alone, but he provided no details of his method; since he did not personally examine most of his twins, the accuracy of his zygosity determinations is questionable.

The use of hospital records alone to select twins for study was also a limiting factor for four other schizophrenia twin studies undertaken at the time of Kallmann's studies. In the United States Aaron Rosanoff and his colleagues collected data from hospital records on twins with schizophrenia. In addition to studying concordance rates, these researchers were also impressed by the number of affected twins in the discordant pairs who had had a history of head trauma or infection preceding the onset of their schizophrenia (Rosanoff et al., 1934). In Sweden Erik Essen-Moller identified from hospital records a group of twins in which one or both had schizophrenia; unlike his predecessors, he personally examined them, used fingerprints and blood typing to confirm zygosity, and followed them for 30 years to confirm that the well twin in the discordant pairs remained well (Essen-Moller, 1970). In England Eliot Slater and James Shields cast a wider net and attempted to identify all twins with schizophrenia and other mental disorders in 10 London county hospitals. They also personally examined the twins, used fingerprints for zygosity ascertainment, and published extensive case histories for each pair (Slater & Shields, 1953). Finally, in Japan Eiji Inouye published data on twin pairs with schizophrenia whom he had identified nonsystematically from psychiatric hospitals and outpatient clinics. He used blood samples to verify zygosity and personally examined all the twins. Inouye was especially interested in the relationship of severity of illness to concordance and believed that the more severe the schizophrenia in the first twin, the greater the chance of the second twin also becoming sick (Inouye, 1961, 1970).

Between 1963 and 1973 three Scandinavian schizophrenia twin studies were carried out and were, in terms of sampling methodology, the best studies ever conducted, using national twin registries, which were maintained in Scandinavian countries for every twin born in each country. Such registries could be compared with psychiatric records to identify virtually every twin who had ever been treated psychiatrically. Pekka Tienari (1963, 1975) worked in Finland, Einar Kringlen (1967) in Norway, and Margit Fischer (1973) in Denmark. Kringlen interviewed all his twins and followed them for many years. Tienari also interviewed most of his twins, but one-third of Fischer's twins had died prior to her study so she had to rely on hospital records and family histories to establish a diagnosis. Kringlen also published more extensive case records for his monozygotic twins than any other researcher had done.

In 1959 a twin registry was also established in the United States utilizing the military records for all twins who served in the military from World War II to the Korean War; later, another registry was added covering the Vietnam War (Kendler & Robinette, 1983). Administered by the National Academy of Sciences and the National Research Council, the registry has several shortcomings. It consists almost exclusively of males and does not include individuals whose onset of schizophrenia took place prior to age 18, because such individuals would not have been accepted into military service. It also includes only those whose illness began while in the service or who later applied for disability from the Veterans Administration; individuals whose illness began after military service but who did not apply for disability were not identified. Finally, the twins were not examined by the researchers; hospital and disability determination records were used to establish the diagnoses.

Another twin study that achieved new standards in diagnostic methodology was that done by Irving Gottesman and James Shields. They applied and extended Eliot Slater's London study, achieving a high reliability in diagnoses for the twins by employing multiple clinicians. Gottesman and Shields's extensive analyses of their own sample as well as previous twin studies have been widely used by researchers in schizophrenia and genetics (Gottesman & Shields, 1972, 1982). They also replicated Inouye's finding that increased severity of schizophrenia in one twin was associated with a higher probability that the second twin would also become affected. In more recent years the Slater-Gottesman-Shields twin sample has been extended by Adrianne Reveley and her colleagues at London's Institute of Psychiatry, and some of the twins have participated in computerized tomography and other biological studies (Reveley et al., 1984).

In addition to the National Academy of Sciences-National Research Council twin registry of military personnel in the United States and the Institute of Psychiatry's twin registry in London, the only other ongoing twin studies of schizophrenia are two studies in Scandinavia. In southern Sweden Goran Eberhard, a student of Essen-Moller's, is following twins born between 1930 and 1946 in which one or both have been diagnosed with schizophrenia. Eberhard and his colleagues are especially interested in trying to predict which of the discordant twin pairs will become concordant, and have carried out biological studies of the twins with this goal in mind (Eberhard, 1981; Eberhard et al., 1989). The other current Scandinavian twin study of schizophrenia is being carried out by Sidsel Onstad and his colleagues in Norway as an extension of Kringlen's work. To date, this group has published data on concordance rates, clinical subtypes, and obstetric complications in these twins (Onstad et al., 1991, 1991a, 1991b, 1992).

With the exception of the most recent studies, all the major twin studies of schizophrenia discussed here were originally conceived to ascertain concordance rates in identical and fraternal twins and thereby determine the importance of genetic factors in this disease. The one exception to this was the study of twins with schizophrenia carried out by William Pollin and his colleagues at the National Institute of Mental Health in the 1960s. This study grew out of psychoanalytic and family interaction theories of schizophrenia that were in vogue at that time. As the researchers stated their hypothesis, "We initially were interested in attempting to exclude genetic and biological factors so as to be able to focus upon psychodynamic, interpersonal phenomena that might have some significant etiologic role with respect to schizophrenia" (Pollin & Stabenau, 1968). They recruited their twins primarily through private psychiatrists, thereby resulting in a sample skewed sharply toward the upper socioeconomic end of the spectrum; the average IQ of the well twins in the discordant pairs was 130 (Rosenthal & Van Dyke, 1970).

The twins studied by Pollin and colleagues were investigated more thoroughly than those in any other previous schizophrenia twin study. The most significant findings were a history of lower birth weight and more obstetric complications in the affected twins in discordant pairs, and more neurological abnormalities in the affected twins (Pollin & Stabenau, 1968; Mosher et al., 1971). The findings, said these researchers, suggested that "the intrauterine experience of one twin, relative to the co-twin, tends to be unfavorable or deficient, leading to a relative physiological incompetence and immaturity at birth and in the neonatal period." Shifting from biological observations to psychological theorizing, the researchers then interpreted their findings as follows: "These [biological] differences may induce attitudes and relationship patterns in the family which accentuate dependency and ego identity problems, and retard self-differentiation in the less favored twin" (Pollin & Stabenau, 1968). It should be noted that Pollin et al. published virtually no data to support their psychological interpretation, despite extensive and intensive analyses of the families. Such an interpretation, which appears absurd in the context of 1990s schizophrenia research, was representative of much 1960s theorizing about this disease.

The twin research that is the subject of this book should be viewed within the historical context of previous studies. Unlike most previous studies, it made no attempt to collect a representative sample of twins in order to compare concordance rates in identical and fraternal twins. Like the Pollin et al. study, it recruited identical twins specifically because they were discordant for schizophrenia, then recruited additional twins discordant for bipolar disorder and concordant for schizophrenia, and twins in which both were normal, in order to compare these groups with the original group.*

The present study departs from the Pollin et al. study in one important respect: We believe that psychodynamic and family interaction theories of schizophrenia have been completely discredited and are no longer worthy of study. The design of our study was exclusively biological, with the assumption that schizophrenia is a brain disease just as multiple sclerosis, Parkinson's disease, or Alzheimer's disease are brain diseases. In this sense the difference between the Pollin et al. study and the present study is the difference between research in the 1960s and research in the 1990s.

How Often Do Both Identical Twins Develop Schizophrenia?

Although we were not specifically addressing the likelihood of the second identical twin developing the disease after the first one has, it is nonetheless an important issue for understanding the genetic contribution to schizophrenia. Since genetics are widely assumed to play a role in the causation of schizophrenia, an understanding of this role has a direct bearing on the interpretation of results from this study. The role of genetics in the causation of schizophrenia will be discussed in Chapter 12. The following serves as a preface to that discussion and also as a summary of the major findings of previous twin studies of schizophrenia.

Most textbooks of psychiatry state that the chances of a second identical twin developing schizophrenia if the first one does is approximately 50%. The statistical method used to arrive at this figure is called the proband method and is favored by geneticists. In the proband method a pair of twins concordant for schizophrenia is counted twice if each of them was ascertained independently in the course of identifying subjects for the study (Gottesman & Shields, 1982; McGue, 1992). An alternate way to measure concordance is by the pairwise method in which there is no double counting of individual twins in concordant pairs; this method is widely used to express concordance rates for diseases other than schizophrenia.

Based on the methods of sampling, determination of diagnoses, and ascertainment of zygosity, the three Scandinavian studies done by Tiernari, Kringlen, and Fischer, which all relied on national twin registries,

---

* Because we are citing the current scientific literature, we use throughout this book the official American Psychiatric Association term "bipolar disorder" to describe the condition more familiarly known as "manic-depressive disorder."

are probably the most accurate twin studies of schizophrenia concordance rates done to date. The studies done by Essen-Moller, Slater and Shields, Gottesman and Shields, Kendler and Robinette (on the National Academy of Sciences–National Research Council registry), and Onstad et al. are probably also acceptable for estimating concordance rates, although each of them has methodological limitations. Table 1.1 shows the concordance rates for identical and fraternal twins with schizophrenia for each of these studies using both the probandwise and the pairwise methods.

It can be seen that the concordance rate for schizophrenia is higher for identical twins than it is for fraternal twins both by the probandwise method (40% versus 15%) and by the pairwise method (28% versus 6%). The fact that the concordance rate in identical twins is three to five times higher than the rate in fraternal twins confirms that genetics plays an

TABLE 1.1
Twin Concordance Rates for Schizophrenia

Study	Identical Twins		Fraternal Twins	
	Probandwise method (%)	Pairwise method (%)	Probandwise method (%)	Pairwise method (%)
Tienari	26 (6/23)	15 (3/20)	13 (6/45)	7 (3/42)
Kringlen	46 (26/57)	31 (14/45)	13 (12/96)	7 (6/90)
Fischer	36 (9/25)	24 (5/21)	18 (8/45)	10 (4/41)
Essen-Moller	50 (4/8)	50 (4/8)	7 (2/27)	7 (2/27)
Slater & Shields	68 (28/41)	65 (24/37)	18 (11/61)	14 (8/58)
Gottesman & Shields	58 (15/26)	41 (9/22)	12 (4/34)	9 (3/33)
Natl. Academy of Sciences–Natl. Research Council	31 (60/194)	18 (30/164)	7 (18/277)	3 (9/268)
Onstad et al.	48 (15/31)	33 (8/24)	4 (1/28)	4 (1/28)
Total Tienari, Kringlen, & Fischer only	39 (41/105)	26 (22/86)	14 (26/186)	8 (13/173)
Total all studies	40 (163/405)	28 (97/341)	15 (62/427)	6 (36/587)

Source: Adapted from Torrey (1992) and McGue (1992).

important role in the causation of schizophrenia. Table 1.1 also shows that the concordance rate for schizophrenia in identical twins is not approximately 50%, as is stated in most psychiatric textbooks, but rather 40% (probandwise) or 28% (pairwise), depending on which method of calculating concordance rates is used. Thus the answer to the question, When one identical twin develops schizophrenia, how often does the second twin also become sick? is either 28% or 40% of the time, depending on the statistical procedure selected.

It is also useful to compare the concordance rates for schizophrenia with the concordance rates for other disorders of the central nervous system. Twin studies for these other diseases have been previously summarized (Torrey, 1992) and the rates are reproduced in Table 1.2. Because twin study concordance rates for other diseases have been calculated as pairwise rates, the pairwise rate is also used for schizophrenia. As can be seen, the pairwise concordance rate for schizophrenia is virtually identical to that for multiple sclerosis and is lower than the concordance rates for such diseases as poliomyelitis and epilepsy. It can also be seen that the pairwise concordance rate for bipolar disorder is 56%, exactly twice the comparative rate (28%) for schizophrenia. This confirms previous data suggesting that genetics play a more important role in the causation of bipolar disorder than it does in schizophrenia.

TABLE 1.2

Pairwise Twin Concordance Rates for Schizophrenia and Other Disorders of the Central Nervous System

Disorder	Identical Twins (%)	Fraternal Twins (%)
Huntington's disease	100 (14/14)	20 (1/5)
Down's syndrome	95 (18/19)	2 (2/127)
Epilepsy	61 (20/46)	10 (13/126)
Mental retardation	60 (18/30)	9 (7/77)
Bipolar disorder	56 (44/79)	14 (16/111)
Cerebral palsy	40 (6/15)	0 (0/21)
Autism	36 (4/11)	0 (0/10)
Poliomyelitis	36 (5/14)	6 (2/31)
Congenital anomalies of the CNS	33 (2/6)	0 (0/5)
Schizophrenia	28 (97/341)	6 (36/587)
Multiple sclerosis	27 (17/62)	2 (2/88)
Parkinson's disease	0 (0/18)	7 (1/14)

Source: Adapted from Torrey (1992).

CHAPTER 2

Are Identical Twins Really Identical?

A TWIN PAIR is born approximately once in every 100 births in the United States. It has long been suspected that twins are conceived more often than they are born, but that one of the fetuses does not survive the early stages of development. Research on women who have had abortions, and new diagnostic equipment such as ultrasound, have further clarified this issue. In one study only one-third of twin pairs diagnosed with ultrasound within the first 15 weeks of pregnancy were actually born as twins; for the other two-thirds, one twin did not live through the early stages of development. Thus for every pair of twins born, it is possible that two other pairs were conceived originally.

There are predominantly two kinds of twins. Two-thirds of all twins are fraternal (dizygotic) twins, which begin when two eggs are fertilized by two sperm. Such individuals share an average of 50% of their genes and, except for sharing a uterus for 9 months, are genetically no more alike than other brothers and sisters. They may be either the same sex or different sexes. The other one-third of twins are identical (monozygotic) twins, which result when one egg is fertilized by a sperm but then divides into two (or more) separate fetuses. These individuals are the same sex, share 100% of their genes, and are therefore genetically identical.

In addition to fraternal and identical twins, there are three other possible kinds of twins, but they occur very rarely. Superfecundation takes place when two of the mother's eggs from the same ovarian cycle are fertilized by two different men and then develop as twins; a few such cases have been documented (Bryan, 1983, p. 16). Superfetation occurs when a single pregnancy has begun, but then a month later the mother's ovary mistakenly releases another egg, which is fertilized and implants in the uterus next to the already-growing fetus; this happens in some mammals but has not been clearly documented in humans. Finally, there is a scenario in which the mother's egg divides *prior* to fertilization, and then each half is fertilized by different sperm, producing children who are intermediate genetically between fraternal and identical twins; rare twins of this type have been recorded (Bryan, 1983, p. 10).

The fetus, which is called a zygote in its earliest stages, becomes lodged in the wall of the uterus and begins to grow. It is surrounded by two membranes, or sacs: an outer chorion and an inner amnion. As seen in Figure 2.1, fraternal twins always have separate chorions and amnions. Identical twins, however, may have either completely separate chorions and amnions (33%), a common chorion but separate amnions (61%), or a common chorion and amnion (6%). Since the chorionic membrane is easily recognizable at the time of birth, it is understandable why there has been some confusion in the past regarding whether a given pair of twins was fraternal or identical. Until recent years it was thought that separate chorions meant that the twins had to be fraternal, when, in fact, one-third of identical twins also have separate chorions. Thus there are many identical twins who believe they are fraternal because a doctor told their mothers at birth that there were two sacs.

FIGURE 2.1
Types of twins showing possible arrangements
of chorion and amnion.

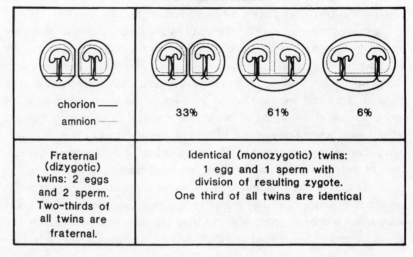

chorion —— amnion ·······	33%	61%	6%
Fraternal (dizygotic) twins: 2 eggs and 2 sperm. Two-thirds of all twins are fraternal.	Identical (monozygotic) twins: 1 egg and 1 sperm with division of resulting zygote. One third of all twins are identical		

Fraternal twins can be any combination of right- or left-handed, just as any two siblings can be. Most identical twins have identical handedness. In occasional pairs, however, identical twins may be opposite handed. These are often referred to as mirror-image twins and may also have skin and hair features that are on opposite sides, such as moles on opposite cheeks or hair whorls on opposite sides of their scalps. It is thought that such mirror-image twins come about when the original zygote divides into two separate fetuses at a slightly later stage of development. This will be discussed further in Chapter 4.

Identical twins are found in approximately the same incidence of 3.5 per 1,000 births everywhere in the world. The incidence of fraternal twins, on the other hand, varies approximately tenfold in different population groups (Little & Thompson, 1988). The United States has an incidence rate of approximately 9.4 per 1,000 for total twin births, according to two large studies, although the rate is higher among African-Americans and lower among Asian-Americans. The Far East has the lowest incidence rate of total twin births, including Japan (average of 5.9 per 1,000 in three studies), Taiwan (5.6), and Singapore (7.8). The rate in European nations varies from Bulgaria (6.5) to Ireland (11.6) and the former East Germany (12.4).

Sub-Saharan African nations have the highest incidence rate of total twin births in the world. Studies have reported a twin incidence rate of 16.3 per 1,000 in Uganda, 16.8 in South Africa, 21.8 in Mali, 27.2 in the Seychelles, and 52.4 in Ghana. Nigeria is generally acknowledged to be the twin capital of the world, with five studies of the Yoruba tribe of 18 million people reporting an incidence rate of 59.4 (range: 47.0 to 76.1). Approximately every third Yoruba household includes a pair of twins, all of whom are named Taiwo ("he who has first taste of the world") and Kehinde ("he who lags behind") regardless of their sex.

The reasons for this wide variation in the incidence of fraternal twinning is unknown, and, in fact, remarkably little is known about the causes of twinning in general. There appears to be a definite genetic predisposition to fraternal twinning, which often runs in families. Identical twinning, on the other hand, only rarely runs in families (Bryan, 1983, p. 15). Fraternal twins also occur more commonly in women who are older and taller and have had several children. Hormones are known to play an important role in twinning, as has been shown by the high incidence of twins and other multiple births following the use of ovulation-stimulating drugs in the treatment of infertility. There has also been speculation that certain chemicals in yams, widely eaten by the Yoruba in Nigeria, may affect women's hormones and that this is the cause of the high rate of twinning among the Yoruba. A recent interesting but unproven theory put forth to explain identical twinning is that there are defective cells in the early-developing zygote, causing it to split in an attempt to slough off the defective cells; the sloughed cells then develop into the identical twin fetus (Bloom, 1992).

It has also become apparent in recent years that the incidence of twinning is slowly declining. The United States, Canada, Europe, Japan, Australia, and New Zealand have all reported a decline in incidence, and there is some evidence for a decrease in Nigeria as well. The reasons for this decline are unknown, but speculation has centered on the widespread use of birth control pills, which affect hormonal cycles and which might interfere with the processes responsible for twinning. Whatever the reason, the rate of twinning (both identical and fraternal combined) in the United States is now said to be approximately 1 in every 100 births rather than 1 in 80 births, the figure cited in most textbooks (Bryan, 1983, p. 22).

Identical Twins May Not Be Identical In Utero

Studies of identical twins have assumed, until recently, that such twins are identical at birth. Not only do identical twins share the same genes, it was thought, but they also share the same uterine environment; therefore, it was reasoned, differences that are found between identical twins later in life must be due to environmental influences to which they are exposed after birth.

Recent studies have forced modifications in this assumption. Identical twins are indeed identical at the time of the original splitting of the zygote, but from that time forward at least four factors may differentially alter the development of one of them. These factors are chromosome or gene changes, differences in circulation and oxygenation, infectious agents, and drugs and chemicals.

Chromosome or Gene Changes

It is a rare but well-documented possibility that chromosomal aberrations or gene mutations may take place in identical twins in one fetus but not the other after initial cleavage of the zygote (Fogel et al., 1965). The twins continue to be identical except for the mutant gene or the altered chromosome. The causes of such gene or chromosome mutations are unknown. Down's syndrome is an example of a chromosome change in which identical twins are usually concordant but in which at least five pairs have been reported with only one twin affected (Benirschke & Kim, 1973; Rogers et al., 1982). Figure 2.2 shows a pair of identical twins in which one has Down's syndrome but the other is normal. Identical twins

FIGURE 2.2
Identical twins in which only one is affected with Down's syndrome.

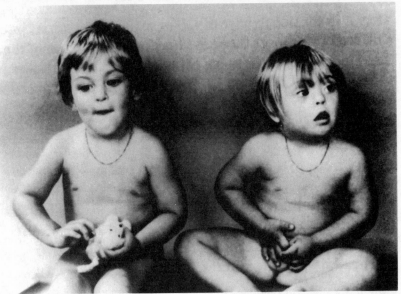

discordant for the fragile X syndrome, another chromosome abnormality, have also been reported (Tuckerman et al., 1985).

Chromosome changes that affect only one of an identical twin pair can sometimes produce bizarre outcomes. One such outcome that has been well documented is identical twins in which one is male and the other is apparently female (Edwards et al., 1966; Nielsen, 1967). This may occur when one of the twins, who were originally both males with XY chromosomes, loses the Y portion of the chromosome thereby becoming XO; such individuals have a condition known as Turner's syndrome and have female physiques and female sex characteristics.

Differences in Circulation and Oxygenation

It has long been recognized that the blood supply of identical twins may be unequal. The reason for this is that the two-thirds of identical twins that share a common chorion may also share some of their blood supply by means of arterial and/or venous anastomoses in the placenta (Price, 1950). The anastomoses allow blood to be shunted from one twin to the other. In the majority of cases this does not result in any significant differences between the twins, but in a minority it does.

Twin pairs in which one twin gets a much more generous blood supply than the other twin are said to have a twin transfusion syndrome. This may be evident at birth when one twin is reddish in color because of its high hemoglobin concentration and large number of red blood cells, while the other twin is pale because of anemia. Such red and white twins are the extreme, but there are less obvious gradations of this phenomenon. As summarized in one textbook, "The striking appearance of red and white babies represents only the tip of the harlequin iceberg" (Burn & Corney, 1988).

Another measure of the twin transfusion syndrome is weight differences at birth, with the donor of the transfusion being lighter. Tan et al. (1979) have suggested that the twin transfusion syndrome be defined as a within-pair (intrapair) weight difference of more than 20% at birth. Using such a definition, twin transfusion syndromes have been documented in approximately 10% of all identical twins. This is almost certainly an underestimation, however, for many cases of twin transfusion syndrome are thought to be most marked in the middle months of pregnancy. In the 5th month, for example, fetuses weigh approximately 300 g, whereas at birth they weigh approximately 3,000 g; therefore, there may have been a marked twin transfusion syndrome in the middle months of pregnancy, which is no longer apparent at birth because the earlier weight difference has been obscured by subsequent weight gain (Morrison, 1949). Cases of twin transfusion syndrome have been documented in which one twin weighed more than twice as much as the other twin at birth (Sydow & Rinne, 1958).

Increasingly, the twin transfusion syndrome is being considered as an important source of prenatal differences between identical twins. The smaller-at-birth twin usually develops more slowly and in some cases remains smaller throughout life (Babson et al., 1964). Studies of intelligence have found that the smaller twin has a lower IQ by an average of 5 points (Munsinger, 1977). The lower hemoglobin concentration in the smaller twin may lead to relative anoxia (decreased oxygen), thereby retarding brain maturation in the lighter twin at critical stages of development.

Bronson Price, who studied the twin transfusion syndrome in great detail, speculated that differences in blood supply and oxygen might affect the twins' "susceptibilities to disease" through differential effects on their immune or endocrine systems (Price, 1950). Sarnoff Mednick, in studies of possible mechanisms leading to schizophrenia, cited work in which different genetic strains of mice were shown to have different susceptibilities to anoxic episodes *in utero*, with some strains developing congenital anomalies with only mild anoxia but other strains acquiring more severe anoxia (Stern, 1960, p. 339; Mednick, 1970).

The twin transfusion syndrome is only one of several possible mechanisms by which one twin in an identical pair may get a better oxygen supply than the other. Anoxic episodes during the birth process are well known, especially in twins in which the placenta begins to shut down after the birth of the first twin but before the second twin has been delivered, thereby reducing the oxygen supply to the second twin.

In the present study of identical twins, a total of 8 out of 63 twin pairs (13%) exhibited the twin transfusion syndrome as defined by one twin weighing at least 20% less than the other. These included 4 pairs discordant for schizophrenia, 1 pair discordant for bipolar disorder, 2 pairs concordant for schizophrenia, and 1 pair of normal controls. In each of the discordant pairs it was the lighter-at-birth twin who later became sick.

Infectious Agents

It is well known that a single twin in a fraternal pair may become infected *in utero* with a bacteria or a virus (Shearer et al., 1972). In one reported case in which a rubella virus was the infecting agent, it was shown that the virus had, in fact, infected both twins, producing a severe rubella syndrome (cataracts, congenital heart defect) in one twin while the other twin remained completely normal (Forrester et al., 1966).

It is less well known that infectious agents can also cause infection *in utero* in only one twin in an identical twin pair. As early as 1924 a case was described in which congenital syphilis was found at birth in only one of an apparently identical twin pair (Penrose, 1937), and additional cases have been subsequently described (Raskin, 1951). In 1986 a pair of identical twins was reported in which only one was infected at birth with the human immunodeficiency virus type 1 (HIV-1), the virus that causes AIDS (Menez-Bautista et al., 1986). A larger study of identical twins born to HIV-infected mothers showed that among 6 twin pairs who were infected, 3 were concordant and 3 were discordant for the virus (Goedert et al., 1991).

Several possible mechanisms may lead to such discordance. In AIDS it is thought that the virus is frequently transmitted to the baby at the time of birth. The firstborn baby is exposed to more trauma in the birth canal as the mother's cervix is being dilated, and this additional trauma might subject it to a greater exposure to infection.

Another possible mechanism involves differential blood supply *in utero*, such as is seen in the twin transfusion syndrome. The twin who gets the poorer blood supply has lower levels of immunoglobulins and is therefore less able to fight infections by invading organisms. In one reported case in which identical twins were born with one weighing 42% less than the other, the lighter twin had only 13% as much immunoglobulin G as the heavier twin and did not catch up until 28 weeks of age (Bryan & Slavin, 1974). Both prior to birth and for the first several weeks of life, the lighter twin was much less able to resist infections. Such discordance in ability to fight infections within identical twin pairs may also lead to the death of the lighter twin in some cases (Abraham, 1967).

Drugs and Chemicals

Like infectious agents, it has long been known that drugs and chemicals may affect only one member of a dizygotic twin pair. For example, one mother who took the anticonvulsant drug phenytoin during pregnancy gave birth to fraternal twins, one of whom had skeletal malformations and severe heart defects characteristic of phenytoin toxicity, while the other twin was completely normal (Loughnan et al., 1973). Other cases have been reported in which one fraternal twin was severely affected by a known teratogen (malforming agent) such as thalidomide (Mellin & Katzenstein, 1962) or alcohol (Chasnoff, 1985) while the other twin was only minimally affected.

Among identical twins, discordance to drug and chemical exposure *in utero* has not been as clearly documented. Fetal alcohol syndrome has been studied in identical twins, and one study of 5 identical twins indicated that all were concordant for the effects of the alcohol (Streissguth & Dehaene, 1990). However, another study reported an identical twin pair in which one twin had severe congenital anomalies while the other was normal; the mother had taken medication during pregnancy, which was thought by the authors to have been teratogenic (Greene et al., 1985).

Given what is known about possible differences in circulation, oxygenation, and weight in identical twins *in utero*, it would be surprising if there were not differential effects of drugs and chemicals on the twins. If the twin had a better circulation, it would be exposed to more of the drug or chemical. If the twin had a poorer circulation, relative oxygen deprivation might make its developing organs more susceptible to damage. In the case just cited in which the mother took medication, for example, there was a 36% difference in birth weight between the twins, and it was the *larger* twin that had the congenital anomalies.

In addition to drugs and chemicals, identical twins may be differentially exposed *in utero* to nutritional factors or hormones that may be critical for development. For example, recent research has shown that a deficiency of folic acid during pregnancy causes neural tube defects, which are severe anomalies of the central nervous system (Czeizel & Dudas, 1992). Similarly, a recent report showed that wartime Dutch women who were severely deprived of food during early pregnancy were more likely to give birth to female children who later had a higher risk for schizophrenia (Susser & Lin, 1992). Hormonal changes in a pregnant woman may also affect identical twins differentially. In one documented case, a mother developed hyperthyroidism during the second month of her pregnancy; on delivery, one twin was hypothyroid, but the other was normal (Fogel et al., 1965). We are only beginning to appreciate how much is going on *in utero* that may cause disease in later years.

Congenital Anomalies of the Brain

Congenital anomalies are one of the few measures available that can be used to assess events taking place before a person is born. The term comes from the Latin *congenitus* and means "born together with"; thus, congenital is a measure of both genetic influence and environmental nongenetic influences that may affect the developing fetus *in utero*. Since identical twins begin life with identical genes, an examination of congenital anomalies among such twins should yield information regarding the relative importance of environmental nongenetic prenatal events. It is known that congenital anomalies can be caused by genetic factors (e.g., polycystic kidneys or polydactyly), chromosomal changes (e.g., Down's syndrome), infections (e.g., rubella or syphilis), and drugs and chemicals (e.g., thalidomide or alcohol). In the vast majority of congenital anomalies, however, the specific cause is unknown.

There have been five major studies of congenital anomalies in twins. Methodologically, the best study prospectively followed the offspring of 55,043 pregnancies in the Collaborative Perinatal Project of the National Institute of Neurological Disorders and Stroke. These children were evaluated extensively until they reached 7 years of age. A total of 615 pairs of twins were included, with zygosity established on 508 of them by both blood groups and detailed placental analysis.

The results of this study, reported by Myrianthopoulos (1975), confirmed previous suggestions that identical (but not fraternal) twins have a higher incidence of congenital abnormalities than do singleton births. Myrianthopoulos pointed out that such results are not surprising since "in itself MZ [monozygotic] twinning can be considered a congenital malformation." Presumably the same factors that produce identical twinning initially continue to operate and may also produce anomalies. He also found that male identical twins were more likely to have congenital anomalies than females, blacks more likely than whites, and those rare twins with a single chorion and a single amnion more likely than other twins. Being a firstborn or secondborn twin did not affect the anomaly rate.

Among the 187 identical twins in the study, 23 twin pairs were concordant for congenital anomalies and 46 twin pairs were discordant, for a concordance rate of 34%. Among fraternal twins, by contrast, 6 twins were concordant and 79 discordant, for a concordance rate of 7%. The fact that the concordance rate is higher for identical twins than for fraternal twins strongly suggests that genes play a role in causing some congenital anomalies, not a surprising finding in view of previous studies suggesting that anomalies such as polycystic kidneys and polydactyly run in families. Of the 23 concordant identical twin pairs, 16 pairs were concordant "for at least one similar malformation" (Myrianthopoulos, 1975), while the remaining 7 had anomalies in different organ systems.

When the Collaborative Perinatal Project data are broken down by organ systems, the pattern of anomalies shows important differences. The identical twin concordance rate for clubfoot was high (75%) compared with the identical twin concordance rate for anomalies of the heart (17%) and the brain (25%). Three identical twin pairs discordant for anomalies of the brain included affected twins with anencephaly, microcephaly, and "a bizarre combination of CNS malformations" (Myrianthopoulos, 1975).

The other four studies of congenital anomalies in twins found results similar to those of the Collaborative Perinatal Project (Record & McKeown, 1951; Stevenson et al., 1966; Hay & Wehrung, 1970; Cameron et al., 1983). The study by Cameron et al. ascertained zygosity with blood studies, but the other three studies used large cohorts of birth records and could only divide the twins into those that were like-sexed and those that were unlike-sexed. We know that approximately 43% of like-sexed twins are identical and 57% are fraternal, whereas all unlike-sexed twins are fraternal (with the exception of rare individuals with XO chromosomes, such as were mentioned previously). Table 2.1 summarizes the data on congenital anomalies of the brain (anencephaly and hydrocephaly) for the five studies and shows that when one identical twin has congenital anencephaly or hydrocephaly of the brain, in the vast majority of cases the co-twin will be normal.

In summary, twin studies of congenital anomalies of the brain clearly suggest that environmental, nongenetic factors play a large role in causing such anomalies *in utero*. Berker et al. (1992), after examining 6 identical

TABLE 2.1
Congenital Anomalies* of the Brain in Twins

		Identical Twin Estimated Concordance Rate	Fraternal Twin Concordance Rate
Myrianthopoulos, 1975	NINDS Collaborative Perinatal Project, 615 twin pairs	25% (1/4)	0% (0/5)
Cameron et al., 1983	England and Belgium, 1,424 twin pairs	50% (1/2)	NA
Hay & Wehrung, 1970	Natl. Cleft Lip and Palate Intelligence Service, 199,700 twin pairs	12%† (6/52)	3% (1/36; unlike-sexed only)
Stevenson et al., 1966	WHO multicenter study, 5,022 twin pairs	44%† (4/9)	0% (0/3; unlike-sexed only)
Record & McKeown, 1951	Birmingham, England, all CNS malformations, 1940–47	14%† (2/14)	0% (0/6; unlike-sexed only)
Totals		17% (14/81)	2% (1/50)

* Anencephaly and hydrocephaly.
†Zygosity in these studies was given only as like-sexed pairs and unlike-sexed pairs. Since it is known that approximately 43% of all like-sexed twins are identical, the number of like-sexed twins discordant for brain anomalies was multiplied by .43, and it was assumed that all the brain anomalies occurred in this group. The actual number of like-sexed identical twins discordant for brain anomalies in these studies was Hay and Wehrung, 106; Stevenson et al., 12; and Record and McKeown, 27. This assumption, therefore, errs on the side of inflating the concordance rate for brain anomalies in identical twins.

twins discordant for hydrocephaly (3 of which had evidence of a twin transfusion syndrome), concluded that "nurture can contribute to strikingly divergent patterns of neurological development. . . . These differences strongly suggest underlying systematic divergent developmental patterns in inter- and/or intrahemispheric cerebral organization." Myrianthopoulos (1975) also concluded that "concordance in twins in general for CNS [central nervous system] malformations is low." Hay and Wehrung (1970) similarly noted: "The literature on congenital CNS malformation contains many individual case reports of nonconcordant MZ [identical] pairs, the conclusion usually being that the genetic contribution to the etiology of these conditions is low." This low concordance rate for congenital anomalies of the brain is surprising in view of the fact that occasional cases of hydrocephaly are known to be genetically transmitted (Edwards, 1961); it suggests that the vast majority of brain anomalies are caused by prenatal environmental influences that selectively affect only one member of the identical twin pair.

There is one other aspect of congenital anomalies of the brain that is of interest in respect to schizophrenia. It is clearly established that an excess number (approximately 5 to 10%) of people who will later get schizophrenia are born in the winter and spring months (Bradbury & Miller, 1985; Boyd et al., 1986). The reason for this is unknown. In 1951 Record and McKeown analyzed their data on congenital anomalies of the central nervous system and reported that individuals with anencephaly (a type of congenital anomaly in which the brain does not develop) were born in a seasonal pattern, with a peak in the winter (November to February) and a low in the summer (May to July); the rate for December was 62% higher than that for May. Since their report, seven additional studies have replicated this seasonal pattern of anencephalic births, but three others have failed to find it (Bailar & Gurian, 1965; Wehrung & Hay, 1970). Hydrocephaly and spina bifida, other congenital anomalies of the central nervous system, show no seasonal birth pattern. Seasonal birth patterns with a winter-spring excess have also been shown for such congenital anomalies as cleft lip, congenital dysplasia of the hip, clubfoot, and hypospadias. It is possible that anencephaly or one of these other congenital anomalies with a winter-spring seasonal excess shares some etiological roots with schizophrenia.

CHAPTER 3

Methodology of the Study

THE IDEA for undertaking this study of identical twins emerged from a 1983 questionnaire distributed to members of the National Alliance for the Mentally Ill (NAMI). The questionnaire sought information on childhood illnesses of individuals who later developed schizophrenia. Among the more than 2,400 replies were 15 pairs of twins. NAMI, which had begun in 1979 as an organization for families of individuals with serious mental illnesses, had approximately 20,000 members at the time and was growing rapidly (it currently has over 140,000 members). Here was an opportunity that had not previously existed to recruit identical twins with schizophrenia and other serious mental illnesses for research purposes.

An application to study identical twins discordant for schizophrenia (one affected, one well) and normal controls (neither affected) was submitted to the National Institute of Mental Health in 1985. It was decided to focus only on identical twins as the most effective means for distinguishing nongenetic and genetic aspects of the disease. The review committee, composed of research psychiatrists and psychologists from university settings, requested that the application be revised to also include identical twins who were concordant (both affected) for schizophrenia. The initial grant was for 4 years, from 1987 through 1990; this was later extended through 1992, with an increase in the number of twins to be studied and the addition of identical twins discordant for bipolar disorder.

Major contributors to the diagnostic research in this chapter included Drs. Irving I. Gottesman and L. B. Bigelow.

Once identified, potential participants were sent detailed information about the research and the testing. If they were still interested, the twins were then asked to send photos of themselves from primary school, which could be used to assess probable zygosity. They were also requested to have their mothers fill out a brief questionnaire regarding how alike they were in appearance as children (e.g., "As children, did people say the twins looked like two peas in a pod?" "As children, were the twins often confused by people outside the family?"). The photos and questionnaires together were used by Irving Gottesman to make a preliminary assessment of zygosity, a method shown to have a high degree of accuracy (Cedorlof et al., 1961). All participants in the study had their zygosity confirmed by the typing of 19 red blood cell antigens (Lykken, 1978) during the study week. All twins who were assessed as being identical by photos and questionnaires were confirmed as being identical by red blood cell antigen analysis.

Potential participants who identified themselves as having schizophrenia or bipolar disorder were asked to sign a record release and have copies of their inpatient and outpatient psychiatric records sent to the investigators. After reviewing these records, a preliminary decision was made regarding the likelihood of the applicant's meeting standard DSM-III-R criteria (American Psychiatric Association, 1987) for these diagnoses. The well twins in the discordant pairs, all normal controls, and some of the affected twins were also asked to complete a Minnesota Multiphasic Personality Inventory (MMPI), which was used to assist with the preliminary diagnosis. Final diagnoses will be discussed later.

Recruitment and Selection Biases

Twins for the study were recruited almost exclusively through NAMI and its companion organization in Canada, the Canadian Friends of Schizophrenics (CFOS), which subsequently changed its name to the Schizophrenia Society of Canada. Additional recruitment was attempted by advertising the project in a professional journal and by using the Vietnam Era Twin Registry set up by the Veterans Administration. These additional attempts yielded only one twin pair for the study.

It should be noted that the present study was the first twin study of serious mental illnesses to recruit its subjects primarily through family organizations. The Scandinavian twin studies used national twin registries; the twin studies of Luxenburger, Rosanoff et al., Kallmann, Slater, and Gottesman and Shields used hospital admissions and hospital records; and the study by Pollin et al. recruited twins by soliciting referrals from psychiatrists in the community. Since the twins in this study were recruited differently from those in previous twin studies, the question arises whether there was any recruitment or selection bias.

One recruitment bias was socioeconomic. The membership of family organizations such as the National Alliance for the Mentally Ill and the Schizophrenia Society of Canada is predominantly middle and upper class; lower socioeconomic families rarely join such support and advocacy organizations. Thus it is not surprising that our sample was also predominantly middle and upper class. The 66 twin pairs who came to Washington to take part in the study were divided into 7 socioeconomic classes, based on their socioeconomic status during their childhood. The twins were distributed from class 1 (highest) to class 7 (lowest) as follows: 1: 15%; 2: 28%; 3: 26%; 4: 23%; 5: 7%; 6: 2%; 7: 0%.

Another recruitment bias was toward chronicity. Families that join support and advocacy organizations are more likely to have affected family members who are more severely and more chronically affected. The individual with schizophrenia who has a good recovery is less problematic for his or her family, so the family is less motivated to join these organizations. At the same time, there was a counterbalancing self-selection bias away from extreme severity of the illness, because the research protocol required affected individuals to be willing and able to travel and cooperate with extensive testing. Those with severe schizophrenia were often perceived by their families as being unable to cooperate with the testing, so the family usually withdrew from consideration in the early stages of discussion.

An important self-selection bias was toward affected individuals who had some insight into their illnesses. Approximately half of all people with schizophrenia have only limited insight and do not realize or acknowledge that they are sick. This is not surprising, since the brain, the organ we use to think about ourselves and assess our needs, is the same organ that is affected in schizophrenia and bipolar disorder. Thus, individuals who deny that they are ill are most unlikely to agree to participate in a research project that assumes they are ill. Not surprisingly, the majority of affected people who took part in the study had good insight into their illnesses, and many did so hoping that their participation would lead to a better understanding of the causes of these illnesses and to improved treatments.

Another self-selection bias was away from those with severe paranoid symptoms. Since individuals with paranoid schizophrenia often have delusions regarding people controlling their thoughts or implanting electrodes in their brains, it is not surprising that many with such symptoms would not agree to participate in extensive testing that included magnetic resonance imaging (MRI) scans, brain blood flow studies, and electroencephalographs (EEGs). The only person to withdraw from the study the day before he was scheduled to fly to Washington was someone with paranoid schizophrenia who was overwhelmed by his delusions.

We also became aware of self-selection factors operating on well twins in the discordant pairs. In virtually every such pair, the well twin conveyed some anxiety about also becoming sick. Many of the well twins who refused to participate in the study did so because they feared that the research would detect evidence of an impending illness in themselves. Some well twins also would not participate because they had hidden from their friends and colleagues the fact that their identical twin was mentally ill. Although stigma against serious mental illness has decreased markedly in recent years, it nonetheless remains an important impediment in research studies such as this. In addition, we were very impressed that the well twins who did agree to participate in the study were unusually altruistic; many of them said that they would agree to virtually any kind of testing if it might help their sick twin.

One additional type of the self-selection of participants was not anticipated by us. During the course of recruiting and selecting twins, five people whom we had identified as possible participants died. In one case the death was from natural causes, but in the other four it was from definite or probable suicide. The deaths served as a sad reminder that schizophrenia and bipolar disorder are very serious, and not infrequently fatal, illnesses (Caldwell & Gottesman, 1992).

In addition to the recruitment bias and self-selection of participants, there were also selection biases of the researchers. Affected individuals whose preliminary diagnosis was unclear, based on hospital records and MMPIs, were not invited to participate, nor were those with known major current drug and/or alcohol problems because of the possibility that these substances would make interpretation of their test results difficult. Also ruled out were twins with preexisting mental retardation, brain trauma, or known organic brain diseases that appeared to be related to the person's mental illness.

All together, during the 6 years of the study, approximately 150 pairs of identical twins and sets of identical triplets in which at least one member had schizophrenia or bipolar disorder were identified in the United States and Canada. Of these, 64 pairs of twins and 2 sets of triplets came to Washington to take part in the study. They came from 27 states, the District of Columbia, and 4 Canadian provinces.

*   *   *

The Problem of Normal Controls

From the inception of the study, it was planned to include identical twins in which both were normal, as controls for the twins in which one or both members were seriously mentally ill. What was not anticipated was how difficult it would be to define "normal" or to recruit identical twin volunteers who met that criterion.

Several recent studies have underscored this problem. In New York 121 volunteers responded to "newspaper advertisements and posted notices" to be normal volunteers "for biological studies" and passed a preliminary structured telephone interview designed to weed out those with any mental illnesses (Halbreich et al., 1989). However, when the volunteers underwent an extensive personal interview (Schedule for Affective Disorder and Schizophrenia [SADS]), 17% "met criteria for diagnoses of current mental disorders," another 36% had past histories of mental illness, and 39% had family histories of mental illness. In a similar study in Baltimore, 53% of volunteer normal controls who had passed a screening telephone interview were found to have a mental disorder (axis I or II by DSM-III-R criteria) on interview (Thaker et al., 1990).

In Columbus, Ohio, "of 51 volunteers who passed a phone screen, nine (17.6 percent) were excluded for major psychopathology" based on a structured interview and another "ten (28.6 percent) had subthreshold diagnoses" (Olson et al., 1990). Similarly, in Philadelphia, among the volunteers for a research project on brain function, 51% were excluded on a screening telephone interview "for having a history of psychiatric, neurologic or medical disease which might affect brain function"; of those remaining who were subsequently interviewed by a structured interview (Structured Clinical Interview for DSM-III-R: Non-Patient Version [SCID:NP]) 50% were similarly deselected (Shtasel et al., 1991). One is reminded of W. Somerset Maugham's comment in *The Summing Up* in which he says: "The normal is what you find but rarely. The normal is an ideal. It is a picture that one fabricates of the average characteristics of men, and to find them all in a single man is hardly to be expected" (Maugham, 1938, p. 20).

To obtain normal control twins for the present study, we initially placed a local newspaper advertisement. We too found considerable psychopathology when we screened the twin volunteers by a preliminary telephone interview and then a follow-up MMPI test. We ended up using only one normal control twin pair recruited in this manner. The other seven were recruited through word-of-mouth by the participating researchers (one pair), by twins who had participated in the study (three pairs), or by members of the National Alliance for the Mentally Ill (three pairs).

A final decision to include a normal control twin pair in the project was made only after they had undergone a SCID:NP for diagnoses on both axes I and II (Spitzer and Williams, 1986) with two experienced clinical psychiatrists (Drs. Torrey and Bigelow). Both clinicians agreed that none of these twins qualified for any diagnosis on axis I or II, and, in fact, they were judged to be remarkably normal, if by normality one means an absence of psychopathology. On the MMPI Dr. Gottesman concurred that none of the normal twins showed evidence of any axis I psychopathology. In 8 of the 16 individual normal twins, he found MMPI evidence suggestive of various traits (paranoid, narcissistic, passive-aggressive, hypomanic, or homosexual), but these were thought to be within normal limits for a control population.

A Week in the Life of the Twin Study

The first twins came to Washington to take part in the study in May 1987, and the final pair came in February 1992. All travel and lodging expenses were covered, they were given a daily per diem for meals, and in some cases they were reimbursed for lost wages, but they were not paid for participating per se.

Twins who arrived in Washington by air or train were met by one of three driver-escorts (NAMI members), who participated over the entire length of the study. The driver-escorts transported the twins to all tests, took them sight-seeing between tests, and generally tried to ensure that they enjoyed their time in Washington. When research funds were sufficient, we also treated them to a social event (a concert or sports event) one evening during their stay. They were housed in a suite with a fully furnished kitchen in the Executive Club Hotel in Arlington, Virginia, a short ride from downtown Washington. Twins were encouraged to bring along other family members to stay with them if they wished, although the study could not pay for their transportation.

The testing was done Monday through Thursday, with Friday used as a backup day in case of testing equipment problems (such as the MRI) or other unforeseen complications. On Monday neuropsychological testing, a videotaped Structured Clinical Interview for DSM-III-R (SCID), neurological examinations, and fingerprinting were done. As part of the interview, an assessment of negative symptoms was done using the Scales for the Assessment of Negative Symptoms (SANS) (Andreasen, 1981). On Tuesday blood was drawn and MRI scans and eye-tracking tests were conducted. On Wednesday EEGs and an examination for minor physical anomalies were done, and blood was drawn using a special technique (aphoresis) that selectively collects lymphocytes and plasma. On Thursday cerebral blood flow studies were conducted using single photon emission computed tomography (SPECT) in the earlier months of the study and positron emission tomography (PET) in the later months. In addition to these standard tests, some twins were asked to consider having a lumbar puncture as an elective procedure. A total of 12 twin pairs (9 discordant and 3 concordant) had this procedure. All research protocols were reviewed by an institutional review board, and the twins (and, in cases where competency was questionable, a parent) signed informed consents for each procedure.

Of the 64 pairs of twins and 2 sets of triplets who came to participate in the study, all except 2 twin pairs were able to complete the testing. They were both concordant twin pairs, in which one was too sick to cooperate (in one case, an affected twin had stopped taking medication two weeks earlier).

The most remarkable aspect of the testing was the extraordinary motivation shown by the participants despite having, in some cases, severe symptoms. Three hours of neuropsychological testing, going without smoking for three hours before blood flow studies, and lying motionless in an MRI scanner for 45 minutes are difficult for people whose brains are functioning normally; for someone with severe schizophrenia or bipolar disorder, completing these tasks approaches the heroic. One measure of the motivation of the participants was the fact that every one of the 130 individuals who were tested (62 twin pairs and 2 sets of triplets) successfully completed an MRI scan.

Bringing this number of seriously mentally ill people to Washington for testing was not without problems. One twin with paranoid schizophrenia, who routinely carries plumbing tools in order to disconnect water supplies suspected of being contaminated, had major problems with metal detectors at the airport security. Another, who carries weapons for delusional reasons, set off the metal detector during a visit to the White House and was quickly surrounded by Secret Service agents. Still another, coming from Canada with no identification, was detained by immigration officials after proudly announcing that he had schizophrenia and was going to Washington for testing. One twin pair and their driver-escort narrowly avoided becoming stranded for 24 hours on a snowbound bridge during a severe snowstorm. The resourcefulness of the driver-escorts, a well-functioning research team, and some luck were all important at these times.

Developmental Histories

Extensive information was collected on the mothers' pregnancies and deliveries; on the twins' developmental, medical, and school histories; and on their family history. Much of this information was obtained by sending a 57-page questionnaire to the mothers or other family members (in two twin pairs their mother had died, and a third pair had been adopted) prior to their participation in the program. Three-quarters of the twins' mothers were also brought to Washington at the time of testing, and the twins' perinatal and developmental data were personally reviewed with them by a senior social worker (Edward H. Taylor). In those cases in which the mother did not come to Washington, the review of perinatal and developmental factors was done by telephone interview. In approximately one-third of the twin pairs, the fathers also accompanied them to Washington at their own expense and were available to supplement the information obtained from the mother. Families were encouraged to bring school records, documents related to the twins' development, and other family records that might be helpful; pertinent ones were photocopied and used to supplement the developmental histories.

Additional information on the development and personality traits of the twins was obtained by having mothers fill out a Personality Inventory for Children (PIC) (Wirt et al., 1981), a 600-item questionnaire described in Appendix D. Each twin also completed a Multidimensional Personality Questionnaire (MPQ) (Tellegen, 1982) at the time of testing, and for well twins, this was supplemented by information from the MMPI, which they had completed previously. Finally, each twin and their mother were asked to complete a questionnaire independently, comparing the twins on 40 personality traits or behaviors for the period covering primary school and the period covering secondary school (e.g., "Which twin got upset more easily?" "Which twin tended to be the leader and tell the other twin what to do?"). Having this rating done by each of the three individuals allowed us to compare their perspectives and to resolve discrepancies in the developmental histories.

The question of accuracy arises in this study—as it does in all studies using retrospective information—regarding the information obtained from the mothers. At least four studies of this question have been carried out, checking histories provided by mothers against known facts that had been independently collected. It has been found that the accuracy of mothers' recollections is highest for quantifiable data such as the child's weight at birth or when the child first walked (Haggard et al., 1960; Goddard et al., 1961). Such behavioral traits as personality characteristics, however, are less accurately recalled (Small et al., 1984). Least accurately recalled by the mother are child-rearing practices, especially when the maternal practices conflicted with the recommendations of standard child-rearing manuals (Robbins, 1963).

No study has been done on the accuracy of maternal recall for identical twins. One might expect that such recall would be improved by having a built-in genetic control twin to act as a baseline for comparisons. On the other hand, in twin pairs in which one twin later becomes sick, the maternal retrospective recall may be distorted by the illness. For these reasons, we sought objective confirmatory information whenever possible.

Final Diagnostic Groups

The final study group of twins who completed the testing consisted of 62 twin pairs and 2 sets of triplets. In one set of triplets, one person was too severely ill to complete the majority of tests; the other two members of this triplet set were included as a pair concordant for schizophrenia (CS-9; see also Chapter 11). In the other set of triplets, one member was diagnosed with schizophrenia, another was well, and the third was thought to have a schizotypal personality disorder at the time of testing; he subsequently became concordant (see Chapter 11). The first two members of this triplet set were included in the study as a pair discordant for schizophrenia (DS-25). For purposes of simplification, the two members of the two triplet sets used in the study will be referred to as "twins."

Altogether, then, 64 twin pairs (including the pairs from the 2 sets of triplets) were included in the study. Final diagnostic groups are detailed in Appendix A and summarized in Table 3.1. Study findings are based on analysis of the data on the groups discordant for schizophrenia, discordant for bipolar disorder, concordant for schizophrenia, and the normal controls. The 8 pairs in the "other" category included twins with a variety of diagnoses such that the pair did not fit cleanly into the discordant or concordant categories at the time of testing and thus were not included in the analyses.

Final diagnoses were arrived at by consensus of the two senior psychiatrists (Drs. Bigelow and Torrey), who did the Structured Clinical Interview for DSM-III-R. Also taken into consideration in arriving at a final diagnosis was the individual's past inpatient and outpatient psychiatric records (in some cases this included telephone interviews with the treating clinicians), interviews with the co-twins and mothers regarding the person's symptoms, the results of the Minnesota Multiphasic Personality Inventory

TABLE 3.1
Final Diagnostic Groups

	Number of Pairs	Mean Age at Time of Testing (range)	Sex (M/F)	Race (Caucasian/ Black/ Hispanic)	Family History for Psychosis	Mean Years Discordant for Illness (as of 3/93)
Discordant for schizophrenia (DS)	27	31 (17–44)	16/11	26/1/0	7/26 (1 unknown)	14.0 (5–30)
Discordant for bipolar disorder (DB)	8	34 (21–52)	1/7	8/0/0	4/8	14.9 (5–30)
Concordant for schizophrenia (CS)	13	30 (22–41)	10/3	10/1/2	2/13	—
Normal controls (N)	8	31 (19–44)	3/5	7/1/0	2/8	—
Other (O)	8	33 (19–50)	6/2	7/1/0	3/8	—

(MMPI), and our informal observations of the twins as we worked with them during the testing. We found informal time spent with the twins often to be as valuable as the more formal time; for example, a subtle thought disorder was sometimes more evident in negotiating to buy popcorn at a baseball game than it was in the structured clinical interview.

The 27 affected twins in the group discordant for schizophrenia included the following clinical subtypes: 11 undifferentiated, 8 paranoid, 3 disorganized, 1 residual, and 4 schizoaffective disorder. Their mean age of onset, defined as the age at which they were first referred to a mental health professional for symptoms related to their developing illness, was 21.1 years (range 11–31). Two of the discordant affected twins (DS-18 and DS-23) had atypical forms of schizophrenia, although they met DSM-III-R criteria for the diagnosis. Two other discordant affected twins had sustained possible brain trauma (DS-7 had possible meningitis or encephalitis in infancy; DS-17 had a severe head injury 10 years prior to the onset of illness). One discordant well twin (DS-8) had sustained anoxia in infancy due to congenital pulmonary stenosis requiring corrective open-heart surgery.

The group discordant for bipolar disorder included 7 affected twins who met criteria for a subtype of bipolar disorder and one (DB-4) whose diagnosis was recurrent major depression with mood-congruent psychotic features. The problem of differentiating such individuals from those diagnosed with schizoaffective disorder will be discussed in Chapter 10. One of the well twins in the discordant bipolar group was born with cerebral palsy.

The Well Co-Twins

How well are the well twins in the discordant groups and what are the chances of some of them becoming sick? It was our intention to keep the discordant groups as diagnostically clean as possible. For that reason twin pairs such as O-2 (well twin diagnosed with personality disorder NOS) and O-3 (well twin diagnosed with schizoid personality disorder) were not included in the discordant group. The only well twins in the discordant groups who, according to the consensus diagnoses of Drs. Torrey and Bigelow, met DSM-III-R criteria for axis I or axis II diagnoses were DS-10 (antisocial personality disorder based on teenage behavior), DS-12 (one past episode of major depression following a major life trauma and a simple phobia for giving blood), DS-13 (developmental disorder NOS in childhood), DB-6 (personality disorder NOS), and DB-8 (avoidant personality disorder). There was a fine line between excluding O-2 and including

DB-6 and DB-8, but the decision rested on the fact that the personality profile of O-2 included some schizotypal features, whereas the profiles of DB-6 and DB-8 did not. In addition, Dr. Gottesman, utilizing MMPI profiles and a review of the videotaped SCID interviews, assigned the following diagnoses to various well co-twins: paranoid personality disorder, antisocial personality disorder, dysthymic disorder and obsessive-compulsive personality disorder, schizotypal personality disorder, antisocial personality disorder, and dysthymic disorder. These additional diagnoses were not supported by Drs. Torrey and Bigelow.

In assessing the well twins in the discordant groups, it is acknowledged that as a group, they exhibited more personality quirks and idiosyncracies than were seen in the normal controls. In selecting the normal controls, we had the luxury of being able to reject any pair in which either twin showed any evidence of such quirks or idiosyncracies on telephone interview or MMPI. The well discordant twins, however, were accepted into the study if the initial information suggested that they probably did not meet criteria for any axis I or axis II diagnosis. There was, in effect, a lower threshold for "normality" among the well twins in the discordant pairs than there was for the normal controls, with the latter more aptly described as "supernormals." The well twins in the discordant groups more closely represent the wide continuum of individuals functioning in the general population.

What are the chances that some of the well twins in the discordant pairs will become sick in the future and the pair will thus become concordant? One pair of twins who had been discordant at the time of their initial participation in the study did in fact become concordant two years later (for a description of this pair, see CS-10 in Chapter 9). The mean number of years that had elapsed since the first twins became sick until the close of the study among our 27 twin pairs discordant for schizophrenia was 14.0 years (range 5–30 years). The comparable figure for the 8 pairs discordant for bipolar disorder was 14.9 years (range 5–30 years). Past follow-up studies of identical twins discordant for schizophrenia have established that the majority of those who do become concordant do so within 5 years following the onset of illness in the first twin (Gottesman & Shields 1972; Belmaker et al., 1974). It seems statistically unlikely, therefore, that more than one or two currently discordant pairs will become concordant. Since we maintain contact with the twins through a newsletter and by personal contact, we would probably find out if this were to happen.

Regarding the concordant for schizophrenia group, it should be noted that in three pairs, one of the twins was diagnosed with schizophrenia and another was diagnosed with schizotypal personality disorder. This is because the three individuals with schizotypal personality disorder technically did not meet full DSM-III-R criteria for schizophrenia at the time of testing, although the evidence strongly suggested that they would have met these criteria if additional data had been available. One of the twins diagnosed with schizotypal personality disorder had had catatonic and bizarre behavior, delusions, markedly blunted affect, probable hallucinations, and six psychiatric hospitalizations, but there was contradictory information regarding his bizarre delusions and hallucinations, so he technically did not meet the full criteria for schizophrenia. Another of the twins diagnosed with schizotypal personality disorder was said to have had paranoid delusions, tangential thought processes, visual hallucinations, probable auditory hallucinations, and one psychiatric hospitalization, but he denied most of these symptoms. The third individual was extremely guarded and suspicious, had blunted affect, mild loosening of associations, an unusual use of words, and had been observed by his family responding to voices, although he denied this. He had been evaluated psychiatrically as an outpatient but had never been hospitalized. On psychological testing (MMPI), he was diagnosed with paranoid and schizoid personality disorder and was judged to be making an obvious effort to minimize his symptoms. Following his participation in the study, his psychotic symptoms became more prominent and he was subsequently treated with antipsychotic medication.

Substance Abuse

Substance abuse was assessed by taking a careful history and by asking the twins independently to compare their own intake with that of their twin. Most twin pairs in this study were teenagers in the 1960s and 1970s, when substance abuse within that age group was at a maximum. Thus it is not surprising that many of the twins in the study met DSM-III-R criteria for past substance abuse, especially cannabis (marijuana). Among the 35 twin pairs in the discordant groups, neither twin in 11 pairs reported using alcohol other than taking an occasional drink or smoking marijuana more than five times. In another 11 pairs, one or both reported using alcohol or drugs more than the minimal amount, but neither met DSM-III-R criteria for abuse or dependence. In the remaining 13 twin pairs, one or both had met DSM-III-R criteria for substance abuse or dependence, most frequently for cannabis abuse during high school years, as follows:

AFFECTED TWIN	WELL TWIN
Amphetamine dependence	Sedative dependence
Cannabis abuse	Cannabis and hallucinogen abuse
Cannabis and alcohol dependence	Cannabis dependence
None	Amphetamine dependence
Alcohol dependence	None
Cannabis and amphetamine abuse	Cannabis, amphetamine, and opioid abuse
Cannabis and alcohol dependence	Cannabis and alcohol dependence
Cannabis dependence	Cannabis dependence
Cannabis dependence	Cannabis dependence
Alcohol and mixed substance dependence	Alcohol dependence
Alcohol dependence	Alcohol dependence
Alcohol dependence	None
Alcohol and amphetamine dependence	Amphetamine abuse

All the reports of substance abuse were in the past except for one twin pair in which both were still dependent on cannabis, one well twin who was alcohol dependent, and another well twin who was suspected of being alcohol dependent.

An important question when considering substance abuse in identical twins discordant for schizophrenia or bipolar disorder is which twin was the heavier user. Among the 11 twin pairs whose substance abuse was reported to be more than minimal but which did not meet diagnostic criteria for abuse or dependence, the affected twin was the heavier user in 2 pairs, the well twin was the heavier user in 2 pairs, and their use was approximately equal in 7 pairs. Among the 13 twin pairs in which one or both met criteria for abuse or dependence, the affected twin was the heavier user in 6 pairs, the well twin was the heavier user in 3 pairs, and their use was approximately equal in 4 pairs. In only 2 twin pairs did substance abuse increase substantially around the time of the onset of illness, and in both cases there was evidence suggesting that early symptoms of illness had begun prior to the increase in their substance abuse.

Family History

Information regarding family history of mental illnesses was collected both by questionnaires and by interviews with the mothers. Special attention was paid to cases in which either a first-degree relative (mother, father, brother, or sister) or a second-degree relative (grandparent, aunt, or uncle) had a history of serious mental illness. On the basis of the information available, these histories were judged to have been either definite (e.g., a person having been hospitalized and diagnosed with schizophrenia) or probable (e.g., a person having had a nonspecific "nervous breakdown" and brief hospitalization).

The number of first-degree or second-degree relatives with a history of definite or probable psychosis was as follows:

TWIN GROUPS	NO. AND % WITH POSITIVE FAMILY HISTORY	
Discordant for schizophrenia		
(1 with family history unavailable)	7/26	27%
Discordant for bipolar disorder	4/8	50%
Concordant for schizophrenia	2/13	15%
Normal controls	2/8	25%
Other	3/8	38%

These data will be discussed further in Chapter 4.

Medication Status

Participants in the twin study were not asked to discontinue their medication for the period of testing because that would have been untherapeutic and would also have severely limited the number who would have been able to participate. Consequently, most of the twins with a diagnosis of schizophrenia or bipolar disorder were taking antipsychotic medication at the time of testing. There were nine affected twins, however, who were not taking antipsychotic medication at the time of testing and had been free of such medication for the following periods:

Discordant for schizophrenia:
    DS-11   2 months
    DS-18   3 years
Discordant for bipolar disorder:
    DB-4   3 months
    DB-8   1 year
Concordant for schizophrenia:
    CS-7 (one twin)   5 years
    CS-12 (one twin)   2 years
    CS-13 (one twin)   5 years

Other:
    O-6 (one twin)   never medicated
    O-7 (one twin)   3–6 months

Current and lifetime total antipsychotic medication intake were calculated for all affected twins. All antipsychotic medications were converted to fluphenazine equivalent units using published recommendations for conversion (Torrey, 1988, p. 188; Inderbitzin et al., 1989). The lifetime total antipsychotic medication intake varied widely among affected twins, ranging from 100 mg to 223,000 mg fluphenazine equivalents.

All affected twins were also questioned regarding past treatment with electroconvulsive therapy (ECT), also known as electroshock therapy. Nine individuals had had previous ECT: 3 discordant for schizophrenia, 0 discordant for bipolar disorder, 4 concordant for schizophrenia (including both members of one twin pair), and 2 in the other diagnosis group.

Statistical Methodology

All data were entered onto a VAX 11/750 computer and analyzed using the Statistical Analysis Software package. In accordance with the study design, data analysis focused on group differences between four independent twin groups: (1) pairs discordant for schizophrenia, (2) pairs discordant for bipolar disorder, (3) pairs concordant for schizophrenia, and (4) normal control pairs. The lack of normality in the within-group distributions of many of the variables of interest suggested the use of nonparametric tests of significance. Two-group comparisons of continuous variables were tested using the Wilcoxon rank sum test or Wilcoxon-Mann-Whitney test, and the differences in observed frequencies of discrete variables were tested using chi-square tests or Fisher's exact test (two-tailed) when the small size of the samples dictated.

Within-pair analyses of the discordant groups were also extensively performed to determine differences between the affected and well twins that could be of etiologic importance. These results were tested for significance using paired t tests, Wilcoxon matched-pairs test, and McNemar's test for matched pairs. Correlations of the findings from various tests were examined to look for relationships that might suggest clinical or etiological subgroups. The correlations were expressed by Spearman rank correlation coefficients or Pearson correlation coefficients and tested for significance by probability values based on the t distribution. Analysis of variance for more than two groups was done using ANOVA and Tukey's studentized range test. Other statistical tests, such as the Jonckheere test for ordered alternatives, were used in special situations. Problems of simultaneous inferences were interpreted by applying the Bonferroni corrective methods.

Information from in-depth case histories of the biographical and clinical findings of each twin participant complemented the quantitative data presented.

CHAPTER 4

When Does Schizophrenia Originate?

T HE IDEA that some cases of schizophrenia originate in events that take place prior to birth or during the delivery of the individual is not a new one. Genes were claimed by many researchers to be important contributors to the cause of schizophrenia in the earliest years of this century. The effects of chemicals and infectious agents, specifically alcohol and syphilis, on the developing fetus were proposed as possible causative factors for schizophrenia by Emil Kraepelin (1919, p. 235). The occurrence of minor physical anomalies, including "malformation of the cranium and of the ears, high and narrow palate . . . [and] deformation of the fingers and toes" (ibid., p. 236) were also cited by Kraepelin as proof that some cases of schizophrenia have prenatal roots. And as early as 1934, "cerebral trauma at birth" was said to contribute to "a large proportion of cases of schizophrenia" by Aaron Rosanoff and his colleagues (Rosanoff et al. 1934).

There has been a recent resurgence of interest in the role played by early developmental processes in the causation of schizophrenia. Neuropathological and neuroradiological studies suggest that many cases of schizophrenia may begin early in life. Past and present studies of minor physical anomalies, dermatoglyphics, and obstetrical complications, to be reviewed

Contributing to the research discussed in this chapter were Drs. Llewellyn B. Bigelow, Particia O. Quinn, H. Stefan Bracha, Thomas F. McNeil, Karin Sjostrom, Ned Higgins, Kenneth C. Rickler, Terry E. Goldberg, James M. Gold, J. Daniel Ragland, and Mihael Polymeropoulos, and Ms. Elizabeth Cantor-Graae.

shortly, also point in this direction. Reports of an increased incidence of schizophrenia among children whose mothers had been exposed to the influenza virus during their pregnancies have also stimulated interest in the prenatal period (Mednick et al., 1988; Barr et al., 1990; O'Callaghan, Sham, et al., 1991). Recent research has suggested that even severe nutritional deficiency during pregnancy may sometimes be related to the causation of later schizophrenia in the offspring (Susser & Lin, 1992).

This chapter examines the identical twins with schizophrenia to determine whether some cases of this disease may indeed originate prior to birth or during delivery. The markers that were studied included genes, minor physical anomalies, finger ridge counts, birth weights, obstetrical complications, and handedness.

Genes and Family History

There is probably no researcher currently studying schizophrenia who does not believe that genes play *some* role in the causation of this disease. As summarized in Chapter 1, the major raison d'être for most previous twin studies of schizophrenia was to ascertain precisely how large an etiological role genes play. Genetic theories have included dominant, recessive, sex-linked, and polygenic models, and these have been thought to interact with such environmental factors as cerebral trauma, infections, anoxia, and stress. Genetic-linkage studies of schizophrenia are currently one of the most generously funded areas of research because it is hoped that such studies will lead to the identification of one or more disease-related genes such as have been found in Huntington's disease.

The present study of identical twins was not intended to be a genetic study of schizophrenia. On the contrary, the inclusion of identical twins discordant for schizophrenia is a strategy designed to minimize genetic contributions in order to identify possible nongenetic causes. Nevertheless, some twins who volunteered for the study did have a family history of schizophrenia or other serious mental illnesses, and it is important to ask whether these twins were different in any way.

As discussed in Chapter 3, the family history for serious mental illnesses was ascertained both by questionnaires filled out by the parents and by direct inquiries during interviews with them. The parents were asked to provide information on all mental illnesses that had occurred among the twins' first-degree (mother, father, brothers, and sisters) and second-degree (aunts, uncles, and grandparents) relatives. Since hospital records of relatives who had been hospitalized were not obtained, presumptive diagnoses were made on the basis of the information supplied by the families. Initially, an attempt was made to have all of the twins' first-degree relatives complete a Minnesota Multiphasic Personality Inventory (MMPI) in order to identify individuals with a schizotypal personality or other schizophrenia spectrum disorders, but this proved to be too intrusive and was therefore abandoned.

Analysis of the family data was done by counting as family history positive any family member with a history of definite or probable schizophrenia, bipolar disorder, or other psychoses (e.g., postpartum psychosis) that did not appear to be caused by known organic factors (e.g., a grandmother with the onset of depression, confusion, and psychotic symptoms at age 76 was not included). The results are shown in Table 4.1.

Among twin pairs discordant or concordant for schizophrenia, 23% (9 of 39) had a family history for psychosis. This is somewhat lower than the 38% (15 of 40) of identical twins with a family history of psychosis reported in Kringlen's (1967) twin study. The low rate of positive family history among the concordant twins (15%, or 2 of 13) is surprising, since Kringlen reported a positive family history in 54% (7 of 13) of his twins concordant for schizophrenia.

The reported percentage of individuals with a family history for schizophrenia or other serious mental illnesses in any study depends on several factors. The most important is ascertainment, and personal diagnostic interviews of all family members will identify cases of serious mental illness that are missed by questionnaires alone. A second factor is the breadth of definition of serious mental illness that is used. Still another factor is the size of the families, with very large families having potentially more psychotic members just on the basis of their numbers; for example, a family with 10 children has 10 times more chance of one of them getting sick than a family with one child. The 26 twin pairs discordant for schizophrenia in our study with known family histories had a mean of 2.4 full brothers and sisters, whereas the 13 concordant twin pairs had a mean of 1.5 full brothers and sisters; thus, having fewer siblings may account in part for the lower number of concordant twins with a positive family history for psychosis. Finally, the rates of positive family history may be biased by self-selection. For example, it is possible that in our study, families with multiple occurrences of psychoses (both twins having schizophrenia and other family members also being mentally ill) might have been less inclined to volunteer for the study because of the stigma associated with these illnesses.

Despite possible limitations in ascertainment and possible self-selection of the participants, it is nevertheless useful to separate the twin pairs discordant for schizophrenia into those with and those without a family history of psychosis and to ask whether there are differences between the two groups. Many researchers assume that a division of schizophrenia into "familial" and "sporadic" (nonfamilial) groups will ultimately yield clues to the cause of the disease (Lewis, Reveley, et al., 1987), although others doubt the usefulness of this strategy (Farmer et al., 1990).

Comparing the 7 pairs discordant for schizophrenia with a family his-

TABLE 4.1
*Family History for Schizophrenia, Bipolar Disorder,
or Other Psychoses*

Diagnostic Group	Number of Pairs Positive	Percentage of Pairs Positive
Discordant for schizophrenia		
(1 unknown)	7/26	26
father with schizophrenia		
father with schizophrenia		
aunt with schizophrenia		
aunt with schizophrenia		
brother and uncle with		
bipolar disorder		
uncle with bipolar disorder		
aunt hospitalized with		
2 "nervous breakdowns"		
Discordant for bipolar disorder	4/8	50
mother with bipolar disorder		
sister with bipolar disorder		
uncle with schizophrenia		
aunt with postpartum psychosis		
Concordant for schizophrenia	2/13	15
grandmother with schizophrenia		
and aunt with bipolar disorder		
grandmother with bipolar disorder		
Normal controls	2/8	25
brother with schizophrenia		
mother with bipolar disorder		
Other twin pairs	3/8	38
sister with schizophrenia		
uncle with schizophrenia		
brother with psychotic depression		

tory of psychosis to the 19 discordant pairs with no apparent family history of psychosis (Table 4.2), no differences were found in sex, race, or age at time of testing. There were also minimal differences between the affected members of these two groups on such clinical measures as age of first referral, acuteness of onset, negative symptoms, neurological abnormalities, total time psychiatrically hospitalized, lifetime antipsychotic

TABLE 4.2
*Family History, Minor Physical Anomalies, Total Finger Ridge Count,
Birth Weight, Obstetrical Complications,
and Non-Right-Handedness*

DS-	FH	MPA	TFRC	BW	OC	NRH
1					OC	
2	FH	MPA				
3						
4	FH					
5		MPA	TFRC		OC	
6						
7			TFRC		OC	
8						
9		[—]				
10						
11			TFRC			
12						
13			TFRC			
14						
15						
16					OC	
17	FH	MPA	TFRC	BW		NRH
18		MPA	TFRC	BW	OC	NRH
19						
20						
21			TFRC	[-]	[-]	
22	FH	MPA				NRH
23	FH		TFRC		OC	
24	FH	MPA		BW		
25						
26	FH					
27	[-]		TFRC	BW	OC	NRH

FH: Family history positive for psychosis in first- or second-degree relative. MPA: Minor physical anomaly score for affected twin is $\geq$ 2 pts. higher than for well twin. TFRC: Total finger ridge count for affected twin is $\geq$ 12% different from well twin. BW: Affected twin was $\geq$ 20% lighter at birth. OC: Total score for obstetrical complications for affected twin was $\geq$ 5 pts. higher than for well twin. NHR: Affected twin is non-right-handed. [-]: Data not available.

intake, or level of function at the time of testing (as measured by axis V on DSM-III-R). The only clinical measure for which there was even a trend toward differences in these two groups was a higher frequency of having an average or better response to antipsychotic medication in the affected twins with a family history of psychosis ($p = .13$, Fisher's exact test).

When the 7 discordant pairs with a family history of psychosis were compared with the 19 pairs with no such history on measures of possible genetic or perinatal liability, the results were as follows. No association was found between family history and total finger ridge counts, birth weight, total obstetrical complication scores, or non-right-handedness. However, the group with a family history of psychosis had a significantly higher average minor physical anomaly score (7.3 vs. 5.1; $p = .05$, Wilcoxon rank sum test). This association could be explained by a gene or group of genes that cause both the symptoms of schizophrenia and the minor physical anomalies (in which case the anomalies would be genetic markers for the disease), or by a gene or group of genes that act as a predisposing factor for an environmental agent (e.g., a virus), which then causes both the disease and the anomalies.

In addition to looking at family history of psychosis, studies of the twins' genes are also being carried out. Although identical twins begin life with identical sets of genes following the initial cleavage of the zygote (as discussed in Chapter 3), it is possible for DNA changes to take place during subsequent development, resulting in the addition or subtraction of DNA on the genes of one twin but not the other. These DNA changes can be identified in the laboratory using minisatellite probes that identify such differences.

In the present study, lymphocytes were collected from all twins and subsequently frozen. A total of 94 minisatellite probes covering all chromosomes were tested on 5 pairs of twins discordant for schizophrenia, as well as on the normal controls. Results so far have found no differences in the genes of the twins (Polymeropoulos et al., 1993). These studies are continuing.

Minor Physical Anomalies

Minor physical anomalies are nonobvious but measurable physical features of the head, hands, and feet thought to be produced by events occurring *in utero*, especially in the first trimester of pregnancy. Examples of such anomalies include low-set ears, a steepled palate, epicanthal eye folds, a curved fifth finger, a wide space between the first and second toes, and the third toe being longer than the second (see Figure 4.1). Occasional minor physical anomalies are found in normal persons, but the association of frequent anomalies with disorders of the central nervous system has been noted since 1902, when Still reported a high incidence of anomalies in a group of hyperactive children. Such an association is not surprising, since both the central nervous system and the tissues in which anomalies are found derive embryonically from the ectodermal cell layer, so both would have developed at the same time.

In recent years there have been five reports of minor physical anomalies occurring excessively in individuals with adult onset schizophrenia and four reports concerning childhood onset schizophrenia and autism. Gualtieri et al. (1982) compared 64 adult inpatients with schizophrenia to 95 normal controls (said to have been "recruited from a variety of locations") and found that the inpatients had a higher mean weighted score ($p < .01$), results that the authors called "quite striking." Guy et al. (1983) compared 40 adults with schizophrenia to published data on normal controls and reported that the affected individuals had a higher mean anomaly score ($p < .001$); an actual control group was not examined in this study. Green et al. (1987) and Green, Satz, Gaier, et al. (1989) compared 67 adult inpatients with schizophrenia to 88 hospital employees and university students and found the mean anomaly score to be significantly higher in the individuals with schizophrenia ($p < .001$). Sharma and Lal (1986) compared anomaly scores for 80 inpatients with schizophrenia to 100 "relatives of the patients who were not known to suffer from any psychiatric or physical illness"; the patients with schizophrenia had significantly higher scores ($p < .005$), with the difference being more marked in female than in male patients. Finally, Lane et al. (1993) compared minor physical anomalies in 58 individuals with schizophrenia and 18 controls and reported that such anomalies were more numerous among the former ($p < .001$).

Among children, Goldfarb (1967) measured anomalies in 29 children ages 6 to 10 with schizophrenia and compared them to 76 normal children within the same age range; he reported that "the schizophrenic children showed a significantly higher mean number of stigmata." Steg and Rapoport (1975) studied 28 children in residential treatment centers with diagnoses of autism, childhood schizophrenia, borderline psychosis, and "atypical child" and compared them to 57 children on a pediatric ward and in a child guidance clinic; the psychotic children had significantly higher mean anomaly scores ($p < .01$). Walker (1977) compared 74 autistic children to an equal number of age- and sex-matched controls and found that the autistic children had more anomalies ($p < .001$). Finally, Campbell et al. (1978) examined 52 autistic chil-

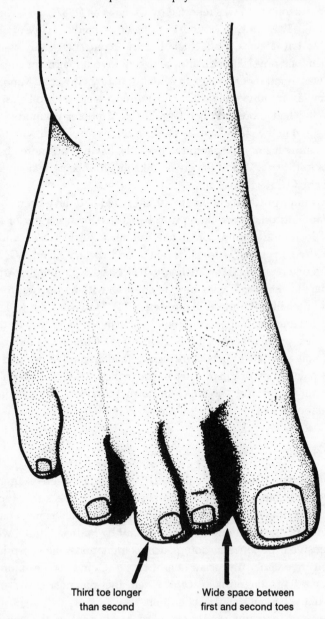

FIGURE 4.1
Examples of minor physical anomalies of the toes.

Third toe longer
than second

Wide space between
first and second toes

dren and 29 normal controls and reported higher anomaly scores for the former group ($p < .05$).

Several findings in the studies of adults are also of interest. An association between the presence of minor physical anomalies and an earlier age of onset for schizophrenia was reported by Green et al. (1987) and Green, Satz, Gaier, et al. (1989) but not found in three other studies (Guy et al., 1983; Sharma & Lal, 1986; O'Callaghan, Larkin, et al., 1991). An association between minor physical anomalies and cognitive impairment in problem solving was found by O'Callaghan et al. but not by Guy et al. Minor physical anomalies in individuals with schizophrenia were said to be associated with having had more childhood problems (a poorer premorbid adjustment, $p < .05$) in the study by Guy et al. and to be associated with having a positive family history for psychosis ($p < .01$), having had more obstetrical complications ($p < .01$), and the greater likelihood of being male ($p < .05$) in the study by O'Callaghan et al.

Many minor physical anomalies are inherited and have been shown to run in families; others are thought to be caused by a variety of *in utero* changes including chromosomal aberrations (e.g., Down's syndrome), infections (e.g., rubella), anoxia, toxemia, and dietary factors. Of special interest is one report of 22 women who had bleeding in the first trimester of pregnancy; of these, 17 gave birth to children with high scores for minor physical anomalies (Quinn & Rapoport, 1974). However, the widespread assumption that anomalies are related exclusively to events in the first trimester of pregnancy has been challenged. Cummings et al. (1982) claimed that anomalies such as increased head circumference and a high steepled palate may originate later in pregnancy. There are no published data on minor physical anomalies in normal identical twins or in twins with schizophrenia.

Present Study

Of the 64 twin pairs in the study, all except 2 pairs were examined for minor physical anomalies. These 2 pairs were omitted because of scheduling problems (they were a discordant pair and a normal control pair). All the examinations except one were carried out by Patricia Quinn, who had had extensive experience in doing such examinations; the exception was examined by another physician taught by Dr. Quinn. The examiner was blind regarding diagnosis, except when the diagnosis was obvious because of the patient's clinical condition.

The examination included a standard assessment of the hair whorl, head circumference, eyes, ears, palate, tongue, fingers, and toes for anomalies (Waldrop et al., 1968). Each item was scored as 0 (normal), 1 (slightly abnormal), or 2 (clearly abnormal), with the maximum possible score being 24. It should be emphasized that many normal people have one or more minor physical anomalies, often inherited from parents or grand-parents, and by themselves such anomalies have no pathological signifi-cance.

The average minor physical anomaly scores for each of the diagnostic groups examined were as follows:

	No. of Twins	Mean Score
Discordant for schizophrenia, affected	26	5.65
Discordant for schizophrenia, well	26	5.23
Concordant for schizophrenia	26	4.85
Normal controls	16	4.57

The most striking aspect of these minor physical anomaly scores for twins is that they are higher than the scores reported for non-twin populations. In studies of non-twins, scores above 4 are usually considered to be abnor-mal (Gualtieri et al., 1982; Guy et al., 1983), yet in the present study the mean score for the normal control twins is 4.57. This suggests that twin-ning itself is associated with increased numbers of minor physical anom-alies.

In the present study, statistical analysis showed no group difference in scores for the affected discordant twins, the concordant twins, and the nor-mal control twins ($F = 1.35$, $p = .27$, one-way ANOVA), and no within-pair difference for the affected and well twins in the discordant pairs ($p = .35$, paired t test). Thus the results in our study failed to replicate the findings of the five studies previously cited. One possible reason for this is that twinning itself produces minor physical anomalies, reflected by the high scores for all groups, and thus obscures anomalies associated with schizo-phrenia. Another possibility is that both twins in the discordant pairs may have experienced the same *in utero* insults, even though only one of them later developed schizophrenia. Note that the affected concordant twins have a lower, though not statistically significant, mean score than the affected discordant twins, which could indicate that the concordant twins have a greater genetic basis to their disease, whereas the discordant twins experienced more *in utero* insults.

The within-pair correlation of minor physical anomaly scores on all twins showed a high degree of similarity ($F = .20$, $p < .000$, intraclass correlation). The highest scores occurred in a discordant pair (DS-15: scores 11 and 10) and a concordant pair (CS-5: scores 10 and 9). Of particular interest were twins in which minor physical anomaly scores were widely discrepant, suggesting that one had been disproportionately subjected to a prenatal insult. The greatest discrepancies in scores among twins with a diagnosis of schizophrenia were 4 points in two discordant pairs; in both pairs the affected twin had the higher score.

In order to ascertain whether the presence of minor physical anomalies is associated with other aspects of schizophrenia, discordant twin pairs in which the affected twin had a score of 2 or more above that of the well twin (n = 6) were compared with the other discordant pairs (n = 20). On most clinical measures, the affected twins in the two groups were similar. There were no significant differences in their ages of first referral for psychiatric evaluation, acuteness of onset, negative symptoms scores (SANS), total time psychiatrically hospitalized, response to medication, lifetime antipsychotic intake, or level of function at the time of testing (as measured by axis V on DSM-III-R). When the 6 affected twins with higher within-pair minor physical anomaly differences were compared as a group against the other 20 discordant affected twins on scores for neurological abnormalities, no significant association was found (5.7 vs. 4.9; p = .58, Wilcoxon rank sum test). However, when the within-pair differences in minor physical anomaly scores and the within-pair differences in neurological abnormality scores were compared for the twins discordant for schizophrenia, a significant correlation was found (r = .38, p = .05, Spearman rank order test), suggesting that there is indeed some relationship between minor physical anomalies and neurological abnormalities in schizophrenia.

When the 6 discordant affected twins with higher within-pair minor physical anomaly scores were compared with the other 20 affected twins on measures of possible genetic or perinatal liability, no significant difference was found for total finger ridge count (120 vs. 133; p = .60, Wilcoxon rank sum test). However, the higher within-pair anomaly score group did differ significantly in having a higher frequency of twins with a family history of psychosis (4 out of 6 vs. 3 out of 19; p = .03, Fisher's exact test); being lighter at birth (2,124 g vs. 2,582 g; p = .02, Wilcoxon rank sum test); and in having a higher frequency of affected twins who were non-right-handed (3 out of 6 vs. 1 out of 20; p = .03, Fisher's exact test). There was also a trend for the higher within-pair anomaly score group to have had greater obstetrical complication scores (6.2 vs. 3.8; p = .08, Wilcoxon rank sum test). These findings thus support the association of minor physical anomalies with a positive family history for psychosis and also with obstetrical complications, both of which were reported by O'Callaghan, Larkin, et al. 1991).

Finger Ridge Counts

The ridges on one's fingers, hands, toes, and feet are collectively called dermatoglyphics, a term that combines the Greek words for skin (*derma*) and carving (*glyphikos*). They *are* literally skin carvings, a permanent record of events that occurred during the first 5 months of development, especially the 4th and 5th months, when that person was still *in utero*. As a window on the past, dermatoglyphics provide us with an important measure for assessing prenatal events that possibly may be linked to the causes of schizophrenia.

Interest in finger and palm print patterns date to antiquity. For centuries they were thought to be linked to patterns of the stars and to predict a person's future. The scientific study of dermatoglyphics began in the 19th century with the fingerprint classification scheme of the Czech biologist Joannes Purkinje and studies of fingerprints by the English geneticist Sir Francis Galton (Plato & Garruto, 1990). It was not until 1880 that it was realized that fingerprints could be instrumental in identifying people, thereby beginning their use in solving crimes. Finger and palm print patterns similar to those found in people also occur in nonhuman primates and can be used for identification of individual animals.

In humans, finger and palm print patterns develop between the 13th and 19th weeks of pregnancy and are completely formed by the 21st week, or the beginning of the 6th month (Mulvihill & Smith, 1969). Thereafter, they cannot be altered except by removing the outer layers of skin. The permanency of dermatoglyphics is illustrated by the fact that they are visible on the hands of some Egyptian mummies after more than 2,000 years (Penrose, 1969).

The primary determinant of a person's finger and palm print patterns is their genes. There are racial differences in these patterns with, for example, Chinese and Javanese people having more whorl patterns on their fingertips than do western Europeans (Penrose, 1969). The importance of this is to emphasize the necessity of having carefully selected control populations when scientific studies are undertaken to look for abnormal patterns in specific diseases.

The other important determinants of finger and palm print patterns are *in utero* events that take place between the 13th and 19th weeks of pregnancy. One *in utero* event that has been clearly documented as causing dermatoglyphic changes is viral infections. Congenital infection with the rubella (German measles) virus has been shown to alter finger and palm prints in approximately half of all individuals who are infected during pregnancy (Achs et al., 1966; Alter & Schulenberg, 1966; Purvis-Smith et al., 1969). Similarly, infection during pregnancy with the cytomegalovirus, a member of the herpes family of viruses, has also been shown to cause dermatoglyphic alterations (Wright et al., 1972; Purvis-Smith et al., 1972). In one especially noteworthy study, both the genetic and the viral (rubella) antecedents of dermatoglyphic alterations were investigated, and a possible interaction of the two was postulated. Specifically, it was said that "those fetuses with a paternal genotype favoring whorl formation are more susceptible to the infection and are more likely to exhibit both raised whorl frequency and clinically significant embryopathy" (Purvis-Smith & Menser, 1973). A possible mechanism whereby a virus may infect the fetal neuroblasts that give rise to the cells controlling dermatoglyphic formation has been proposed (Moore & Munger, 1989).

In addition to schizophrenia, dermatoglyphic patterns have been claimed to be altered in a wide variety of diseases, including Down's syndrome, Turner's syndrome, Klinefelter's syndrome, Wilson's disease, Huntington's disease, epilepsy, psoriasis, Alzheimer's disease, mitral valve prolapse, celiac disease, childhood cancers (e.g., leukemia and retinoblastoma), and childhood crib deaths. The dermatoglyphic pattern of Down's syndrome is so distinctive that it has been said that "a correct diagnosis of this syndrome can almost always be made from a good set of prints of the hands and feet" (Penrose, 1969). In other conditions the pattern is less clearly diagnostic. The interpretation of such studies has been confounded by the use of inappropriate control groups, the wide range of patterns found in normal individuals, and the measurement of different dermatoglyphic patterns in different studies, such as the frequency of loops, whorls, and arches in fingerprints; total finger ridge counts; the width of the angle in the triradius where the ridges come together at the base of the fingers; abnormal creases on the palms; and comparisons of the right and left hands.

Studies of dermatoglyphic patterns in adult individuals with schizophrenia were begun in the 1930s by researchers interested in the genetics of the disease. More than 20 such studies have been carried out in countries ranging from Germany (Schlegel, 1948), Italy (Kemali et al., 1972), Sweden (Beckman & Norring, 1963), England (Mellor, 1968), and Yugoslavia (Turek, 1990) to India (Murthy & Wig, 1977), Australia (Singh, 1967), Chile (Rothhammer et al., 1971), Mexico (Zavala & Nunez, 1970) and the United States (Raphael & Raphael, 1962; Rosner & Steinberg, 1968; Stowens et al., 1970; Polednak, 1972). Studies have also been carried out on children with schizophrenia and other forms of childhood psychosis (Shapiro, 1965; Sank, 1968; Hilbun, 1970). The vast majority of such studies have reported that the dermatoglyphic patterns of individuals with adult and childhood schizophrenia differ from patterns found in normal controls, although a few studies have concluded the opposite (Veliscu et al., 1968; Slastenko et al., 1976). Interpretation of the results of these studies and comparison of the studies with each other are exceedingly difficult because of the lack of adequate control groups and the measurement of different dermatoglyphic patterns in different studies.

In recent years there has also been an interest in how dermatoglyphic patterns vary between the right and left hands in individuals with schizophrenia. Most animals have certain asymmetries that are thought to be genetically determined, such as the heart being placed on the left side in humans. Other asymmetries thought to be under genetic control are randomly distributed, for example, whether a whorl pattern on the third finger is on the right or the left hand. This pattern of random asymmetry is referred to as fluctuating asymmetry. Researchers have reported alterations in the fluctuating asymmetry of dermatoglyphics in individuals with schizophrenia in four separate studies (Markow & Wandler, 1986; Rickler et al., 1989; Markow & Gottesman, 1989; Mellor, 1992), but not in a fifth study (Cannon et al., 1993). The 1989 study by Markow and Gottesman is especially interesting since it showed alterations in fluctuating dermatoglyphic asymmetry in twins with schizophrenia, using the twins studied in England by Eliot Slater. Such alterations in fluctuating dermatoglyphic asymmetry have been cited as support for the genetic nature of the disease (Markow, 1992).

Present Study

In this study a preliminary analysis was done on a variety of dermatoglyphic measures including palmar creases; size of the digits; the relative frequency of loops, whorls, and arches; the width of the atd angle; fluctuating asymmetry; and total finger ridge counts. The first two measures, when combined into a composite "hand maldevelopment score," showed modest promise as a clinical means for distinguishing affected from well twins (Bracha, Torrey, & Bigelow, 1991; Bracha, Torrey, Bigelow, Lohr, et al., 1991). However, it was the total finger ridge counts that most clearly distinguished the affected from the well twins and that was therefore used for primary analysis (Bracha et al., 1992).

Finger ridge counts were calculated by drawing a line between the core of the fingerprint and the triradial point, then counting the number of ridges that crossed this line. This is illustrated in Figure 4.2, which shows a lower count for the affected twin. The total finger ridge count is the sum of the individual counts for all 10 digits. The counts were done by a trained research assistant who was not aware of the diagnosis of any individual twin or of the identity of the co-twin. Ridge counts were then repeated by a medical geneticist. An intraclass correlation coefficient between the two investigators was computed to be .98, indicating a high degree of reliability of the ridge counts.

Identical twins are known to have finger ridge counts that are almost identical. One study reported an intraclass correlation of .96 for finger ridge counts for normal identical twins (Bouchard et al., 1990), compared with .49 for first-degree relatives and .05 for randomly selected individuals (Slater, 1953; Holt, 1961; Nylander, 1971). Among the 7 normal control twins in our study, there also was an intraclass correlation of .96, and the largest within-pair difference in total finger ridge counts was an 11% difference.

When there are wide differences between the finger ridge counts in identical twins, it suggests that the physical size of the twins was unequal during the 4th and 5th months of pregnancy, at which time the finger ridges are developmentally completed. Such discrepancies in size may be due to unequal blood supply such as is found in the twin transfusion syndrome (see Chapter 2), retarded growth in one twin for other reasons, edema, infection, or any other condition that selectively affects only one of the twins at that particular stage of development. Thus a twin who was deleteriously affected might have been smaller (e.g., due to retarded growth) or larger (e.g., edema due to infection) than the co-twin in the 4th and 5th months. We therefore considered within-pair differences in total finger ridge counts to be notable if the twin who later developed schizophrenia deviated substantially from the co-twin's score in either direction—higher or lower.

In our initial analysis the affected twins and the well twins in the pairs discordant for schizophrenia were compared. We found significant within-pair differences between the two groups both for within-pair absolute total finger ridge counts ($p = .008$) and for within-pair percentage total finger ridge counts ($p = .006$, Wilcoxon rank sum test used for both) (Bracha et al., 1992). In other words, the finger ridge counts of a subgroup of the identical twins discordant for schizophrenia were significantly less "twin-like" than normal control twins.

We next identified the individual twin pairs whose total finger ridge

FIGURE 4.2

Finger ridge count in identical twins discordant for schizophrenia.
Ridges are counted along a line from the core to the triradial point.

Well Twin
Ridge count=12

Twin with Schizophrenia
Ridge count=9

count differences lay outside the usual range. Since the maximum within-pair difference among our 7 normal controls was 11%, we considered all discordant twins with a within-pair total finger ridge count of 12% or greater to be abnormal. Among the discordant twins there were 9 such pairs (Table 4.2) with a mean within-pair percentage difference of 22% (range 12 to 52%). These 9 pairs were then compared with the 18 discordant pairs with within-pair percentage differences of less than 12%.

On clinical measures there were no significant differences between the two groups, including measures of age of first referral, acuteness of onset, negative symptoms scores (SANS), neurological abnormalities, total time psychiatrically hospitalized, response to medication, lifetime antipsychotic medication intake, and level of function at the time of testing. Correlations with MRI brain structural changes will be described in Chapter 6.

On measures of possible genetic or perinatal liability there were also no significant differences between the two groups for family history of psychosis, minor physical anomaly scores, or non-right-handedness. However, the group with greater within-pair percentage differences in total finger ridge counts did have a significantly lower mean birth weight (2,148 g vs. 2,609 g; p = .01, Wilcoxon rank sum test) and a higher mean score for total obstetrical complications (8.8 vs. 2.9; p = .006, Wilcoxon rank sum test). Some association between finger ridge count and birth weight is to be expected, since the finger ridge count is largely determined by the size of the fetus during the 4th and 5th months of pregnancy. And since low birth weight is one of the obstetrical complications, some association between finger ridge counts and obstetrical complications would also be expected.

Birth Weight

The birth weight of a newborn baby is a composite outcome of many factors operating throughout the course of pregnancy; as such, birth weights provide a window through which to view the events of pregnancy. The genetic contributions of both parents are important factors, as are the mother's nutrition and smoking habits during the pregnancy. Infections, diabetes, toxemia, and other complications of pregnancy may also markedly alter the weight of the newborn. The length of the pregnancy is one of the most important determinants, especially since 75% of a baby's birth weight is gained in the last 3 months of pregnancy. Given these many variables, the birth weight of any individual newborn must be considered in the light of all the events of that pregnancy.

Twins are known to grow at the same rate as singletons *in utero* until approximately the 6th month (Bryan, 1983, p. 39). At birth, however, twins weigh an average of 500 g (1 lb 2 oz) less than singletons because, according to Bryan, "between 20 and 30% of twins are born before the 37th week and are, therefore, preterm" (1983, p. 87). It is also known that the average weight for identical twins is less than that for fraternal twins, although the reason for this is not known (Corney et al., 1972). The most important cause of weight differential in identical twin pairs is the twin transfusion syndrome, discussed in Chapter 2, in which the blood supply from one gets shunted to the other, thereby causing one to grow faster than the other.

The first detailed study of birth weights in individuals who later developed schizophrenia was done in 1947 by Herbert Barry in Boston. He asked the mothers of 308 "young psychotic patients" (the diagnoses were not further specified) how much their children had weighed at birth and found that many of these children had been excessively *heavy*. Since 6% of the mothers reported that their children had weighed 5.4 kg (12 lbs) or more at birth, Barry himself acknowledged that this was "presumptive evidence of exaggeration" (Barry, 1947).

Three subsequent studies compared the birth weights of individuals who developed schizophrenia with those of their siblings. Using birth weights obtained from mothers' recall, Pollock et al. (1966) found no significant difference between 33 individuals with schizophrenia and their siblings. Using birth weights obtained from birth records, Lane and Albee (1966) reported that 52 individuals with schizophrenia weighed an average of 170 g (6 oz) *less* than their siblings and that this difference was statistically significant (p < .01, chi-square). Woerner et al. (1971) also used birth records to compare the weights of 34 individuals with schizophrenia with their siblings and found that the former averaged 164 g less (p < .10, chi-square, not significant), virtually identical to the findings of Lane and Albee.

There is a suggestion, then, that people who develop schizophrenia may have been slightly lighter at birth than their siblings. If lighter birth weight is related to schizophrenia, however, it could be postulated that very low birth weight babies should have a higher incidence of developing this disease. In the only research reported on this question to date, Smith et al. (1992) in Vancouver followed up 501 low-birth-weight babies and compared them with 203 full-birth-weight babies. In preliminary results, they reported having identified 9 individuals with schizophrenia, bipolar disorder, or psychotic depression from the low-birth-weight group and only 1 from the full-birth-weight group. A similar research project is being carried out in England.

Birth weight studies of twins in which one or both develop schizophrenia have provoked lively controversy. Slater and Shields (1953) concluded in their twin study that "birth weight . . . seemed to be almost without effect." Gottesman and Shields (1976), in a review of the former's results as well as other twin studies, stated categorically that "systematically ascertained twin samples do not support the hypothesized role of birth weight differences in discordant pairs" (p. 49).

On the other side of the controversy, the findings of the Pollin et al. (1966) twin study provided support for the idea that low birth weight may be a risk factor for schizophrenia. In that study, birth weights were published for 14 pairs of discordant identical twins, including members of 2 sets of triplets (Pollin & Stabenau, 1968). Subsequent follow-up found that 2 of the 14 pairs had become concordant (Belmaker et al., 1974), leaving data for 12 discordant pairs. In 10 cases the twin who later developed schizophrenia was lighter at birth, and in the other 2 cases the well twin was lighter. The mean birth weight for the 12 affected twins was 2,088 g, and for the well twins it was 2,297 g, a difference of 209 g (7.4 oz).

For the purposes of the present study, weight differences in individual twin pairs are more important than weight differences among diagnostic groups. Among identical twins a weight difference of more than 20% is considered to be presumptive evidence of the twin transfusion syndrome (Tan et al., 1979), as discussed in Chapter 2. It is generally recommended that weight differences between twins be expressed as a proportion of the weight of the larger twin. When the Pollin et al. (1966) study is looked at in this light, only one pair in that study had a weight difference greater than 20%, and that pair was actually two members of a set of triplets in which the individual who developed schizophrenia was 33% lighter than the well triplet (Pollin et al., case number 5, discussed in Chapter 11). All other Pollin et al. twin pairs had weight differences of 15% or less.

Two more recent studies of birth weights in twins with schizophrenia have been carried out. In London Lewis, Chitkara, et al. (1987) collected birth weights from maternal reports on 13 identical twin pairs discordant for psychosis. In 6 cases the affected twin had been lighter, in 4 cases the well twin had been lighter, and in 3 cases they were equal. The most impressive finding from this study was that among the 4 twin pairs in which the *well* twin was lighter, the difference was over 20% in 3 of the pairs, thus appearing to be examples of twin transfusion syndromes in which the twin who remained well had a poorer blood supply. Lewis et al. also compared the weight differential for twin pairs discordant for psychosis with twin pairs concordant for psychosis and found a trend ($p = .07$) for the differences to be greater in the discordant pairs.

The other recently reported study of birth weights in twins was the Norwegian study of Onstad et al. (1992). Among 15 identical twin pairs discordant for schizophrenia, they found the affected twin to have an average weight of 50 g (1.76 oz) less than the well twin, which is not statistically significant. Since individual weights were not provided in this study, within-pair weight differences cannot be assessed.

Present Study

Birth weights in the present study were obtained from the mothers; in at least half of all twin pairs, these weights were verifiable with birth records or records of childhood kept by the mothers. Birth weights were not available for one discordant pair whose mother was deceased and for one pair in the "other" category who were born at home.

The mean birth weights of twins in the discordant, concordant, and normal control groups were as follows:

	No. of Twins	Average Birth Wt. (g)
Discordant, with schizophrenia	26	2,484
Concordant, with schizophrenia	26	2,525
Discordant, well	26	2,567
Normal controls	16	2,521

The mean weights were similar for all groups. Among the 26 discordant pairs, the affected twin was lighter by an average of 83 g (3 oz), which is not statistically significant. In 12 pairs, the twin who became sick was lighter, in 12 pairs the twin who remained well was lighter, and in 2 pairs their weight was even.

When the within-pair birth weight differences were analyzed, it was found that in 4 of the pairs discordant for schizophrenia, the twin who later developed schizophrenia was more than 20% *lighter* at birth (Table 4.2), presumptive evidence of having had a twin transfusion syndrome. These were as follows:

	Well Twin Birth Wt. (g)	Affected Twin Birth Wt. (g)	Percentage Difference
DS-17	2,694	1,760	35
DS-18	2,948	1,728	41
DS-24	3,602	2,776	23
DS-27	2,694	1,928	28

In none of the discordant pairs was the *well* twin more than 20% lighter, as was found in the study done by Lewis, Chitkara, et al. (1987). A weight difference of more than 20% was also found in 2 of the 13 concordant pairs and in one normal control pair.

In order to ascertain whether the 4 affected twins who were 20% or more lighter at birth were different in any way, these 4 were compared with the 22 affected twins who were not 20% or more lighter at birth. On clinical measures, there were no significant differences between the two groups for age of first referral, acuteness of onset, negative symptom scores (SANS), neurological abnormalities, response to medication, or level of function at the time of testing. Although the 4 lighter twins were younger at the time of testing (mean age 26.5 years vs. 31.4 years for the others), their length of illness was similar (mean of 8.0 years vs. 9.9 years for the others). The 4 affected twins who were much lighter at birth were less likely to have had lifetime antipsychotic medication (9,100 mg equivalents vs. 29,700 mg equivalents; $p = .10$, Wilcoxon rank sum test) and of having spent significantly less time hospitalized (0.3 years vs. 1.3 years; $p = .02$, Wilcoxon rank sum test). Thus these 4 affected twins who had been notably lighter at birth had had a more *benign* disease course than the other affected twins.

Comparison of the two groups on measures of possible genetic or perinatal liability showed no significant differences for family history of psychosis. There were nonsignificant trends for the 4 affected twins who were born lighter to have higher scores for minor physical anomalies (7.5 vs. 5.5; p = .10, Wilcoxon rank sum test) and to be more likely to have a total finger ridge count 12% or more different from their co-twins (3 out of 4 vs. 5 out of 22; p = .07, Fisher's exact test). An association between birth weight and total finger ridge count would be expected, since the ridge counts are largely determined by the size of the developing fetus. The lighter-at-birth twins also had a significantly higher mean score for obstetrical complications (10.0 vs. 3.7; p = .02, Wilcoxon rank sum test), an association that is also predictable, since low birth weight is counted as an obstetrical complication. Finally, the lighter-at-birth twins were significantly more non-right-handed (3 out of 4 vs. 1 out of 22; p = .006, Fisher's exact test).

Following up the trend reported by Lewis et al. for discordant twins with schizophrenia to have a greater within-pair difference in birth weight than do concordant pairs, the average differences were calculated for this study. It was found that the average birth weight difference for the discordant twin pairs was 11.6%, and for the concordant twin pairs it was 9.9%; thus there was only a slight insignificant trend in the same direction as reported by Lewis and his colleagues. The average difference for the 8 normal control pairs was 8.8%.

Overall, how important is birth weight in schizophrenia? The majority of studies of singleton and twin births have suggested that individuals who later develop schizophrenia have a tendency to be lighter at birth, although the weight differences are minimal. The present study found that in 4 of 26 pairs of twins discordant for schizophrenia, the twin who later became sick was more than 20% lighter at birth. The importance of this finding, however, is thrown into doubt by the Lewis et al. study, in which 3 of 13 of the *well* twins in pairs discordant for schizophrenia were more than 20% lighter at birth. The data, then, suggest that low birth weight is not a very important factor in most cases of schizophrenia, although there may be individual cases in which it may contribute to, or be a marker for, the disease.

Obstetrical Complications

The possibility that obstetrical complications may contribute to the cause of schizophrenia has been studied extensively for the past 25 years. The first controlled study of these complications in adult onset schizophrenia was done by Pollack et al. (1966), in which 33 affected individuals were compared with an equal number of their normal siblings (obstetrical data were obtained retrospectively from the mothers). Those with schizophrenia tended to have had "more frequent and more severe" complications, but the trend did not achieve statistical significance. In 1973 this same group of researchers published another study comparing 46 people with schizophrenia with 37 of their normal siblings. Obstetrical data, obtained from maternal recall and birth records, showed that the affected ones had had more pregnancy complications ($p = .03$) and more birth complications ($p < .02$) (Woerner et al., 1973).

Three Scandinavian studies followed, all using midwife and hospital birth records to eliminate possible bias in maternal recall. In Sweden McNeil and Kaij (1978) compared the records of 54 individuals with schizophrenia with 100 matched normal controls and reported more obstetrical complications in the affected ones, although the difference was not statistically significant. They concluded that "obstetric complications are risk-increasing factors to be taken seriously in the etiology of schizophrenia." In Denmark Jacobsen and Kinney (1980) compared the birth records of 34 individuals with schizophrenia who had been adopted, 29 other schizophrenics who were not adopted, and 63 normal controls. Those with schizophrenia (both adopted and not adopted) had experienced significantly more obstetrical complications ($p < .05$) and more severe complications ($p < .005$), especially prolonged labor. Also in Denmark Parnas et al. (1982) compared the records of 12 people with schizophrenia (and whose mothers had also had schizophrenia) with 39 normal controls. They found that "there is a tendency . . . toward more and worse complications in schizophrenics," but the trend was not statistically significant.

In recent years there has been a flurry of interest in the question of obstetrical complications in individuals who develop schizophrenia, with one American and five European studies. DeLisi et al. (1987) in New York compared the obstetrical histories of 123 individuals with schizophrenia in families that had two or more affected siblings with 148 well siblings from the same families. Using histories obtained from the mothers, the researchers found that 24% of affected individuals versus 13% of well siblings had "complications associated with their births" ($p < .025$). Lewis et al. (1989) in England, also using obstetrical information obtained from the families, compared 207 individuals with schizophrenia with 203 inpatients diagnosed with neuroses and reported that the former had had significantly more pregnancy and birth complications ($p < .001$). Eagles et al. (1990) in Scotland blindly rated the birth records of 27 people with schizophrenia and the records of their unaffected siblings and found that the "schizophrenics had significantly more obstetric complications than controls ($p < .02$)," with premature rupture of the membranes being especially frequent.

The most recent study of obstetrical complications in individuals with schizophrenia was an Irish study done by O'Callaghan et al. (1992). The hospital birth records of 65 individuals with schizophrenia were blindly compared with an equal number of matched controls. Affected individuals were significantly more likely to have had obstetrical complications ($p = .03$) and more severe complications ($p = .03$), with fetal distress being frequently reported.

Two other recent studies found no statistically significant relationship between obstetrical complications and a diagnosis of schizophrenia. Done et al. (1991) identified mentally ill adults born in 1958 during the British perinatal mortality survey. A variety of pregnancy and birth complications were combined to form a single estimate of probability regarding whether the child would be stillborn or die within the first month of life. The researchers found that individuals with schizophrenia had a modestly higher number of risk factors than did controls or individuals with neuroses, but that the increase fell far short of statistical significance ($p = .40$ for narrowly defined schizophrenia and $p = .24$ for broadly defined schizophrenia). McCreadie et al. (1992) in Scotland also reported no statistically significant difference when 54 individuals with schizophrenia were compared with 114 of their siblings regarding obstetrical complications (based on maternal recall); 35% of those affected "had at least one definite obstetric complication" compared with 29% of their siblings.

In summary, since 1966 there have been 11 controlled studies of obstetrical complications in non-twin individuals who later developed adult onset schizophrenia. Seven of these studies reported a statistically significant increase in obstetrical complications in the affected individuals (4 used hospital records and 3 were based on maternal recall). Another 2 studies reported a clear trend in this direction but were not statistically significant. The other 2 studies reported negative results.

Turning to studies of obstetrical complications in twins with schizophrenia, it is important to remember that twins per se are an obstetrical complication; therefore, insofar as obstetrical complications contribute to the cause of schizophrenia, one would expect the incidence of schizophrenia to be higher in twins than in singleton births, as Rosanoff et al. (1934) predicted. Rosenthal (1960), reviewing older studies, concluded that there was no evidence that schizophrenia occurs more often in twins; there is, however, surprisingly little data on this issue, and it should be considered an open question.

Reviews of obstetrical complications in past twin studies have been done by Pollin and Stabenau (1968) and McNeil and Kaij (1978). The former collected data on 86 pairs of identical twins discordant for schizophrenia "in which the evidence for diagnosis and zygosity has appeared reasonably compelling"; for twin pairs in which there were known birth complications, in 18 of 23 cases it was the affected twins who had had the complications. McNeil and Kaij's review included many of the same twins as had been included by Pollin and Stabenau (specifically those of the Slater and Shields, Kringlen, and Tienari studies), as well as twins studied by Gottesman and Shields and by Inouye, and it concluded that "obstetric complications are a risk-increasing factor to be taken seriously in the etiology of schizophrenia."

Among the identical twins discordant for schizophrenia, in 6 of the 7 cases actually studied by Pollin et al. in which there was "any birth complication," it had occurred in the affected twin. According to their summary, "The five twins in which there is well-documented evidence of cyanosis at birth are all index [affected] schizophrenic twins. The preponderance of neonatal medical complications such as infectious episodes, occurred in the index twins" (Pollin & Stabenau, 1968). Another schizophrenia twin study that specifically looked at obstetrical complications was the English study carried out by Reveley et al. (1984). Among 12 identical twins discordant for schizophrenia, there had been birth complications (breech birth, use of forceps, "a blue baby," or low birth weight) in 5 of the 12; in each case these had occurred in the affected twins. Onstad et al. (1992), in a study that included 16 identical twins discordant for schizophrenia, reported that birth complications occurred in 7 of the pairs but that the *well* twin had been "weakest at birth" more often than the affected twin. Overall, however, the net weight of previous twin studies is similar to that for non-twin studies in suggesting that obstetrical complications occur with excess frequency in individuals who later develop schizophrenia.

Present Study

Information on obstetrical complications in the present study was obtained from the mothers, as summarized in Chapter 3. Such maternal recall is limited by the fact that the mother is being asked to recall events of a pregnancy and birth that occurred 20 or more years previously, and by possible selective remembrance of events that *she* believes to be related to the subsequent development of schizophrenia in her offspring. One study of maternal recall of pregnancy and birth reported that such recall is accurate for events such as miscarriages but poor for events such as X rays and medications (Tilley et al., 1985). A more recent study comparing maternal recall with the hospital records was more optimistic and concluded that "maternal recall can be a surprisingly accurate source of obstetric information in relation to research on schizophrenia" (O'Callaghan, Larkin, & Waddington, 1990).

One would assume that using medical records of the pregnancy and delivery would be a more accurate source of information than maternal recall, but they also have limitations. Obstetrical and midwife records are often surprisingly sparse, reporting only major events such as toxemia, whereas mothers may recall events that were not recorded. Furthermore, Thomas McNeil (1988) personally attended 200 births in Sweden and compared his observations of birth and neonatal complications with those recorded in the medical records. He found that "some of the information recorded in medical records, even in the excellent Swedish obstetrical system, is incorrect and could lead to inaccurate interpretation of the role of [obstetrical complications] in the development of later pathology." For our study, we obtained the hospital obstetrical records for 8 pairs of our twins, which provided surprisingly little information, and in no instance did the information conflict with the mothers' recall.

The information on obstetrical complications we obtained from the mother was transferred onto standardized forms by a physician with obstetrical training who was unaware of the diagnoses of the individuals. These data were then analyzed by Thomas McNeil, Karin Sjostrom, Elizabeth Cantor-Graae, and their colleagues at the University of Lund in Sweden, all of whom were also unaware of the diagnoses of the individuals. A scoring scale was devised for categorizing each obstetrical event on a 6-point scale with respect to its potential to cause somatic damage (especially to the central nervous system) in the offspring. In cases in which supplementary information was required from the mother to clarify any given obstetrical event, it was obtained by the principal investigators and then transferred to Dr. McNeil and his colleagues in a manner that ensured their continued blindness to the diagnosis.

The 6-point scale for categorizing obstetrical events ranged from level 1 ("not harmful") to level 6 ("great harm or deviation"). Scores were summarized for each individual twin for pregnancy complications, labor, delivery complications, and neonatal complications (from the moment of birth until the end of the 1st month following delivery). Most of the data analysis used events categorized at levels 4 ("clearly likely harmful"), 5 ("clearly greatly harmful"), and 6 ("great harm or deviation"). Examples of obstetrical events categorized at those levels are as follows:

Pregnancy complications: bleeding during pregnancy, toxemia, diabetes in mother

Labor and delivery complications: prolonged labor, forceps delivery, delayed delivery of second twin

Neonatal complications: difficulty breathing, prematurity, life-threatening infection in newborn

The results of an analysis by diagnostic groups showed that discordant twin pairs had the highest mean number of total obstetrical complications (2.33), followed by concordant pairs (1.60), and then normal control pairs (0.71). The differences were statistically significant ($p = .008$, Jonckheere test for ordered alternatives) and are consistent with previous studies (summarized earlier) suggesting that individuals who later develop schizophrenia have had more obstetrical complications than those who do not develop schizophrenia. Complications of labor and delivery, especially prolonged labor and precipitous delivery, were especially marked among the discordant twins and were the main factors distinguishing the discordant pairs from the concordant pairs ($p = .02$, Wilcoxon-Mann-Whitney test, one-tailed). The finding of more obstetrical complications among discordant twins than among concordant twins with schizophrenia is in agreement with the findings recently reported by Onstad et al. (1992) in their twin study.

When the affected twins in the discordant pairs were compared as a group to the well twins in these pairs, there were no significant differences in obstetrical complications. A perusal of the individual pairs, however, readily identified some pairs in which the affected twin had had more complications than the well twin. In 7 of the 26 discordant pairs (obstetrical data were not available on the 27th pair), the affected twin had a total obstetrical complication score 5 points or more higher than the well twin (Table 4.2). The affected twins in these 7 pairs were compared with the affected twins in the other 19 to see whether there were any distinguishing features for the former group.

There were no clinical differences between these two groups on any measures, including age of first referral, acuteness of onset, negative symptom score (SANS), neurological abnormalities, total time psychiatrically hospitalized, response to medication, lifetime antipsychotic medication intake, or level of function at the time of testing. Three previous studies had reported that individuals with more obstetrical complications experienced schizophrenia onset at an earlier age (Owen et al., 1988; Lewis et al., 1989; O'Callaghan, Larkin, Kinsella, et al., 1990), and as early as 1934, Rosanoff et al. had predicted such an association; however, another study had not found this (McCreadie et al., 1992). Our findings showed no difference in the mean age of first referral for the affected twins who had had more obstetrical complications compared to the affected twins with fewer complications. Likewise, Parnas et al. (1981) and Kinney, Woods, et al. (1991) had previously reported a direct association between obstetrical complications and neurological abnormalities in schizophrenia, but in the present study neurological mean scores were virtually the same for the two groups. Finally, a relationship between having had more obstetrical complications and having a more severe form of schizophrenia was reported by Wilcox and Nasrallah (1987b) but was not found by McNeil (1988) or in our study.

Among schizophrenia researchers, there has been much interest in the relationship between family history of psychosis and obstetrical complications because of the theory that schizophrenia related to obstetrical complications may be a nongenetic form of the disease; in such cases, one would not expect to find a positive family history. Five earlier studies have reported that individuals with schizophrenia who had more obstetrical complications were less likely to have a family history of this disease (Reveley et al., 1984; Lewis et al., 1989; Schwarzkopf et al., 1989; O'Callaghan, Larkin, Kinsella, et al., 1990; Persson & Dalen, 1992), whereas four other studies found no such relationship (McNeil, 1988; Nimgaonkar et al., 1988; Reddy et al., 1990; McCreadie et al., 1992). The present study also found no relationship between obstetrical complications and family history of psychosis.

There was also no significant association between obstetrical complications and either minor physical anomalies or non-right-handedness. There was, however, a trend for the affected twins with more obstetrical complications to have been lighter at birth (2,236 g vs. 2,552 g; $p = .10$, Wilcoxon rank sum test), but this is to be expected, since low birth weight was counted as an obstetrical complication.

In our study the only measure of genetic or perinatal liability to schizophrenia associated with obstetrical complications at a statistically significant level was total finger ridge count. The 7 affected twins with higher within-pair scores for obstetrical complications, compared with the other 19 affected twins, had a lower mean total finger ridge count (75 vs. 151; $p = .008$, Wilcoxon rank sum test) and also were more likely to have a 12% or greater within-pair ridge count difference (5 out of 7 vs. 3 out of 19; $p = .01$, Fisher's exact test). This suggests that there is some relationship between obstetrical complications and finger ridge counts in schizophrenia.

Birth order of the twins discordant for schizophrenia was also examined. Studies of twins have shown that second-born twins have a higher perinatal mortality because of anoxia, which occurs when the second birth is delayed (Bryan, 1983, p. 71). In the present study 15 of the discordant twins who developed schizophrenia had been firstborn and 12 had been second-born. Thus birth order does not appear to be an important factor in determining liability to schizophrenia in twins, a conclusion that is consistent with previous twin studies of this disease.

The mother's history of having had any miscarriages (spontaneous abortions) or stillbirths was also examined in the twins discordant for schizophrenia. MacSweeney et al. (1978) reported that women who gave birth to children who later developed schizophrenia had had twice as many miscarriages as a control population. In our study 25 mothers of the twins discordant for schizophrenia had had a total of 85 live births (counting the twins as a single birth). Miscarriage rates in the general population are known to be approximately 1 per every 10 live births, so these mothers would have been expected to have had 8.5 miscarriages. In fact, the 25 mothers reported having had a total of 12 miscarriages and 1 stillbirth, a nonsignificant trend in the same direction as the results reported by MacSweeney et al.

We examined one other perinatal measure. As was mentioned in Chapter 2, it is clearly established that people who develop schizophrenia are born disproportionately in the winter and spring months of the year (Bradbury & Miller, 1985; Boyd et al., 1986). For this reason, we looked at the month of birth for the 27 discordant and 13 concordant twin pairs. Because of the small number of twins to be divided over 12 months, we divided them into summer-fall (June to November) and winter-spring (December to May) births. It was found that 14 of the 40 twins in which one or both have schizophrenia had been born in the summer-fall months and 26 had been born in the winter-spring months. Comparing this distribution with all births in the United States for the years 1964 to 1968 (Lyster, 1971), it was found that among our twins with schizophrenia, there were more winter-spring births, consistent with previous studies of seasonality in schizophrenia, but that this excess was not statistically significant ($p = .14$, chi square).

Handedness and Mirror Imaging

The handedness of individuals is a topic of both considerable interest and confusion. Studies have shown that between 90 and 95% of the population are right-handed, with the others being left-handed or mixed-handed (ambidextrous). Left-handedness is slightly more common in males. Longevity is also a determining factor; 10 to 14% of high school and university students are left-handed, but this decreases to 3% for people aged 55 to 64 and to 1% for those aged 76 to 100 (Fennell, 1986). Handedness also differs somewhat by ethnic groups.

One confusing aspect of this trait is that there are degrees of right- or left-handedness. A person may do most things with one hand, but a few things with the other hand. The measurement of handedness becomes even more confusing when footedness (which foot is used to kick a ball) and eyedness (which eye is used to look through a telescope) are also measured. Correlations among handedness, footedness, and eyedness are now known to be much lower than was previously thought (Plato et al., 1985).

It should be noted that handedness is only one aspect of the lateralization of brain function in humans. Pamela Taylor noted in an excellent review that "man is a highly lateralized animal" with motor control, perceptual skills, many cognitive functions, language, and some aspects of the control of emotions, all more or less lateralized to either the right or the left hemisphere. Taylor speculated that increasing lateralization is an indication of higher evolutionary status, although she noted that "even some single-celled organisms show simple lateral asymmetries" (Taylor, 1987).

Of special interest for researchers concerned with schizophrenia and bipolar disorder is the fact that, for unknown reasons, the left hemisphere normally lags behind the right hemisphere in intrauterine growth, so that by the 6th month of pregnancy, the right hemisphere (which some researchers believe to be more involved in bipolar disorder) has achieved almost full size, whereas the left hemisphere (which researchers believe to be more involved in schizophrenia) lags considerably in its growth. That has led to speculation that an insult to the brain (e.g., a viral infection) that occurs at a particular time in pregnancy might have more effect on either the right or the left side of the brain in a developing fetus because that hemisphere was growing more rapidly at the time of the insult. This could theoretically lead to either bipolar disorder if the right hemisphere was more affected, or schizophrenia if the left hemisphere was more affected.

The reason that 90 to 95% of individuals are right-handed is unknown. Genes certainly play a major role. One study, for example, found that the offspring of two left-handed parents have a 27% chance of being left-handed (Fennell, 1986). It is also widely believed that insults to the brain *in utero* may affect handedness; for instance, in most persons the left hemisphere is dominant and determines right-handedness, but if the left hemisphere is damaged during development, it would increase the chances that the right hemisphere would assume dominance, in which case the person might be left-handed. This insult-to-the-brain hypothesis has been widely cited as a cause of left-handedness despite the paucity of research data to support it (Hicks et al., 1979).

There is also a learned aspect to handedness, as shown by a recent study in which young children acquired some of their handedness by imitating their mothers (Michel, 1992). Sometimes handedness can also be changed, as when teachers in the past insisted that left-handed students write with their right hands. Assessing the importance of this learning aspect of handedness is exceedingly difficult, however, because hand preference is not clearly established until a child is 8 or 9 years old; prior to that, handedness sometimes shifts back and forth between the right and left.

Certain professions are said to be associated with left-handedness, especially music and architecture. The advantages of left-handedness for playing professional baseball are well known, especially the southpaw pitchers and ambidextrous switch hitters, who may be able to market their unusual lateralization of motor function for contracts worth millions of dollars. Both gifted children and learning-disabled children have also been said to include a disproportionate number of left-handers. Some diseases thought to occur more commonly in left-handers are mental retardation, autism, migraine, epilepsy, and rheumatoid arthritis.

Schizophrenia has also been said by some researchers to affect a disproportionate number of left-handers (Gur, 1977) or people with ambiguous handedness (Green, Satz, Smith, et al. 1989). Other researchers, however, have not found this to be true (Kameyama et al., 1983), and one study even found less than the number of expected left-handers among a sample of individuals with schizophrenia (Taylor et al., 1980). The assessment of handedness in schizophrenia is complicated by the fact that right-left confusion is not uncommon in this disease, so the assessment of handedness must be based on observed actions and not merely on self-reports by the person who is affected.

Twin Handedness

If handedness in schizophrenia is a confused research area, handedness in twins with schizophrenia is doubly confusing. One reason for this is that handedness in twins, in general, is an area of lively controversy; as summarized by Elizabeth Bryan in *The Nature and Nurture of Twins*, "over no aspect of twinning has there been more disagreement than over laterality" (Bryan, 1983, p. 125). The main source for the controversy is that left-handedness occurs more frequently than expected in twins. Since the incidence of left-handedness among singletons is up to 10%, in any given twin pair the probability of at least one twin being left-handed should be 20% or less. The majority of studies, however, have found the incidence of left-handedness in twins to be approximately 25% (Segal, 1989). There are thought to be at least two reasons for this.

The first is that twins experience more trauma both *in utero* and during the birth process than do singletons, thus making them more liable to brain damage. If the brain damage occurs in the left hemisphere, it could theoretically lead to both left-handedness (because the right hemisphere would then become dominant) and schizophrenia (which is thought to involve the left hemisphere). Malcolm Weller in London recently reported a case of identical male twins in which the one with schizophrenia was left-handed and had some weakness of his right arm, and EEG abnormalities were more marked on the left half of his brain. All of this suggested that the affected twin had experienced some kind of insult to the left brain. He had been the second twin, born 30 minutes after the first, during which time anoxia or other brain insults may have taken place (Weller, 1990).

The other explanation for the increased incidence of left-handedness in twins is mirror imaging, discussed in Chapter 2. Whereas the brain-damage factor applies to both identical and fraternal twins, mirror imaging is a phenomenon unique to identical twins. The term is commonly used to indicate identical twins in which one is right-handed and the other left-handed and who also have external skin features on opposite sides (e.g., hair crowns on opposite sides, so that they part their hair accordingly, or congenital skin blemishes on opposite sides). The twins are said to be literally mirror images, as if each were facing a mirror when standing face-to-face. Many families use the term *mirror image* twins for any identical twins who are opposite handed, even if they do not have any hair or skin markers.

Although some researchers have expressed doubt whether mirror imaging actually exists (e.g., Bryan, 1983, p. 126), most believe that it does. The mechanism thought to be responsible for this phenomenon is the splitting of the fertilized zygote slightly later than usual after lateralized asymmetry has become fixed in the zygote (Newman, 1928). If splitting takes place before the asymmetry becomes fixed, each of the two new zygotes develops its own asymmetry; if asymmetry has already taken place, however, then splitting the zygote is like dividing a walnut that had formed a small node on one side in the plane of cleavage.

It appears that there are differing degrees of mirror imaging, probably depending on the precise timing of the splitting of the zygote. Opposite handedness is one degree, and some of the excess left-handers found among identical twins are almost certainly the product of mirror imaging. Opposite-sided hair crowns and birthmarks are the product of the embryonic ectodermal (outer cell) layer and is probably the next degree of mirror imaging. In rare instances, the internal organs of identical twins are on opposite sides of the body, referred to as *situs inversus*, suggesting that the embryonic endodermal (inner cell) layer has also been affected.

An intriguing case of schizophrenia in mirror-image identical twins was recently reported by Lohr and Bracha (1992). The first twin was right-handed and had symptoms of classical schizophrenia. The second twin was left-handed, with a mixed clinical picture of both affective and schizophrenic symptoms; she was diagnosed as having schizoaffective disorder on one occasion and bipolar disorder on another. Mirror imaging was confirmed by examining their fingerprint patterns. In addition, on a computerized tomography (CT) scan of their brains, it was found that there was a mirror asymmetry to their occipital lobes, suggesting the possibility of *situs inversus* of the brain. The brain, along with the skin, originates from the ectodermal cell layer. There was apparently no suggestion of *situs inversus* of other internal organs, which originate from the endodermal cell layer. The authors of this case speculated that the twins' different clinical symptoms might have been caused by a common insult to the left brain. For the first twin, this caused schizophrenia, which is thought to be associated with left-brain damage, but for the second twin, the brain insult caused more affective symptoms because, due to mirror imaging, her laterality was reversed.

One of the most controversial findings that has emerged from the study of handedness and schizophrenia in twins has been that of Charles Boklage (1977). Utilizing data from twins with schizophrenia previously studied by Slater, Shields, and Gottesman, Boklage divided them into right-handed and non-right-handed. He found that non-right-handedness occurred more often in identical than in fraternal twins, and that in identical twins discordant for schizophrenia, it was the twin with schizophrenia who was more likely to be non-right-handed. If true, this implies that the cause of some cases of schizophrenia might be associated with the process of lateralization. Boklage's findings have been widely cited by researchers to support a theory that schizophrenia's origins are developmental.

Subsequently, two other research groups examined twins with schizophrenia to try to replicate Boklage's findings. Luchins and his colleagues (1980) used data from the Pollin et al. (1966) National Institute of Mental Health twin study, while in England Shon Lewis et al. (1989) used another collection of twins with schizophrenia. Neither research group was able to replicate Boklage's findings, thus throwing his results into doubt. One of the aims of the present study was to further test Boklage's findings.

Present Study

Handedness, footedness, and eyedness were determined for 55 twin pairs in this study using a standard test, the Edinburgh Inventory (Oldfield, 1971). For 9 other twin pairs, only handedness was assessed by observing their hand preference for writing and by obtaining information from their mothers. Information on the handedness of each mother and father was also collected by self-report. Individuals with mixed handedness were assigned with left-handers to a category called non-right-handers for data analysis.

The first question we asked was whether non-right-handedness is more common in our twin population than in non-twin populations. The incidence of having at least one member non-right-handed among twin pairs in each of the study groups was as follows:

Discordant or concordant for schizophrenia: 10/40 (25%)
Discordant for bipolar disorder: 3/8 (38%)
Discordant or concordant for other diagnoses: 2/8 (25%)
Normal controls: 2/8 (25%)

Thus the incidence of non-right-handedness among twin pairs in our study was remarkably similar to the 25% rate reported for all twins, and there was no increased incidence of non-right-handedness among twin pairs with schizophrenia.

We next looked at the twins discordant for schizophrenia to see whether it was the twin with schizophrenia who was usually non-right-handed, as Boklage had found. Among the 5 discordant twin pairs in which one was right-handed and the other non-right-handed (in the 6th pair both were non-right-handed), the twin with schizophrenia was non-right-handed in 3 cases, but the well twin was non-right-handed in the other 2; thus little support was found for Boklage's theory. He had also claimed that twins discordant for schizophrenia in which one is non-right-handed tend to have a clinically less severe form of disease. We therefore compared our 6 discordant affected twins with a non-right-hander in the pair against the other 21 discordant affected twins on two measures of disease severity: total years of hospitalization and level of function at the time of testing (axis V on the DSM-III-R diagnostic scale). There was no significant difference on either measure, which also did not support Boklage's findings.

Working with the discordant pairs, we also compared the 4 affected twins who were non-right-handed (Table 4.2) with the other 23 affected twins who were right-handed to ascertain possible differences between the groups. Clinically, no significant differences were found for age of first referral, acuteness of onset, negative symptom scores, neurological abnormalities, total time psychiatrically hospitalized, response to medication, lifetime antipsychotic medication intake, or level of function at the time of testing.

When the two groups were compared on indicators of possible genetic or perinatal liability, there was no difference in the family history of psychosis. A nonsignificant trend was found for an association between non-right-handedness and having a higher mean occurrence of minor physical anomalies (7.5 vs. 5.3; $p = .10$, Wilcoxon rank sum test) and also having greater within-pair percentage differences in total finger ridge counts (3 out of 4 vs. 1 out of 23; $p = .09$, Fisher's exact test). Statistically significant associations were found between non-right-handedness and low birth weight (3 out of 4 vs. 1 out of 23; $p = .005$, Fisher's exact test). Being non-right-handed was also associated with having a higher mean total obstetrical complication score (9.5 vs. 3.8; $p = .04$, Wilcoxon rank sum test).

We also looked at the self-reported histories of handedness in mothers and fathers of the non-right-handed twins to see how important genetics appeared to be. Of the 5 twin pairs in which one twin was non-right-handed (data were not available on the other pair because they had been adopted), only one parent reported being non-right-handed. Thus in our small study population, parental handedness did not appear to play a large role in the determination of non-right-handedness.

Finally, we looked at the phenomenon of mirror imaging in all of our twins by asking them which side they part their hair on and whether they have any birthmarks. Among the 15 twin pairs in all diagnostic groups in which one was right-handed and the other non-right-handed (in the other 2 pairs both were non-right-handed), there was additional evidence of mirror imaging in 10 pairs. In most of the twins this consisted of parting their hair on opposites sides to correspond with their hair crowns, but 1 pair was judged as being mirror images because they have congenitally curved fifth fingers on opposite hands. In the other 5 twin pairs there was no evidence of mirror imaging other than their opposite handedness.

In summary, the assessment of handedness and mirror imaging in our 64 pairs of identical twins has verified the increased incidence of non-right-handedness in twins in general, but no support was found for theories that link the cause of schizophrenia to the development of brain laterality. There are suggestions, however, that the increased incidence of non-right-handedness in some of the twins in the present study may be related to low birth weight or obstetrical complications, which might have caused brain changes.

Is There a Perinatal Form of Schizophrenia?

For many years it has been assumed that there is a genetic form of schizophrenia, and that individuals with this form of the disease are more likely to have a family history of the disease. However, attempts to identify clinical markers characteristic of the genetic form of schizophrenia have been largely unsuccessful. The question may now be raised whether there is also a perinatal form of the disease.

We studied five possible markers of perinatal liability: minor physical anomalies, finger ridge counts, birth weight, obstetrical complications, and non-right-handedness. For finger ridge counts and obstetrical complications, statistically significant group differences were found that separated the affected twins from normal controls. Furthermore, there was a significant correlation between total finger ridge counts and obstetrical complications in the affected twins, suggesting that there is a relationship between them. Minor physical anomalies did not correlate with either of these two markers but were associated significantly with family history; in other words, affected twins with a family history of psychosis had a higher frequency of minor physical anomalies. Low birth weight and non-right-handedness were also significantly associated in affected twins, perhaps due to a common *in utero* insult that produced both conditions.

Note, too, that none of the 5 possible markers of perinatal liability were associated with clinical aspects of the disease, such as age of onset, negative symptoms, level of function, or response to medication. This is analogous to the failure of the presumed genetic form of schizophrenia—those with a family history of serious mental illness—to be associated with clinical aspects of the disease. It suggests that dividing patients with schizophrenia by clinical categories is not likely to be useful in identifying those who have perinatal or genetic roots.

In addition to the group differences, we also looked at the occurrence of possible markers of perinatal liability in the individual affected twins. As Table 4.2 illustrates, there is a clustering of these in specific twins. Some overlap should be expected, since total finger ridge count is partially dependent on the size of the individual *in utero* and thus with birth weight, and low birth weight was included as one measure of obstetrical complications. However, the clustering of these possible markers of perinatal liability in specific individuals exceeds what would be expected by chance and suggests that there is indeed a perinatal form of schizophrenia.

How large is this presumed perinatal group? Looking at Table 4.2, one can see that there are 6 affected twins with only 1 perinatal marker, 5 with 2 markers, and 1 each with 3, 4, and 5 markers. If we arbitrarily establish 2 or more markers as the minimum criteria for perinatal liability, then the perinatal group would include 8 out of the 27, or 30% of the affected twins. It is interesting that the 3 affected twins, in which the total within-pair finger ridge count exceeding 12% was the only marker of possible perinatal liability (DS-11, 13, and 21), were the only 3 in which the affected twin had a *higher* count than the well twin; in the other 6, the affected twin in each case had a *lower* count. This suggests that a lower total finger ridge count may be more important as a perinatal marker of schizophrenia than a higher count.

Another interesting observation is that 7 of the 8 twins in the perinatal group were born in January through April. Although the numbers are too few to be meaningful, it does suggest the possibility that the perinatal form of schizophrenia may account for the known excess of winter and spring births in this disease.

On reflection, it is surprising to find that a perinatal form of schizophrenia appears to be identifiable from a retrospective study. Our ability to measure the events of pregnancy and delivery, especially early pregnancy, are in fact very limited. Pregnancy is similar to a closed nation such as Albania was during the cold war: we could measure earthquakes and major insurrections that took place, but we had no way to measure minor uprisings that might have had long-term consequences. That a perinatal form of schizophrenia is identifiable at all suggests that what we are able to see may be merely a portion of the whole. As McNeil (1988) perceptively summarized the situation: "If [obstetrical complications] data include as much 'noise' as they might appear to, then the relationship between the true perinatal trauma and the development of schizophrenia may be much stronger than our statistical findings indicate."

In examining the perinatal form of schizophrenia, it should be noted that there is no single pregnancy or birth complication that stands out either in the present study or in previous studies. Eagles et al. (1990) found an unusually high number of women in their study who had had premature rupture of the membrane (their waters broke more than 24 hours before the onset of labor), but other studies have not found this. McNeil (1988) has postulated that decreased oxygen supply to the baby is the common denominator of obstetrical complications contributing to the development of schizophrenia. The recent finding by O'Callaghan et al. (1992) of excess cases of "fetal distress" among children who later develop schizophrenia is consistent with this.

The idea that decreased oxygen supply *in utero* or during delivery may make some individuals more likely to develop schizophrenia is one that has interested researchers for over 20 years. Sarnoff Mednick initially proposed this hypothesis in 1970, specifically citing the hippocampal area of the brain as being very susceptible to anoxia, and others have subsequently enlarged on this idea (Lewis, Owen, et al., 1989). Since recent neuropathological and imaging studies of individuals with schizophrenia have also pointed toward involvement of the hippocampal area, Mednick's hypothesis appears to have been prescient.

The Problem of Chickens and Eggs

Mednick's theory, like other speculations regarding obstetrical complications and schizophrenia, assumes that anoxia is a *cause* of the brain changes that lead to susceptibility to the disease. An alternative formulation was put forth in 1988 by Robert Goodman, who suggested that "the PBCs [pregnancy and birth complications] are effects rather than causes of a schizophrenia liability"; that is, anoxia is not a chicken but merely one of the eggs, with schizophrenia being another egg. Rather than being a *cause* of schizophrenia, anoxia at birth and schizophrenia are both *effects* of earlier, preexisting, but still unidentified, pathogenic factors.

The possibility that obstetrical complications that are observed in individuals who later develop schizophrenia may be effects rather than causes gained credibility from the studies on cerebral palsy done under the collaborative Perinatal Project of the National Institute of Neurological Disorders and Stroke (NINDS) (Nelson & Ellenberg, 1986). In that study, pregnant mothers were carefully monitored to try to determine what events of pregnancy and delivery were associated with the development of cerebral palsy in the children born from the pregnancies. The researchers found, much to their surprise, that predictors of cerebral palsy were factors that began during *pregnancy*, not during *delivery*, and that both anoxia and cerebral palsy appeared to be effects of these earlier factors. In other words, in most cases anoxia during delivery does not apparently cause cerebral palsy; rather, the anoxia is a marker for preexisting pregnancy events that cause it. This sequence of events had in fact been proposed by an earlier researcher on cerebral palsy in 1897 when he wrote: "One has to consider that the anomaly of the birth process, rather than being the causal etiologic factor [for cerebral palsy], may itself be the consequence of the real prenatal etiology" (Paneth, 1986). This early researcher was none other than Sigmund Freud, who did research on cerebral palsy prior to taking up psychoanalysis. It would be an irony indeed if Freud's real contribution to psychiatry turns out to be a theory he developed for cerebral palsy rather than the psychoanalytic theory with which his name is associated.

As attractive as may be the hypothesis that obstetrical complications in schizophrenia may be effects rather than causes, it has one central shortcoming: It does not identify the nature of the chicken. *What* is occurring during pregnancy that may produce both the birth complications and the later development of schizophrenia? Is it one or more genes that lead to both outcomes, or a genetic predisposition to nonspecific factors? Do nonspecific factors disrupt the developmental process of the central nervous system during specific critical periods of pregnancy? Could infection of the fetus by viruses or other pathogens lead to both the perinatal complications and the schizophrenia? We will return to these questions in Chapter 12.

CHAPTER 5

Are Individuals Who Develop Schizophrenia Different as Children?

VER SINCE the early years of this century there have been suggestions that some individuals who develop schizophrenia are "different" as children. The definitions of "different" have varied from
developmentally slower and neurologically more impaired to behaviorally
withdrawn and asocial, but the concept of "different" has continued to
recur over the years. Although there is also no consensus on what proportion of individuals who later develop schizophrenia are different as children, most observers agree that it is less than half.

Emil Kraepelin in 1919 was among the first to make this observation.
He noted that "in a considerable number of cases definite *psychic peculiari-
ties* have come under observation in our patients from childhood up." In
such cases, said Kraepelin, personality changes take place in childhood
"many years before the real onset of dementia praecox [schizophrenia]"
(Kraepelin, 1919, pp. 236–237).

The first systematic study of this phenomenon was carried out by
Kasanin and Veo in Boston in 1932. They examined school records and
interviewed the teachers of 35 people with adult-onset schizophrenia.
They reported that for 8 of these individuals "everybody in the school
noticed that these children were odd, peculiar and queer"; 12 others had
been "sensitive, shy, bashful, passive"; 10 had had "a slight personality

Contributing to the research discussed in this chapter were Drs. Llewellyn B. Bigelow,
Kenneth C. Rickler, Patricia O. Quinn, H. Stefan Bracha, and Thomas F. McNeil, and Ms.
Elizabeth Cantor-Graae.

problem"; and the remaining 5 had seemed perfectly normal (Kasanin & Veo, 1932).

Another strategy for studying this question has been the use of child guidance clinic records, retrospectively examining the records of children who had been evaluated there and who later developed schizophrenia. The problem with this strategy is that children who are referred to a child guidance clinic are a select group who may already be showing early symptoms of schizophrenia. In 1958 O'Neal and Robins in St. Louis published a retrospective study of the records of 228 individuals with schizophrenia who had been examined in a child guidance clinic 30 years earlier; compared with "control subjects selected from public school records," the ones who developed schizophrenia had experienced a higher frequency of "severe infectious diseases in the first 2 years of life" ($p < .05$), had been slower to walk ($p < .05$), and had nonsignificant trends of higher occurrences of retarded development and hearing problems (O'Neal & Robins, 1958).

A similar retrospective study of child guidance clinic records was carried out by David Ricks and his colleagues in Boston. They noted that "withdrawal, apathy, and passivity" were especially common among the records of individuals who later developed chronic schizophrenia. Signs of neurological dysfunction were also prominent: "Slow motor development, poor co-ordination, unusual gait, tremor, hyperactive reflexes, and other symptoms suggesting neurologic impairment occurred in nearly 20 per cent of the pre-schizophrenic records, as compared to about 10 per cent of the controls." These researchers also found that "about 25 per cent" of the children who later developed schizophrenia had had delayed development of speech compared with 10% of the controls (Ricks & Nameche, 1966; Ricks & Berry, 1970).

Among the best-known studies of childhood antecedents of schizophrenia are those of Rachel Gittelman-Klein and her colleagues in New York who studied "premorbid asociality." Using scales rating such traits as social isolation and peer relationships, these researchers have shown that approximately one-third of individuals who later develop schizophrenia have preadolescent "premorbid asociality" (Gittelman-Klein & Klein, 1969). Such people tend to develop a chronic form of schizophrenia. One study of adults with schizophrenia showed a significant association between the traits of "premorbid asociality" and retarded development in the first 5 years of life (Torrey & Beemer, unpublished data). Another study indicated an association between "premorbid asociality" and enlarged brain ventricles on computerized tomography (CT) brain scans (Weinberger et al., 1980). Personality characteristics suggesting "premorbid asociality" were also noted by Watt and his colleagues in the primary school records of girls, but not boys, who later developed schizophrenia (Watt, 1978; Watt & Lubensky, 1975).

More recent studies have found additional evidence that some individuals with schizophrenia are different as children. Lynn DeLisi and her colleagues in New York collected developmental childhood histories for 100 individuals with schizophrenia who were being admitted to a psychiatric hospital for the first time. Compared with controls, the individuals with schizophrenia had experienced a higher rate of delayed development in speaking in sentences ($p < .05$) and in reading skills ($p < .001$) (DeLisi et al., 1991). In London Alice Foerster et al. (1991) found that males with schizophrenia being admitted to a psychiatric hospital had an increased number of "pre-morbid schizoid and schizotypal traits" and poorer "pre-morbid social adjustment" compared to admissions with bipolar disorder. Also in London, Timothy Crow and his colleagues, using prospectively collected data from people born in 1958 in the British Perinatal Mortality Survey, found that individuals who later developed schizophrenia, when tested at ages 7 and 11, showed an excess of speech, reading, and incontinence problems, and displayed more hostility and behavioral problems than those who had not developed schizophrenia (Crow et al., 1992; Done et al., 1993). In another English study, Aris Ambelas, retrospectively examining child guidance clinic records for individuals who later developed schizophrenia, also found that they had a high rate of developmental problems "in the areas of speech, language and reading" (Ambelas, 1992).

Perhaps the most impressive evidence in this investigation has come from the research of Walker and Lewine at Emory University and Barbara Fish and her colleagues at U.C.L.A. Dr. Walker collected home movies from families with more than one child, one of whom had developed schizophrenia as an adult, and then asked university students to try to identify which child would become sick. As the authors summarized their findings: "Although none of the subjects had any psychiatric disorder in childhood, the preschizophrenic children were reliably identified by the viewers. . . . Recorded observations about the preschizophrenic children noted less responsiveness, eye contact, and positive affect and poorer fine and gross motor coordination" (Walker & Lewine, 1990).

Fish and several other researchers, employing a novel strategy for studying schizophrenia, have followed from birth the offspring of mothers who have schizophrenia. Since it is projected that approximately 10% of such offspring will themselves develop the disease, it was hoped that by prospectively following this high-risk group, some early indicators of future disease might be detected.

In many high-risk studies the offspring have reached an age at which they will develop schizophrenia if they are going to. In 1992 Fish and colleagues summarized the evidence, showing that some of the children destined to develop schizophrenia had had "pandysmaturation," which included abnormalities of development (e.g., transient lags in developmental milestones such as walking) and retardation of skeletal growth (Fish et al., 1992). Fish believes that the "pandysmaturation" is inherited. Other studies of high-risk children who later develop schizophrenia are also finding evidence of early neurological dysfunction.

In summarizing the literature showing that people who develop schizophrenia are different as children, Offord and Cross (1969) suggested that "schizophrenic patients should be divided into two groups, those who have difficulty in childhood before the onset of the overt schizophrenia illness and those who do not." The former are characterized in childhood by "an increased evidence of scholastic difficulty, poor peer-group adjustment [and] evidence in childhood of minimal brain damage." The percentage of individuals with schizophrenia who showed such premorbid characteristics varies from study to study but appears to be in the range of 25 to 40%. Despite this, however, it is difficult to use such data to predict the development of schizophrenia in any given child (Hanson et al., 1990).

Identical twins in which one later develops schizophrenia afford a unique opportunity to examine questions about early development, since the well twin represents a genetic control. It is important to remember, however, that twinning itself affects development. Twins tend to be premature and lower in birth weight, thereby slowing their motor development. And because at least one-third of twins initially communicate in their own personal between-twin language, their regular language development is often retarded compared with non-twin children of the same age (Bryan, 1983, pp. 126–130).

Most twin studies of schizophrenia have not addressed the developmental issue directly, although individual case histories of twins who participated in such research suggest that some of the twins who developed schizophrenia were indeed different as children. For example, in an identical twin pair reported by MacSweeney (1970), the twin who later developed schizophrenia was "more difficult to manage . . . he cried more, was wilder in his behavior and tended to smash things up" prior to age five. In a pair of identical twins reported by Gottesman and Shields (1972, p. 78), the twin who later became sick was "always quiet and shy, retiring, nervous, frightened, and lacking in self-confidence" as a child. Similarly, the affected twin in one of Tienari's discordant identical twin pairs "played with his fingers markedly longer than normal . . . [and] was lonely and timid" (Tienari, 1963, p. 58).

Two twin studies have provided developmental data on a large number of identical twins in which one later developed schizophrenia. In Kringlen's study of Norwegian twins, many of the twins who developed schizophrenia were retrospectively identifiable in childhood by having been "more retarded psychomotorically, more lonely and reserved, more sensitive, more obsessional, more dependent, more nervous, [and] more submissive in the twinship" (Kringlen, 1967, p. 119). In reviewing this and previous twin studies, Kringlen concluded that "it must now be considered as a well-established fact that the schizophrenic twin was *even in childhood* less strong psychologically than the non-schizophrenic partner" (ibid., p. 122).

The other twin study that addressed the developmental issue was the American study of Pollin and colleagues. They found that "in the clearly schizophrenic group, five of seven control twins were the first to walk" (Pollin et al., 1966). Behaviorally, the twin who later developed schizophrenia was more likely to have had the following traits as a child: submissive, sensitive, serious-worrier, obedient-gentler, dependent, quiet-shy, and neurotic (Stabenau & Pollin, 1967). Pollin et al. also reviewed previous twin studies of schizophrenia and reported that the earlier studies showed childhood behavioral traits in the twins that developed schizophrenia that were virtually identical to their own findings.

Present Study

We used a variety of sources of information to assess the personalities of the twins at different stages of development. As summarized in Chapter 3, these included extensive questionnaires such as the Personality Inventory for Children (see Appendix D), retrospective comparisons of the twins with each other, and interviews with the mother (and sometimes also the father) after the questionnaires had been reviewed. All interviews and ratings of premorbid developmental traits were done by Edward Taylor, the senior social worker, and were completed while Dr. Taylor was still blind to the results of all other tests.

In the 27 twin pairs discordant for schizophrenia, comparison of early childhood traits in the twins who later became affected and those who remained well showed few significant differences when they were compared *as groups*, although trends were almost invariably in the expected direction. Primary and junior high school grades, reading skills, and peer relationships were very similar. In primary school, 3 affected and 3 well twins (including both members of 2 pairs) required special education classes for reading or other learning problems; in junior high school, 4 affected but only 1 well twin required such classes. There were nonsignificant trends for the affected twins to have shown more disruptive behavior in both primary school and junior high (7 affected vs. 2 well twins; $p = .14$, Fisher's exact test) and for the affected twins to have been perceived by teachers as being less highly motivated (8 affected vs. 2 well twins; $p = .08$, Fisher's exact test).

Another measure of early childhood development is leadership within the twin pair, and we sought information on this for the preschool, primary school, and high school years. Previous studies of twins discordant for schizophrenia have suggested that the twin who remains well is much more likely to have been the leader of the two in childhood. Among our twins during primary school, the well twin was the leader in 15 pairs, the affected twin was the leader in 9 pairs, they were equal in 2 pairs, and data were insufficient to make a judgment in 1 pair. Thus there is a trend in the same direction as in previous studies, but it is not statistically significant ($p = .09$, McNemar's chi-square for matched pairs).

Despite the paucity of statistically significant *group* differences in childhood developmental traits between affected and well twins, it became clear early in the study that there were *individual* twin pairs in which the twin who would later develop schizophrenia was clearly different. Among the 27 twin pairs, in primary school 4 affected twins (15%) had been shy and withdrawn and had had very few friends, the personality traits that are classically associated with premorbid asociality. Another 4 affected twins (15%) had been unusually aggressive, argumentative, and/or exhibited odd behaviors. Learning problems and signs of neurological dysfunction had also been found among many of these 8 affected twins. A description of these 8 twins follows:

> DS-2: At age 5 the affected twin became much more aggressive and argumentative, and continued to be so until the onset of her illness at age 14.

> DS-7: From early childhood the affected twin was noted to be very clumsy and said by his father to "trip over his own shadow." At age 8 he began having problems concentrating in school and to become increasingly quiet and withdrawn. He was seen by a pediatrician who prescribed methylphenidate (Ritalin) with some improvement. He was diagnosed with schizophrenia at age 19.

> DS-13: At age 5 both twins were noted to be extremely shy and withdrawn. After repeating kindergarten, both were placed in a special class for children with learning disabilities. They later returned to regular classes and graduated from high school. The affected twin was diagnosed with schizophrenia at age 19.

> DS-17: At age 5 both twins were noted to have difficulty reading and concentrating, and at age 8 both were labeled as "borderline

dyslexic." The affected twin was more shy, quiet, and dependent, but also got upset more easily and was more argumentative. He had problems with enuresis (bed-wetting) until age 7, 3 years longer than his twin. He was diagnosed with schizophrenia at age 22.

DS-18: The affected twin's developmental milestones (walking, talking, toilet trained) were considerably later than those of his brother. He was also much less coordinated; for example, he had problems throwing a ball or riding a bike. Behaviorally, he was shy and withdrawn, and occasionally exhibited odd behavior, such as a phobia of stairs. At age 8 the quality of his drawings was said to deteriorate. He was diagnosed with schizophrenia at age 14.

DS-19: At age 5 the affected twin was noted by his kindergarten teacher to have "a strange gait" and to lose his previous ability to tie his shoes. He also was said to be socially immature and was asked to repeat the year. In primary school he required speech therapy for one year, had reading problems, and was less coordinated than his brother; for example, he could not do a somersault. He was also recalled as having been intolerant of noise, sometimes holding his hands over his ears. At age 9 he began having occasional outbursts of screaming in the classroom and became more withdrawn. At age 11 he missed much of the school year because of these problems. However, he was not diagnosed with schizophrenia until age 26.

DS-23: At age 3 the affected twin developed a hand-washing compulsion and strong fear of germs, which persisted throughout childhood. Both twins were shy and socially withdrawn although academically successful. The affected twin was diagnosed with schizophrenia at age 29.

DS-24: The affected twin started walking one month after his brother. At age 5 he was referred for speech therapy because of "baby talk." In school he had difficulty concentrating, could not sit still, and was diagnosed as "borderline hyperactive." Later in primary school he had temper tantrums and inappropriate aggressive outbursts. He was diagnosed with schizophrenia at age 22.

The co-occurrence of behavioral, learning, and neurological problems in these children is impressive. One reason for this is that such problems tend to interact with each other, so that a child with behavioral problems may have more difficulty learning to read, or a very clumsy child may be ridiculed by peers, leading to social withdrawal. Beyond such interactions, however, one is left with an impression with many of these children that their behavioral, cognitive, and neurological problems may have all been part of a nonspecific cerebral dysfunction in childhood that manifested itself later in life as schizophrenia. The overall picture is similar to the "pandysmaturation" syndrome described by Fish et al. (1992) in some of the children they studied who later developed schizophrenia.

The Concept of Divergence

As our research project progressed and it became clear that a subgroup of affected twins had been different as children, we sought ways in which this subgroup could be objectively delineated. No single behavioral, cognitive, or neurological measure adequately defined the difference, so a combined measure of "divergence" evolved. Divergence utilizes the twin who remained well as a baseline control against which to compare the twin who developed schizophrenia. It takes advantage of the identical twin paradigm insofar as both twins experienced similar family events (e.g., a divorce or death) and both have identical genes, so when one twin diverges markedly and permanently from the other in behavioral, cognitive, and/or neurological skills, such divergence may be indicative of a change in cerebral function.

We defined divergence as the age at which the twin who later became sick began markedly and permanently to diverge from the twin who remained well behaviorally, cognitively, and/or neurologically. Instead of asking the question "when did the affected twin become sick," we asked "when did the affected twin become *different*." A decision on the age of divergence was made by Dr. Taylor on the basis of all the information available on the developmental histories, and was completed while he was still blind to all test results.

Using the above criteria, it was determined that 7 affected twins had had an early age of divergence (by the age of 5), and that all others diverged at age 13 or older, usually within the 2 years preceding the onset of their illness (Figure 5.1). The 7 affected twins with an early age of divergence were DS-2, 7, 17, 18, 19, 23, and 24, described previously. Information was available from school records or other relatives, which corraborated the parental history in 5 of these 7 twins. The 8th affected twin described previously, DS-13, did not qualify as having had an early divergence because her co-twin had also been shy and withdrawn with learning disabilities. Only one other affected twin was seriously considered as possibly having had an early age of divergence. In twin pair DS-5

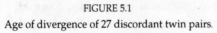

FIGURE 5.1

Age of divergence of 27 discordant twin pairs.

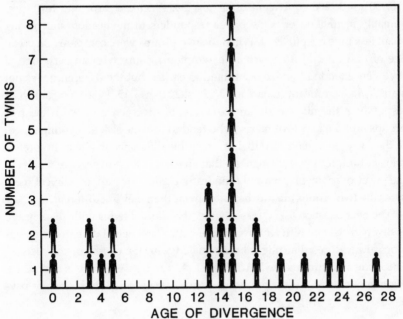

the affected twin had been 2 to 6 weeks slower in developmental milestones, and at age 4 had begun to twirl her hair and suck her thumb for
extended periods, in contrast to her sister. During their school years,
however, there were apparently no recognizable differences between
them, so they did not meet the criteria for *permanent* change.

As can be seen in Figure 5.1, the distribution of age of divergence is
bimodal, with 7 affected twins (27%) meeting the criteria for early divergence and 20 affected twins having had a later age of divergence. The first
question asked was whether schizophrenia in the twins with an early age of
divergence differed in any way from the disease in twins with later divergence. When the affected twins in the two groups were compared on clinical
measures, there was virtually no difference in the mean age at time of testing, years discordant at time of testing, acuteness of onset, headache at time
of onset, neurological abnormalities, or negative symptom score as measured by the SANS (Andreasen, 1981). There was a tendency for the affected
twins with an early age of divergence to have a better response to antipsychotic medication (5/5 vs. 13/20 average or better responders), to have
spent less total time hospitalized (0.5 vs. 1.4 years), and to be functioning
better at the time of testing (42.7 vs. 39.5 on axis V). The only clinical com-

parison that achieved statistical significance, however, was a lower mean lifetime antipsychotic medication intake for the early divergence group (10,500 vs. 36,400 equivalent units; $p = .04$, Wilcoxon rank sum test), presumably a function of being better responders to medication and having spent less time hospitalized. When the two groups were compared on mean age of first referral for psychiatric symptoms, those with an early age of divergence tended to have been referred earlier, but the difference was not statistically significant (mean age 18.7 vs. 22.0; $p = .15$, Wilcoxon rank sum test). Given the marked difference in age of divergence between the two groups and the excess of males (who tend to become sick at a younger age) in the early divergence group, however, this difference in age of first referral is not impressive and suggests that an early age of divergence results in the onset of schizophrenia only modestly earlier. Overall, on clinical measures the two groups are much more similar than they are different.

The next question asked was whether the affected twins with an early age of divergence were different from those with a later age of divergence on etiological measures that might be associated with the causes of the disease. The results are summarized in Table 5.1. As can be seen, there is a trend for the twins with an early age of divergence to have a family history of psy-

TABLE 5.1
Comparison of Affected Twins with Early Age of Divergence and Later Age of Divergence

	Early Divergence $N = 7$	Later Divergence $N = 20$	Statistical Significance
Family history of psychosis	4/7	3/19	$p = .06$, Fisher's exact test
Male	6/7	10/20	$p = .18$, Fisher's exact test
Mean minor physical anomaly score	7.0	5.2	$p = .13$, Wilcoxon rank sum test
Total finger ridge count >12% difference	4/7	5/20	$p = .18$, Fisher's exact test
Birth weight lighter by >20%	3/7	1/20	$p = .04$, Fisher's exact test
Mean total score for obstetrical complications	8.0	3.5	$p = .06$, Wilcoxon rank sum test
Firstborn	5/7	10/20	$p = .41$, Fisher's exact test
Born Jan. to April	5/7	7/20	$p = .18$, Fisher's exact test

chosis ($p = .06$). They were also more likely to be male ($p = .18$), to have a higher occurrence of minor physical anomalies ($p = .13$), to have greater differences in total finger ridge counts ($p = .18$), to include the twins who were markedly lighter at birth ($p = .04$), to have had more obstetrical complications ($p = .06$), and to have been born between January and April ($p = .18$). Although only the birth-weight measurement achieved statistical significance, the uniformity of the results is impressive in suggesting that the affected twins with an early age of divergence may be etiologically different.

Another question asked was whether the twins with an early age of divergence in childhood are the same as the twins identified in Chapter 4, who had suggestions of a genetic or perinatal predisposition. The results of the comparison would suggest that these are the same twins. This is confirmed in Table 5.2, which lists the twin pairs individually. All affected twins with an early age of divergence except one (DS-19) had either a family history of psychosis (1 twin), perinatal problems (2 twins), or both (3 twins). The only affected twin with an early age of divergence but with neither a family history of psychosis nor perinatal problems (DS-19) had the onset of behavioral, cognitive, and neurological problems almost simultaneously, at approximately age 5.

In summary, the present study suggests that for a subgroup of individuals who are affected with schizophrenia, the disease has biological roots that go back to childhood. This subgroup does not appear to be clinically distinct (e.g., on negative symptom scores or neurological abnormalities) but may be etiologically distinct on factors pertinent to the cause of the disease. Emil Kraepelin, in fact, arrived at a similar conclusion when he suggested that "the psychic abnormalities which precede the real onset of dementia praecox [schizophrenia] already represent in part at least the action of the cause of the disease, even if they can be traced back into the first years of the patient's life" (Kraepelin, 1919, p. 238). Establishing an age of "onset" of disease for this subgroup of patients is extremely difficult because, as Kraepelin also noted, "all sorts of insidious changes have already for years been developing imperceptibly" (ibid., p. 210). This subgroup of individuals might be said to have pre-schizophrenia of childhood.

Is Childhood Pre-schizophrenia Related to Childhood Onset Schizophrenia?

Since the findings of our study as well as other studies have suggested that some individuals who get schizophrenia as adults have had pre-schizophrenia or early manifestations of the disease in childhood, it is

TABLE 5.2
Genetic Predisposition, Perinatal Predisposition, Childhood Problems, Head Trauma, and Physical Illnesses in Affected Twins

	Genetic Predisposition (family history of psychosis)	Perinatal Predisposition (defined in Chap. 4)	Childhood Problems (divergence by age 5)	Head Trauma and Physical Illnesses Preceding Onset
DS- 1				
2	+		+	
3				"Flulike syndrome"
4	+			
5		+		Enlarged lymph nodes
6				
7		+	+	Severe illness in infancy
8				
9				
10				Head trauma
11				Head trauma
12				
13				
14				
15				Abdominal pains
16				
17	+	+	+	Head trauma (severe)
18		+	+	
19			+	
20				
21				
22	+	+		Mononucleosis 1 year earlier
23	+	+	+	
24	+	+	+	
25				Viral illness with rash
26	+			
27	[–]	+		

logical to ask whether this antecedent condition is related in any way to childhood onset schizophrenia, which has been defined as "childhood psychoses, beginning after 5 years of age, with symptoms comparable with those found in adult forms of schizophrenia" (Beitchman, 1985). Recent studies have clearly differentiated this condition from infantile autism, which is said to begin before the age of 3. In the DSM-III-R system of classification currently in use, childhood schizophrenia is subsumed under the broader category of schizophrenia and is assumed to be an early, although comparatively rare, variant of the adult disease (Russell et al., 1989; Green et al., 1992).

A comparison of the affected twins with pre-schizophrenia in the present study and children with childhood onset schizophrenia reveals many similarities. Males predominate among our affected twins with pre-schizophrenia; in childhood onset schizophrenia males also predominate by a ratio of approximately 2:1 (Beitchman, 1985; Russell et al., 1989). A family history of psychosis was found in 4 out of 7 of our affected twins, and genetic factors have also been found to be prominent in childhood onset schizophrenia (Hanson & Gottesman, 1976; Beitchman, 1985; Green et al., 1992).

In addition, an excess of minor physical anomalies was found among our affected twins with pre-schizophrenia; studies of minor physical anomalies in children with childhood onset schizophrenia have also found them to be prominent (Goldfarb, 1967; Steg & Rapoport, 1975). Increased obstetrical complications occurred in the present group, and there are suggestions that they may also be increased in childhood onset schizophrenia (Pollack & Woerner, 1966; Beitchman, 1985), although not all studies have found this (Green et al., 1984). Among the affected twins with pre-schizophrenia in our study there is a suggestion of a winter-spring birth seasonality (5 of 7 twins were born between January and April); studies of childhood onset schizophrenia, although often confounded by the inclusion of autism, have also shown an excessive number of winter and spring births (McNeil et al., 1971; Bolton et al., 1992). Finally, dilatation of the cerebral ventricles on CT and MRI scans is found in some cases of schizophrenia (Chapter 6), as well as in some cases of childhood onset schizophrenia (Woody et al., 1987; Hendren et al., 1991).

A final point of comparison is the long-term course of these disorders. In the present study the 7 affected twins with manifestations of pre-schizophrenia tended to respond better to medication, had spent less time psychiatrically hospitalized, and functioned better at the time of testing compared to the affected twins with no manifestations of pre-schizophrenia. This trend was surprising because it was contrary to what we would have predicted. Recent studies of childhood onset schizophrenia have also reported a surprisingly favorable outcome for some children. Bender (1973) found that 38% of such patients had "made a social adjustment as adults." Eggers (1978) reported that 20% of his patients "recovered completely" and another 30% "reached a relatively good social adjustment." Kydd and Werry (1982) followed up 10 children and concluded that "the outcome in childhood schizophrenia may be more favorable than generally assumed."

In summary, there appear to be many similarities between the affected twins in the present study who have manifestations of pre-schizophrenia and individuals who have childhood onset schizophrenia. One group may be said to have a latent form of schizophrenia in childhood, whereas the other group has a manifest form of the disease. It is possible that they are alternative outcomes to common genetic, *in utero,* or early childhood biological antecedents and that they thus share a common etiology. If this is so, then is adult onset schizophrenia, in which there are no childhood manifestations, another outcome of these same antecedents or is it a separate disease altogether?

Does Divergence Also Apply to Non-twin Individuals with Schizophrenia?

The use of divergence in identical twins to establish more firmly that some individuals who later develop schizophrenia were different in childhood is one of the more important findings to emerge from our study. If divergence is a valid concept only among identical twins, however, then it will obviously be of limited utility. During the course of the study we wondered whether divergence might also be applied to non-twins, and using siblings and peers as a point of reference, a preliminary study was carried out to ascertain this.

At the annual meeting of the National Alliance for the Mentally Ill (NAMI) in 1990, a two-page questionnaire was distributed to attendees. The people who filled out the questionnaires were asked to state their relationship to the person affected, to complete a brief checklist of symptoms, and to check the predominant diagnosis given the affected person. We restricted our analysis to those individuals who had been predominantly diagnosed with schizophrenia or schizoaffective disorder and in whom at least 3 of the following 4 symptoms were checked: (1) hearing voices, (2) delusions, (3) jumbled (illogical) thought processes, and (4) catatonia.

The remainder of the questionnaire requested information regarding family history for serious mental illnesses, age of first referral to a mental health professional, age of first psychiatric hospitalization, whether the affected person had ever been referred for psychological or neurological testing while in elementary school, whether the affected person had ever been referred for special education while in elementary school, questions regarding problems during pregnancy, and questions regarding possible divergence. These last two questions were phrased as follows:

1)   During pregnancy, delivery, and the first month of life of your son/daughter who later developed schizophrenia or schizoaffective disorder, did anything unusual happen?_____yes(1)_____no(2). (If you had bleeding during pregnancy, please indicate approximately which month(s).) If yes, please describe:

_____

_____

2)   Some people who get schizophrenia or schizoaffective disorder appear to behave within a normal range until a few weeks or months before symptoms of their illness appear. Other people who get sick have exhibited for many years behaviors that make them clearly different from their brothers/sisters/peers even though symptoms of their illness do not appear until later. Thinking back on the childhood of your son or daughter, which group did he/she fall into? (Choose one.)

_____Behavior was clearly different from brothers/sisters/peers by the age of 5 years even though symptoms of illness did not begin until later.

_____Behavior became clearly different from brothers/sisters/peers between ages 6 and 12 years even though symptoms of illness did not begin until later.

_____Behavior was within a normal range until age 13 years or older.

If you checked (a) or (b), please also tell us at what age your son/daughter was first noticeably different (your best guess) and *how* he/she was different:

_____

_____

Replies to the problems-during-pregnancy-and-delivery question were rated on a 0 (no problems) to 6 (severe problems) scale by one of us (E.F.T.) using the criteria developed by McNeil et al. (Chapter 4) and without knowledge of the respondents' answers to other questions.

A total of 671 completed questionnaires were received that met all criteria just outlined. It was estimated by us that the respondents represented approximately half of all possible respondents at the NAMI meeting, and it was not possible to ascertain in what ways our sample may have been biased. The families were only told that it was a research questionnaire on development, and at the time none of our twin study findings on divergence had yet been published or presented.

In terms of divergence, 24% of the parents reported that the behavior of their son or daughter had been "clearly different from their brothers/sisters/peers by the age of 5." This is close to the 30% of the affected twins in the discordant pairs in the present study who were reported to be different from their co-twins. In the questionnaire study 14% of parents reported that their son/daughter became "clearly different from brothers/sisters/peers between ages 6 and 12," and in 62% their "behavior was within a normal range until age 13 years or older." Thus the responses were not as cleanly bimodal as were the results of divergence in the twins, but they are in the same direction.

Correlations between the age of divergence and scores for problems during pregnancy and delivery were highly significant. Mothers of individuals whose behavior had become "different" by age 5 reported having had pregnancy and delivery complications that were almost twice as severe as mothers of individuals whose behavior was "within a normal range" until age 13 or older (pregnancy complication score of 2.4 vs. 1.4; p <.0001, t test). Looked at another way, 46% of the offspring of mothers with the most severe pregnancy and delivery complications (scores 4–6) had behavior that made them "different" by age 5, whereas only 22% of these offspring had behavior that was "within a normal range" until age 13 or older.

The children whose behavior had become "different" by age 5 were compared to those whose behavior had been "within a normal range" until age 13 or older on several other measures. The early divergence group had been referred to a mental health professional significantly earlier (mean age 15.2 vs. 19.6; p <.0001, t test) and had been hospitalized significantly earlier (mean age 20.1 vs. 21.4; p <.009, t test). Not surprisingly, the early divergence group were also more likely than the later divergence group to have been referred for psychological or neurological testing (52% vs. 7%) or referred for special education (36% vs. 8%) in elementary school. There was also a nonsignificant trend for the early divergence group to have a family history for major mental illness (p = .11, chi-square). No significant correlations were found between the age of divergence and sex, order of birth, season of birth, or total years hospitalized.

On almost every measure, the individuals who were said to become "different" between ages 6 and 12 had values midway between the two groups discussed.

In summary, the results of our preliminary questionnaire on non-twins who developed schizophrenia or schizoaffective disorder are congruent with the concept of divergence derived from the twin study. There appears to be a subgroup of 24 to 30% of individuals who develop schizophrenia—both twins and non-twins—who are recognizably different on behavioral grounds by the age of 5. For at least some of this group, these behavioral changes are associated with problems that occurred during pregnancy and delivery. Controlled studies of this association are needed.

Are Some Cases Caused by Head Trauma or Illness?

Ever since the early years of this century, there has been speculation that some cases of schizophrenia might be caused by head trauma or physical illnesses, especially infections. Emil Kraepelin, in his 1919 treatise, mentioned both possibilities, but also noted methodological problems inherent in proving causation in such cases. Episodes of head trauma, said Kraepelin, "are in any case so frequent that they can only quite exceptionally be made use of for establishing a cause" (p. 241). He also said that the possibility that "infections in the years of development that might have a causal significance cannot in its indefiniteness be either proved or disproved" (ibid., p. 240). In the intervening years, studies have suggested that head injuries do occur more commonly preceding schizophrenia than in control populations (Davison & Bagley, 1969; Wilcox & Nasrallah, 1987a) and that cerebral viral infections may be responsible for some cases of schizophrenia (Menninger, 1922; Torrey, 1986).

In previous schizophrenia twin studies, head trauma and physical illnesses have also been cited as possible etiological factors. Rosanoff et al. (1934) claimed that 5 of their 9 identical twin pairs, in which only one twin had developed schizophrenia, were "of traumatic or infectious origin." The evidence for causality in some of their twins was weak (head trauma with unconsciousness for "a few minutes," which occurred 46 *years* prior to the onset of schizophrenia), but in other twins causality appeared plausible (head trauma with unconsciousness for two weeks followed immediately by personality change and the onset of schizophrenia 1 year later). Pollin and Stabenau (1968) in their twin study reported that the affected twins in the discordant pairs had had a higher occurrence of childhood central nervous system illnesses compared to the well twins (5 cases to 2 cases); these included one affected twin who had had meningitis at age 9 and another who had had severe Rocky Mountain spotted fever at age 3. Slater and Shields (1953, p. 190) also described a pair of identical twins in which the one who developed schizophrenia had had life-threatening meningitis at age 4 and after that "he was always a bit slower, a bit scatter-brained."

In the present study we attempted to assess the importance of head trauma and physical illnesses that took place prior to the onset of schizophrenia by including questions in our routine history about head trauma, seizures, routine childhood illnesses, mononucleosis, and any other serious injury or illness. For the affected twins we asked specifically about physical illnesses that occurred preceding or concurrent with the onset of schizophrenia. When serious trauma or illnesses were reported, we obtained the medical records whenever possible.

The results are shown in Table 5.3. Head trauma with unconsciousness occurred in 3 affected and 4 well twins; however, all 3 of the twins who later developed schizophrenia were hospitalized following their head trauma, whereas none of the 4 well twins were hospitalized.

The most severe head trauma occurred in an affected twin (DS-17) who at age 12 was in a vehicular accident, with resulting immediate seizures, unconsciousness for 1 week (during which he had some decerebrate posturing and hyperreflexia), hospitalization for 3 weeks, and then complete recovery over 3 months. Although such severe head trauma might be suffi-

TABLE 5.3

Head Trauma and Physical Illnesses in 27 Identical Twins Discordant for Schizophrenia

	Affected Twins	Well Twins
Head trauma with unconsciousness		
with hospitalization	3	0
without hospitalization	0	4
Seizures		
nonfebrile	1	0
febrile	0	3
Routine childhood illnesses	Equal	Equal
Major childhood illnesses	1	1
Mononucleosis	5	3
Physical illnesses preceding or concurrent with onset of schizophrenia	4	——

cient to cause the symptoms of schizophrenia, the relationship of the head trauma and schizophrenia in this case is unclear because the young man had no personality change following the injury, got better grades than his co-twin in high school, and did not exhibit any symptoms of schizophrenia until age 22. At the time of testing, this twin was one of the least cognitively impaired of all affected twins on neuropsychological tests.

Furthermore, this affected twin had shown other indicators of increased liability to schizophrenia prior to his head trauma. He had a family history for psychosis, more minor physical anomalies and a 13% lower total finger ridge count than his twin, weighed 35% less than his twin at birth following a complicated delivery (forceps used for an occiput posterior presentation), and was left-handed. In childhood he had also had enuresis for 3 years longer than his twin, had been labeled as "borderline dyslexic," and had been shyer and quieter than his twin. Indeed, there are so many possible predisposing factors for schizophrenia in this affected twin that there is no way to know which ones are most relevant and precisely what role the head trauma may have played in the causative chain of events.

The other 2 affected twins with a history of head trauma suffered less severe injuries. One of them (DS-10) fell off his bike at age 12, was unconscious for "a few minutes," but was then hospitalized for 3 days for observation because of "disorientation." The other (DS-11) fell at age 6, was unconscious for "3 to 5 minutes" and subsequently hospitalized for 2 days for observation.

Among the 4 well twins who reported a history of head trauma, the most serious occurred in a 14-year-old girl (DS-2) who was thrown from a horse, was unconscious for 2 hours, said to be "blind" for the following week, and stayed home from school, although she was not hospitalized. The other 3 well twins with head trauma included 1 (DS-3) who fell from a roof and was unconscious "for a very brief period," 1 (DS-4) who "passed out for a few minutes" following a motorcycle accident, and 1 (DS-14) who was unconscious for 20 minutes following a bicycle accident. As noted, none of the 4 well twins were admitted to hospitals for observation following their injuries, in contrast to the 3 affected twins, who were all admitted.

No affected twin had had either a febrile or a nonfebrile seizure prior to the onset of illness, except for the twin (DS-17) who had had seizures immediately following his severe head trauma. In the general population, approximately 1 out of 25 children have a history of having had a febrile seizure. A comparison of routine childhood illnesses showed virtually no differences between the affected and well twins. One affected twin (DS-7) survived a life-threatening illness in infancy, which was said to be viral in origin, possibly encephalitis or meningitis (discussed in Chapter 4). One well twin (DS-8) was diagnosed with pulmonary stenosis at age 2 months and subsequently had open-heart surgery to repair the defect. Regarding mononucleosis, 5 affected twins (DS-5, 16, 21, 22, and 26) and 3 well twins (DS-19, 26, and 27) were said to have had symptoms of this disease, although in the majority of cases it was not confirmed by blood tests. In one of the affected twins (DS-22) the mononucleosis occurred 1 year prior to the onset of schizophrenia, and this case was confirmed by blood tests.

Four other affected twins had a history of having had a physical illness immediately preceding or accompanying the onset of their schizophrenia. The most interesting such case (DS-3) was a man with no known preexisting indicators of liability or risk for the disease. At age 27 he experienced a severe flulike syndrome that lasted for 1 month and incapacitated him. Three months later he began having paranoid ideas, complained of a "vision," and then slowly developed a full schizophrenia syndrome over the following 2 years.

In another case (DS-5) a young woman developed persistently enlarged lymph nodes in her neck at age 17, with negative blood tests for mononucleosis. The symptoms of schizophrenia began a few months later with headaches, irrational fears, premonitions, inappropriate giggling, bizarre behavior, and subsequent psychiatric hospitalizations. Another twin (DS-15), who developed symptoms of schizophrenia at age 20 over a period of 3 months, complained of abdominal pains for several weeks during the onset of her disease. Finally, a 14-year-old twin (DS-25) became psychiatrically ill immediately following a "viral illness" that included "red spots" on his arms, legs, and trunk. He became depressed, withdrew from his friends, and began having auditory hallucinations.

What is the relationship of these episodes of head trauma and physical illnesses to the onset of schizophrenia? One can argue that many of them are no more than chance occurrences, more likely to be remembered by parents because they took place preceding the onset of the schizophrenia. On the other hand, the number of them is impressive and consistent with the reported findings in the previous twin studies of Rosanoff et al. (1934) and Pollin and Stabenau (1968). Their precise etiological role, if any, remains to be delineated.

Viral and Immunological Studies

From the inception of our twin study, we had planned to look for evidence of possible past viral infections and immune dysfunction in the affected twins. For that reason plasma, lymphocytes, and (in those who agreed) cerebrospinal fluid were collected. Several studies are under way using these samples. Specimens have also been stored for future analysis, and lymphocytes from some twins have been transformed so that they can also be used in genetic studies.

Viruses have been suggested as being the cause of some cases of schizophrenia since the early years of this century. The evidence includes an excess number of births in the winter and spring months of people who later develop schizophrenia; an increased number of people who later develop schizophrenia whose mothers were exposed to the influenza virus during pregnancy; an increased number of cases associated with urban crowding, which could facilitate transmission of a virus; and the fact that some cases of known viral encephalitis have clinical symptoms similar to schizophrenia (Torrey, 1986; Torrey & Kaufmann, 1986; Torrey & Bowler, 1990). Previous attempts to identify viruses or viral antibodies in samples from individuals with schizophrenia have yielded conflicting results.

In the present study a variety of viral research projects are under way. The most promising, to date, is the finding of antibodies in the plasma of 10 of 25 (40%) of the affected discordant twins with schizophrenia to pestiviruses (derived from *pestis,* Latin for plague) (Yolken et al., 1993). This group of viruses are well known as animal pathogens but have not previously been found in humans. They are members of the Flavivirus family, which also includes the group B arboviruses (arthropod-borne viruses, many of which cause encephalitis in humans), rubella, and hepatitis C. None of the 25 well co-twins among the discordant pairs reacted to the pestivirus antigen, and 1 of the 16 normal control twins reacted to it. Cerebrospinal fluid from 6 of the twins reacted the same as the plasma (3 positive and 3 negative). Initial studies with the bipolar twins found that 3 of the 8 (38%) of the affected twins also reacted to this antigen, and none of the 8 well co-twins did. Pestiviruses are especially interesting to schizophrenia researchers because the pestivirus that infects cattle is known to be transmitted *in utero,* but most cows do not develop symptoms for several years. It is also known to be strongly neurotropic and to have a special affinity for neurons in the hippocampus (Fernandez et al., 1989).

Immunologic abnormalities have also been reported since the early years of this century in some individuals with schizophrenia, but the results have been conflicting (Rapaport & McAllister, 1991). Recent studies have focused on subsets of lymphocytes and peripheral autoantibody production, both of which are known to be abnormal in many immune diseases. Whether such abnormalities are caused by immune alterations from autoimmune disease or by immune activation from a viral infection is not known.

Our study found the twins with schizophrenia to have significantly higher levels of serum-soluble interleukin-2 receptors compared to the well twins (Rapaport et al., 1993). Elevations of these interleukin-2 receptors have previously been described in individuals with schizophrenia (Ganguli & Rabin, 1989; Licinio et al., 1991) and are also known to occur in autoimmune disorders and infections. In another finding from the present twin study, a preliminary analysis of lymphocyte subsets found an elevation of CD5+CD19+ lymphocytes in the discordant twins with schizophrenia compared to the well co-twins (Sambunaris et al., 1993), which also suggests immune dysfunction in these individuals. These studies are continuing.

Can We Predict Who Will Get Schizophrenia?

The results of this study confirm previous research suggesting that individuals with adult onset schizophrenia have more genetic, perinatal, and childhood indicators of disease liability than do individuals who do not have schizophrenia. For some indicators of liability there are statistically significant differences between groups, and for other indicators there is a clustering of liability indicators in certain affected twins. Does this mean that these indicators of liability can be used to predict specifically who will get schizophrenia if a sufficient perinatal and childhood history is available?

The answer is clearly no. The associations we have discussed, which link various perinatal and childhood measures to the development of schizophrenia, are statistical measures only and have virtually no predictive value for individual cases. Genetically, only approximately 10% of those who have a parent with schizophrenia will themselves develop the disease. For minor physical anomalies in the present study, two *well* twins had minor physical anomaly scores 3 points higher than their affected co-twins. Within-pair total finger ridge counts were virtually equal in the majority of twins discordant for schizophrenia. Birth weight had no significant association except in the four cases in which one twin was ≥20% lighter; even here, however, there were four other twin pairs in which the *well* twin was 16 to 18% lighter. In the case of obstetrical complications, in one twin pair (DS-6) the affected twin had had a completely uncomplicated delivery while the well twin, who was second-born, was delivered breech after a delay of 43 minutes. In another pair in which both were delivered breech, it was the *well* twin who sustained a fractured femur from the traumatic delivery. Non-right-handedness was also not a predictor of which twin would get schizophrenia, for there were two twin pairs in which the affected twin was right-handed and the well twin was non-right-handed.

In childhood, only 4 of the 27 affected twins exhibited markedly shy and withdrawn behavior, thought to be an early sign of impending disease; there were other pairs, however, in which the well twin had been slightly more shy and withdrawn. School grades were strikingly similar between affected and well twins, as were reading and speech problems. Leadership within twin pairs in childhood was assumed more frequently by the well twin, but the difference was not statistically significant. Suggestions of neurological dysfunction, such as delayed developmental milestones or lack of coordination, were perhaps the single most reliable predictor of which twin would later become affected, but neurological markers accounted for only 8 out of the 27 affected twins.

The lack of predictive ability in individual cases for perinatal and childhood indicators of liability can perhaps best be summarized by twin pair DS-2, which has a family history of psychosis. In this pair, one twin was 18% lighter at birth; had difficulty breathing following birth; was more shy and quiet than her co-twin, who was the leader; and had a head injury resulting in unconsciousness for 2 hours and was said to be "blind" for a week after. This twin remains completely *well* at age 44 while her co-twin, to whom none of these things happened, has had schizophrenia since the age of 14.

CHAPTER 6

Does Schizophrenia Change the Structure of the Brain?

D
OES SCHIZOPHRENIA change the structure of the brain? John Haslam noted that it did as early as 1798, but it has taken almost 200 years to prove that he was right. Haslam, one of the first physicians to describe schizophrenia, noted that on autopsies many of his patients had enlarged ventricles in their brains (Waddington, 1984).

It was not until the introduction of pneumoencephalography early in this century, however, that brain structures could be studied in living subjects. In this procedure, air is injected into the ventricular spaces in the brain to temporarily replace the cerebrospinal fluid and thereby permit X-ray outlines of the adjacent structures. In 1927 the first pneumoencephalography study was carried out on 19 individuals with schizophrenia, and 18 of them were said to have enlarged ventricles. Over the next 35 years several additional studies reported similar results, but they were largely ignored because there was little interest in biological aspects of schizophrenia at that time.

The introduction of computerized tomography (CT) scans in 1974 initiated a veritable revolution in research on brain structure. CT scans, which use X rays, were supplemented 10 years later by magnetic resonance imaging (MRI) scans, which use magnetic fields and radio waves, thus

Contributing to the research discussed in this chapter were Drs. Daniel R. Weinberger, Richard L. Suddath, George W. Christison, Manuel F. Casanova, Katalin Vladar, Laura Marsh, Jeffrey R. Zigun, Douglas W. Jones, Richard Coppola, Nicholas W. Carosella, Michael S. Myslobodsky, Thomas F. McNeil, H. Stefan Bracha, Patricia O. Quinn, Kenneth C. Rickler, and Lewellyn B. Bigelow, and Ms. Alycia J. Bartley, Ms. Jennifer J. Kulynych, Ms. Elizabeth Cantor-Graae, and Mr. Mark Zito.

enabling the brain to be visualized, without the danger of radiation. MRI imaging technology continues to improve, with three-dimensional reconstructions and volumetric assessments now possible.

CT and MRI scans have proved conclusively that schizophrenia does change the structure of the brain. The most commonly observed abnormality is mild to moderate dilatation of the lateral and third ventricles, now shown to occur in schizophrenia in over 100 controlled studies (Hyde et al., 1991). These studies have established that the dilatation is not an effect of medication taken by patients, for it was seen in the pneumoencephalography studies before such medication was available and it is seen in studies of newly diagnosed patients before they have taken any medication. The studies also suggest that the ventricular dilatation is static, present at the onset of the schizophrenia and not progressing further. In addition, mild to moderate ventricular dilatation is also found in some patients with brain tumors, stroke, multiple sclerosis, Alzheimer's disease, and bipolar disorder, as well as occasionally being present in normal individuals with no known brain pathology; thus it is a nonspecific finding.

Another clearly established abnormality in brain structure in schizophrenia is decreased size of the hippocampus and amygdala, critical components of the limbic system. At least seven separate research groups have reported this finding using MRIs, and several other researchers have reported neuropathological and neurochemical changes in the hippocampus and amygdala on autopsy studies (Hyde et al., 1991). It seems likely that damage to these structures is related to the symptoms of schizophrenia. Other parts of the limbic system also show changes on neuropathological and neurochemical studies; for example, dopamine D-2 receptors have been shown to be increased in the nucleus accumbens.

Several other structural differences have been reported in the brains of individuals with schizophrenia, but they have not been as clearly established as ventricular dilatation and changes in the hippocampus and amygdala. Some reports suggest that the brain in schizophrenia shrinks or atrophies slightly, thereby making the sulcal spaces surrounding the brain appear more prominent.

There have also been reports of abnormal gyral or sulcal patterns on the surface of the brain, asymmetries of the Sylvian fissure, reversed asymmetry of the frontal and occipital lobes, abnormalities in the basal ganglia (e.g., increased dopamine D-2 receptors in the caudate and putamen), abnormalities of the frontal lobe (e.g., increased glutamate receptors), abnormalities of the cerebellum (e.g., atrophy of the vermis), abnormalities in the size or shape of the corpus callosum, and abnormalities of brain-tissue density. Some of these abnormalities are suspected as being secondary to medication (e.g., atrophy of the cerebellar vermis) or to other brain changes in schizophrenia (e.g., the shape of the corpus callosum may be changed by ventricular dilatation), but others may be integral to the disease process.

Correlation Between Changes in
Brain Structure and Schizophrenia

Ever since the initial CT scan study of schizophrenia in 1976, there has been an ongoing and lively controversy among researchers whether brain structural changes in schizophrenia are associated with clinical or developmental aspects of the disease. Family history is one such area of inquiry, and in 1987 Lewis and colleagues reviewed 10 studies comparing brain structural changes (specifically ventricular dilatation) and the presence or absence of a family history of schizophrenia. They reported that 6 studies found more ventricular dilatation in patients with a negative family history, 1 study found the opposite, and 3 studies found no relationship (Lewis, Reveley, et al., 1987).

Ventricular dilatation is the measure used most often to represent brain structural changes in schizophrenia, and various studies have claimed that it is associated with neuropsychological impairment, negative symptoms, poor response to medication, disordered smooth eye pursuit movements, and EEG abnormalities (Zigun & Weinberger, 1992). Contradictory studies are equally prominent, but none of these associations has been clearly established. Recently, Buchanan et al. (1993) reported that negative symptoms in schizophrenia correlate with enlargement of the right caudate (part of the basal ganglia) on MRI, but not with the size of the hippocampus and amygdala. Much research in this area is in progress, but it remains an open question whether brain structural changes in schizophrenia correlate with any specific group of clinical symptoms and represent a clinical subgroup, or whether the brain structural changes are an inherent part of the schizophrenia disease process and are found on a continuum of severity in most or all affected individuals. A 1991 analysis of all CT and MRI studies done up to that time suggested that the continuum hypothesis was more likely than the subgroup hypothesis (Daniel et al., 1991).

There have also been attempts to relate changes in brain structure to developmental aspects of schizophrenia. A history of having had obstetrical complications was found by Owen et al. (1988) to be significantly associated with a combination of dilated ventricles and widening of the cortical sulci (but not with either measure individually). Similarly, a history of having had an abnormal delivery and the presence of left-handedness were reported as being significant predictors of ventricular dilatation, using multiple regression analysis (Pearlson et al., 1989). "Unusual events of pregnancy" were significantly related to ventricular dilatation of a specific portion of the ventricles (the ventricular horn) in another study (Degreef et al., 1991). Three other studies, however, reported no significant relationship between obstetrical complications and ventricular dilatation (DeLisi et al., 1988; Nasrallah et al., 1988; Hubner et al., 1988). Low birth weight alone was said to be associated with ventricular dilatation in one study (Silverton et al., 1985), and left-handedness was reported to be associated with it in yet another study (Katsanis & Iacono, 1989).

Overall, then, it remains unclear whether there is any consistently predictable relationship between structural changes in the brains of individuals with schizophrenia and clinical or developmental variables. Many of the associations that have been reported as being statistically significant do not appear to be robust, and the majority of them have been contradicted by other studies. Ventricular dilatation is the measure of brain structure used in virtually all of these studies because it is comparatively easy to measure and was the only structure that could be reliably measured on CT scans, but it is possible that if other measures of brain structure are used, stronger relationships may emerge.

Previous Twin Studies

Because CT and MRI scanning technology has been available only in recent years, few of the previous schizophrenia twin studies included them. The first twin study of schizophrenia using CT scans was reported by Adrianne Reveley and her colleagues in 1982. They initially studied 11 identical twin pairs in which neither twin was sick in order to establish norms for brain structures in identical twins. They found the within-pair ventricular size to be remarkably similar ($r = .98$, $p < .001$). They then compared the normal twins with 7 identical twins discordant for schizophrenia and found that "the mean intrapair differences for ventricular area and VBR [ventricle/brain ratio] were approximately six times greater in the MZs [monozygotic twins] discordant for schizophrenia than in normal MZs" (Reveley et al., 1982).

Several other aspects of this study are of interest. In 6 of the 7 twins discordant for schizophrenia, the affected twin had larger ventricles than the well twin. Furthermore, as a group, the well twins in the discordant pairs had ventricles that were midway in size between the affected twins in the discordant pairs and the normal control twins in which neither was sick, suggesting the possibility of a common cerebral insult to both twins but affecting one more than the other. Reveley et al. also noticed that the 2 discordant pairs with the least within-pair difference in ventricular size were the only 2 twin pairs with a family history of "major psychiatric illness" (not further defined). They therefore undertook a study of additional twins and verified an inverse association between ventricular dilatation and family history; in other words, more ventricular dilatation was found in twins with no family history of major psychiatric illness (Reveley et al., 1984). Additional CT studies of these twins have reported that "the left hemisphere was relatively less dense than the right hemisphere" in the twin with schizophrenia compared to the well co-twin or to normal controls (Reveley et al., 1987).

Two of the twin pairs studied by Reveley and her colleagues are of special interest because they are so similar to twins that were included in the present study. In one pair the well twin "had epilepsy and spastic hemiparesis," while the affected twin had neither (Reveley et al., 1982). In our study a pair discordant for bipolar disorder (DB-1) also presented with the well twin having had cerebral palsy since infancy, while the affected twin had no evidence of this. Reveley et al. (1982) also described a pair discordant for schizophrenia in which both twins had had dyslexia. Both twins in one of our pairs discordant for schizophrenia (DS-13) also suffered from dyslexia and learning disabilities and had been placed in a special class in primary school.

Lewis et al. (1990) reported the results of MRI scans on an unusual pair of 38-year-old identical twins discordant for schizophrenia. Twin A had had a complicated delivery, cerebral palsy from infancy, and a complex partial seizure disorder starting in his teenage years, but he had remained psychiatrically normal. Twin B had had a less complicated delivery and neither cerebral palsy nor seizures, but at age 22 he had developed schizophrenia. On MRI twin A had evidence of right temporal lobe damage and marked right ventricular dilatation. Twin B, by contrast, had no evidence of MRI pathology despite having schizophrenia. Lewis et al. speculated that the brain damage suffered by twin A might have protected him from developing schizophrenia. It seems equally likely that both twins suffered a common *in utero* brain insult that resulted in cerebral palsy and seizures in one and schizophrenia in the other. It is also interesting that this identical twin pair is the third such pair reported in which one has cerebral palsy and the other has schizophrenia, similar to the two described earlier.

Finally, preliminary MRI results have been reported for 7 identical pairs discordant for schizophrenia studied by Bacic and Mahnik (1991) in Yugoslavia. They found that "small anterior hippocampi and enlarged lateral and third ventricles are consistent neuropathological features of schizophrenia" and concluded that "their cause is, at least in part, not genetic."

Present Study

We were able to obtain MRI scans on every twin who took part in the study. In the initial phases, 5-mm-thick slices were used, and in the latter phases, we obtained 2-mm-thick slices; the technical details of the MRI scans have been published elsewhere (Suddath et al., 1990). The scan time varied between 45 and 60 minutes, depending on the protocol being used. As mentioned earlier, undergoing an MRI of the brain is a difficult procedure for normal people, especially those with any degree of claustrophobia; for the mentally ill it is much more difficult, and the efforts put forth by our twins to complete this test were most impressive.

Our initial analysis was done on the first 15 twin pairs discordant for schizophrenia and 7 normal control pairs. Placing the MRIs of the pairs discordant for schizophrenia side by side, Daniel Weinberger was able to pick blindly the twin who had schizophrenia by visual inspection alone in 12 pairs; in 2 other pairs the MRIs appeared to be virtually identical, and in 1 pair he selected the wrong twin as being the affected one. The criteria used to differentiate the twins on visual inspection were relative ventricular dilatation and widening of sulcal spaces. In most cases the differences within the twin pair were not dramatic, and it was only by having an identical twin as a control that the affected twin was identifiable. In a few twin pairs the differences between the twins were immediately obvious. Figure 6.1 shows MRIs from 4 twin pairs with varying degrees of greater ventricular dilatation in the affected twin.

FIGURE 6.1

MRI scans from 4 identical twins discordant for schizophrenia showing varying degrees of increased ventricular dilation in the affected twin compared to the well twin.

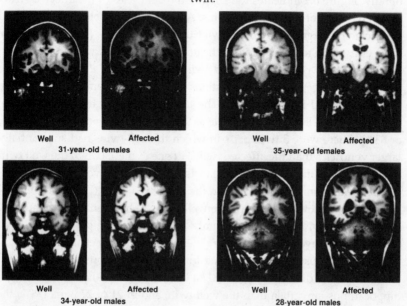

The MRIs were then blindly subjected to formal measurement by two separate raters, both of whom independently measured three structures and obtained similar findings (intraclass correlation coefficient of .99; $p < .0001$). The following structures were measured: lateral ventricles, third ventricle, prefrontal region gray and white matter, temporal lobe gray and white matter, amygdala, and anterior hippocampus. The results of this initial study were reported in the *New England Journal of Medicine* (Suddath et al., 1990).

As summarized in the report, the main finding from the study "was that evidence of anatomical changes in the brain was present in almost every twin with schizophrenia." Within pairs, the twins with schizophrenia had larger left ventricles (14 of 15 pairs), larger right ventricles (13 of 15 pairs), larger third ventricles (13 of 15 pairs), smaller left anterior hippocampi (14 of 15 pairs), smaller right anterior hippocampi (13 of 15 pairs), and reduced left temporal lobe gray matter (14 of 15 pairs). The finding that structural brain differences exist in almost every twin pair discordant for schizophrenia suggests that the brain pathology in this disease is on a continuum, rather than being dichotomous with one subgroup showing differences but another subgroup not showing differences. There was also found to be no significant association between these anatomical differences and age of onset of illness, duration of illness, or total lifetime intake of antipsychotic medication in this group of 15 affected discordant twins.

The twin study was subsequently enlarged to 27 pairs discordant for schizophrenia and the data were analyzed. All measurements were done blindly. Figure 6.2 indicates the sizes of the ventricles of the affected twins as a percentage of their well co-twins. Among the ventricles, the left lateral ventricle was larger in the majority of the affected twins (17 of 27 pairs, or 63%) and was a slightly better indicator of which twin was affected than the right lateral ventricle (affected twin larger in 13 of 27 pairs, or 48%), thus supporting previous suggestions that the left hemisphere is more severely affected in this disease. The third ventricle, a midline structure, was equal to the left lateral ventricle as an indicator (larger in 17 of 27 pairs, or 63%). There were 3 twin pairs in which the *well* twins had substantially larger ventricles than the affected twins; in one of these (DS-8) the well twin had had congenital pulmonary stenosis, which may have caused the ventricular dilatation due to anoxia. In the other two pairs (DS-22 and DS-23) there was no known reason for the well twins to have enlarged ventricles, but occasionally, people in randomly selected normal populations have been found to have enlarged cerebral ventricles (Buckley et al., 1992).

Figure 6.3 illustrates similar data for the hippocampus-amygdala complex. In 22 of 27 discordant pairs (81%) the affected twin has a smaller right hippocampus-amygdala than the well twin, and in 21 of 27 pairs (78%) the

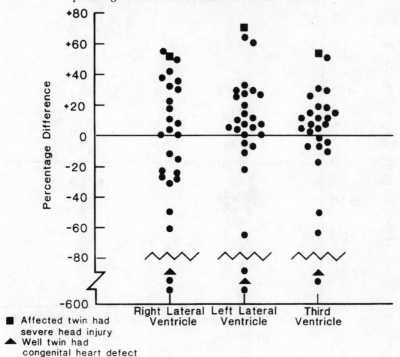

FIGURE 6.2

Cerebral ventricular size in identical twins discordant for schizophrenia; percentage difference of affected twin minus well twin.

affected twin has a smaller left hippocampus-amygdala than the well twin. In most cases the difference in size of the hippocampus-amygdala between the affected and well twins was modest and ranged between 2 and 20%. The findings for the right and left sides were virtually identical, suggesting that damage to the hippocampus-amygdala complex in schizophrenia is bilateral. It is also apparent that such damage is found in most affected individuals on a continuum and not merely in a subgroup. Reduction in size of the hippocampus-amygdala appears to be a better predictor of which twin is affected with schizophrenia than is enlargement of the cerebral ventricles.

Twin pairs in which the findings were not in the expected direction for one ventricle tended to have findings not in the expected direction for the other ventricles as well. Similarly, three of the twin pairs with findings not in the expected direction for the hippocampus-amygdala on one side had similar findings on the other side. Two twin pairs had findings not in the expected direction for both the ventricles and the hippocampus-amygdala.

In order to ascertain whether the changes in brain structure are related to other aspects of schizophrenia, the difference in size of the ventricles

FIGURE 6.3

Hippocampus-amygdala size in identical twins discordant for schizophrenia:
percentage difference of affected twin minus well twin.

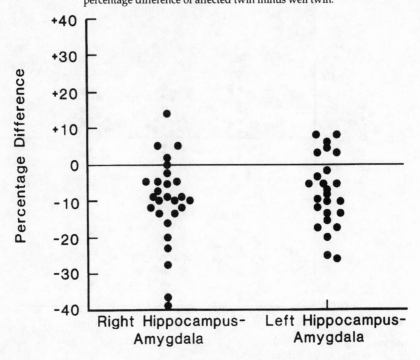

(right, left, and third) and of the hippocampus-amygdala (right and left)
were compared to a variety of clinical and developmental measures in the
affected twins. Because of the large number of variables tested, the Bonferroni correction was used and resulted in a threshold of statistical significance of $p < .003$. This conservative threshold was used because the study
did not begin with a priori assumptions about what such correlations
should be. Utilizing this threshold, four statistically significant correlations emerged from these comparisons, as shown in Table 6.1.

1)   The smaller the left hippocampus-amygdala in the affected twin
relative to the well co-twin, the later was the age of first referral for
psychiatric evaluation ($r = -.56$, $p = .002$, Spearman rank order correlation coefficient).

2)   The smaller the right hippocampus-amygdala in the affected twin
relative to the well co-twin, the lower was the total finger ridge count
($r = .58$, $p = .002$, Spearman rank order correlation coefficient).

3)   The larger the left ventricle in the affected twin relative to the well
co-twin, the lower was the birth weight of the affected twin ($r = -.59$, p

TABLE 6.1

Correlations Between Brain Structure and Clinical or Developmental Variables

	Left Hippocampus-Amygdala	Right Hippocampus-Amygdala	Left Ventricle	Third Ventricle
Age of first referral	$r = .56$, $p = .002$**; indirect		$r = -.37$, $p = .06$*; indirect	
Age of divergence				$r = .62$, $p = .0008$; indirect
Minor physical anomaly score	$r = .42$, $p = .03$*; direct			
Total finger ridge count (TFRC)		$r = .58$, $p = .002$**; direct		
Obstetrical complications score		$r = -.45$, $p = .02$*; indirect		
Birth weight				$r = -.59$, $p = .002$**; indirect

*Significant at trend level.

**Significant at $p < .003$ as suggested by Bonferroni correction.

= .002, Spearman rank order correlation coefficient). This replicates findings previously reported by Silverton et al. (1985).

4) The larger the third ventricle in the affected twin relative to the well co-twin, the earlier was the age of divergence (as defined in Chapter 5) ($r = -.062$, $p = .0008$, Spearman rank order correlation coefficient).

In addition to these statistically significant correlations, three other interesting correlation trends emerged.

1) The smaller the left hippocampus-amygdala in the affected twin relative to the well co-twin, the lower the minor physical anomaly score ($r = .42$, $p = .03$).

2) The smaller the right hippocampus-amygdala in the affected twin

relative to the well co-twin, the higher the obstetrical complications score ($r = -.45, p = .02$).

3) The larger the left ventricle in the affected twin relative to the well co-twin, the earlier the age of first referral ($r = -.37, p = .06$).

What can be made of these correlations? One salient aspect of them is the relative *paucity* of correlations between the structural changes in the brain and clinical aspects of schizophrenia. Except for the age of first referral and age of divergence, no significant correlations were found between structural changes in the brain and such clinical measures as negative symptom scores (SANS), neurological abnormality scores, current level of function (axis V on DSM-III-R), or total lifetime intake of antipsychotic medication. The significant correlation between the size of the left hippocampus-amygdala and the age of first referral was an inverse one, suggesting that the structural changes in the brain did not make the person more liable to have an earlier age of onset.

There is some indication that structural changes may be related to developmental aspects of schizophrenia, but the nature of that relationship remains to be clarified. The correlations between a smaller right hippocampus-amygdala and both lower finger ridge counts (statistically significant) and higher obstetrical complication scores (trend) suggest that developmental factors may be important in this structural change. As was discussed in Chapter 4, total finger ridge counts and obstetrical complications scores were found to be significantly related to each other in these twins. The statistically significant correlation between a larger left lateral ventricle and lower birth weight is also consistent with this hypothesis.

On the other hand, the statistically significant correlation of a smaller left hippocampus-amygdala with a *lower* minor physical anomaly score suggests that minor physical anomalies are *not* markers of structural changes in the brain. Furthermore, no significant associations emerged between the ventricular or hippocampus-amygdala changes and a family history of serious mental illnesses. The relationship between dilated lateral ventricles and negative family history was scrutinized especially closely, since this association had been previously reported for both twin (Reveley et al., 1984) and non-twin (Lewis, Reveley, et al., 1987) study populations. In our study the affected twins with no family history for serious mental illnesses had larger lateral ventricles, but this did not approach statistical significance ($p = .3$, Wilcoxon rank sum test).

In addition to the analysis of the cerebral ventricles and hippocampus-amygdala complex, the MRIs of the twins in the present study were examined for a variety of other abnormalities; many of these studies are still in progress. A preliminary study has been done on the superior temporal gyrus, which is anatomically proximate to the hippocampus, and the results appear promising for distinguishing affected from well twins. The basal ganglia have also been examined; no significant differences were found in the caudate nucleus, but the volume of the right (but not the left) lentiform nucleus was found to be significantly *larger* in the affected twins (Vladar, Zigun, et al., 1992). Iron concentration in the globus pallidus was also assessed using T2 weighted MRI images, and no differences were found between affected and well twins (Carosella et al., 1989).

Surface markings of the brain have also been studied in the twin MRIs. A preliminary analysis of the lateral and superior cortical surface revealed that the degree of similarity of gyral patterns was greater in normal control identical twins than in the twins discordant for schizophrenia, but these differences were not statistically significant (Weinberger, Zigun, et al., 1992). The length and angle of the Sylvian fissure was also examined. In normal identical twin pairs, the Sylvian fissure on the left side is longer than that on the right side. In this study both the affected twins and the well twins in the discordant pairs showed this normal asymmetry, and there was no significant difference between them (Bartley et al., 1993). A shape analysis was also carried out on the temporal lobes, and the affected twins were found to have more shape distortions than the well twins. These results were reported as being "consistent with bilateral focal or multifocal distortions of the temporal lobes of patients with schizophrenia" (Casanova et al., 1992).

Finally, studies have been carried out using the twin MRIs on the septum pellucidum and corpus callosum. A small but significant increase in septal size was found in the affected twins ($p = .002$) (Myslobodsky et al., 1990). Septal defects were also examined, but no significant differences were found between the affected and well twins (Vladar, Ljaljevic, et al., 1992). The corpus callosum was analyzed for area, thickness, length, and shape. Contrary to some previous reports, no differences were found between the affected and well twins on area, thickness, or length (Casanova, Sanders, et al., 1990). The shape of the corpus callosum, however, did differentiate the affected from the well twins, but further analysis revealed that the shape differences were caused by the greater ventricular dilatation in the affected twins (Casanova, Sanders, et al. 1990; Casanova, Zito, Goldberg, Abi-Dargham, et al., 1990).

John Haslam Was Right

Does schizophrenia change the structure of the brain? The evidence now appears overwhelming that it does, and that John Haslam was indeed correct in his observations 200 years ago. The structural changes are often subtle, but they appear to be present to some degree in the majority of people who are afflicted with this disease, not just those in a subgroup. Furthermore, the structural changes appear to be on a continuum, with varying degrees of severity, and do not appear to be related to any clinical measures, with the exception of age of onset. They also are not associated with either an absence or a presence of a family history for serious mental illnesses, so they represent neither a nongenetic subgroup nor a genetic subgroup.

Given the structural changes that occur in the majority of individuals with schizophrenia, can these now be used for diagnostic purposes? Unfortunately, they cannot, for two reasons. First, the changes are subtle in many affected people and only become evident when an identical twin control is available for purposes of comparison. Second, the structural brain changes in schizophrenia are statistically significant for groups but not predictive for individuals. This was illustrated for us most dramatically by one of our pairs discordant for schizophrenia (DS-22) (Figure 6.4). The *well* twin, a successful 41-year-old corporate executive with no evidence of any mental illness, was found to have cerebral ventricles *five times* larger than his affected twin brother, who has had severe schizophrenia for 20 years—the opposite of what is found in most such twins. There is no known reason for the well twin to have dilated ventricles in this case, and

FIGURE 6.4
MRI scans of identical twins discordant for schizophrenia, in which the well twin has markedly enlarged cerebral ventricles and the affected twin has ventricles within normal limits.

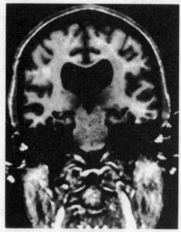 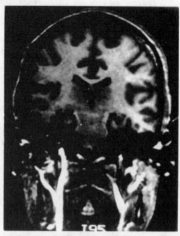

Well twin   Affected twin

such cases are occasionally discovered during MRI studies of normal people (Buckley et al., 1992). It is noteworthy in this case that even though the well twin had much larger ventricles, the affected twin nonetheless had a smaller hippocampus-amygdala on both the right (22% smaller) and on the left (17% smaller), consistent with his diagnosis of schizophrenia.

CHAPTER 7

Does Schizophrenia Change the Function of the Brain?

D OES SCHIZOPHRENIA change the function of the brain? In a literal sense, the question is tautological, because the symptoms that constitute schizophrenia—delusional thinking, loose associations, and auditory hallucinations, for example—are indicative of brain dysfunction. In a nonliteral sense, however, the question implies brain functions *other than* those involved in causing the symptoms of the disease. Among the brain functions most studied in schizophrenia (and the focus of this chapter) are metabolic function, cognitive function, neurological function, and eye-tracking function. We also included electroencephalograms (EEGs) to assess electrical brain function in our battery of tests, but, as noted in the Preface, analysis of these data is still in process.

Observations on altered brain function in schizophrenia are not new. Theories regarding altered metabolic function of the brain, including decreased blood supply to specific areas, were prominent throughout the 19th century. Cognitive function in schizophrenia was studied by Eugen Bleuler and others in the earliest years of the 20th century. Altered neurological function, including involuntary arm movements, tongue movements, and tremors, were also described in patients with schizophrenia by

Contributing to research discussed in this chapter were Drs. Karen F. Berman, Douglas W. Jones, Daniel R. Weinberger, Richard L. Suddath, David G. Daniel, Anisa Abi-Dargham, Susan M. Resnick, Terry E. Goldberg, James M. Gold, J. Daniel Ragland, Constance Carpenter, Kenneth C. Rickler, Thomas M. Hyde, Robert Litman, Llewellyn B. Bigelow, H. Stefan Bracha, Patricia O. Quinn, and Thomas F. McNeil, and Ms. Jill L. Ostrem and Ms. Paula Domenici.

Emil Kraepelin at the beginning of the century. In addition, Kraepelin described nystagmus (involuntary lateral movement of the eye pupil), while Diefendorf and Dodge in 1908 reported eye-tracking abnormalities similar to smooth-pursuit eye tracking more recently under study (Stevens, 1974). What *is* new is the markedly improved technology now available to study brain function in schizophrenia, and it is this technology that has produced a renaissance of interest in this type of research.

Metabolic Function

The new technology for studying brain metabolic function, including blood flow patterns, has been one of the hallmarks of contemporary brain research. Modern studies of cerebral blood flow began with the use of nitrous oxide in the 1940s, then received a substantial boost in the 1960s when radioactive tracers came into use. An example is xenon-133, a radioactive isotope of xenon gas that emits gamma rays. When inhaled, the gas diffuses throughout the body, including the brain, and its rate of diffusion can be measured by gamma ray detectors positioned around the head. The result is a two-dimensional composite record of regional cerebral blood flow, usually abbreviated simply as rCBF.

Because rCBF provides only a two-dimensional image, it has a limited ability to localize metabolic changes to specific regions of the brain. For this reason, a method was developed to produce multiple two-dimensional cerebral blood flow images, which could then be reconstructed into a three-dimensional picture. This is the single photon emission computed tomography (SPECT), which uses radioactive isotopes of xenon, iodine, or technetium. A major limitation of SPECT, however, is that measurements are more accurate from brain surface structures and less accurate from deep structures, which are of greatest interest in schizophrenia.

Positron emission tomography (PET) was developed to provide improved spatial resolution so that metabolic changes could be localized to relatively small areas in the brain, including the deeper structures. PET uses a cyclotron to produce isotopes of oxygen, fluorine, or carbon, which can measure either oxygen or glucose metabolism in the brain. It is, however, a very expensive procedure that requires an intravenous and sometimes an intra-arterial line, so it is also an uncomfortable procedure. Both SPECT and PET can measure specific neurotransmitter systems as well. Newly developed techniques for combining PET with MRI scans promise to produce three-dimensional brain maps of specific cerebral metabolic functions in the near future.

Past Studies

The most clearly established brain metabolic change in people with schizophrenia is decreased blood flow to the frontal lobe (Berman et al., 1993). This hypofrontality, as it is referred to, is seen most clearly when the person is asked to do a task that demands frontal lobe functions. One task commonly used in PET studies is the Wisconsin Card Sorting Test, which requires abstract problem solving (see Appendix B). In normal individuals this test elicits an increase in blood flow to the frontal region, whereas in individuals with schizophrenia there is usually no increase. Several studies have been done with patients who have never been treated with antipsychotic medication; since the results are similar to studies of patients on medication, the hypofrontality seen in schizophrenia does not appear to be a drug effect. Recent studies have also suggested that hypofrontality may correlate with having larger brain ventricles on MRI scans (Berman et al., 1987) and with having more negative symptoms of the disease (Andreasen et al., 1992; Wolkin et al., 1992; Liddle et al., 1992).

In addition to the frontal lobe differences, recent PET studies have also suggested that there are metabolic changes in the medial temporal lobe. Tamminga et al. (1992) studied 12 drug-free individuals with schizophrenia and found that they had a significantly lower metabolic rate in the hippocampus as measured by glucose metabolism. Similarly, Friston et al. (1992) found alterations of cerebral blood flow in the parahippocampal region in 30 severely affected individuals. With rapidly improving technology for making such measurements, it is likely that increasingly, specific cerebral metabolic changes will be described in schizophrenia.

Present Study

Approximately one-third of the twins were studied, each by rCBF, SPECT, and PET. The tests proved to be difficult to do for many of the affected twins, both because they required abstention from nicotine and caffeine for at least 3 hours prior to the tests and because the test procedures require continuous cooperation. In addition, the technical aspects of the SPECT procedures proved to be very complex and somewhat unreliable, so cerebral metabolic information was unusable for twins tested by this method.

The most extensive analysis of cerebral metabolic function in the twins thus far completed is rCBF, carried out on 10 pairs discordant for schizophrenia, 8 pairs concordant for schizophrenia, and 3 pairs of normal controls. In the 10 discordant pairs, it showed that in every pair, the affected twin was more hypofrontal than his or her co-twin (in other words, had less blood flow to the frontal area) while performing the Wisconsin Card

Sorting Test. As summarized in the report on these findings, "These data indicate that in virtually every case in this sample, something had happened to the brain of the schizophrenic twin to make it more hypofrontal. . . . A decrement in prefrontal function from a patient's individual potential is frequently, if not universally, present in this illness" (Berman et al., 1992).

A question that frequently arises regarding cerebral blood flow studies in schizophrenia is whether the hypofrontality that is observed is a medication effect. A study of persons with schizophrenia who had never been treated with antipsychotic medication also reported hypofrontality, making it unlikely that medication is the cause (Raese et al., 1989; Rubin et al., 1991). We examined a possible medication effect in the 8 twin pairs concordant for schizophrenia. These pairs had widely differing within-pair total lifetime antipsychotic medication intake, which varied from 24% to 253%. In 6 of the 8 pairs, however, the twin who had had the *least* exposure to antipsychotic medication was the most hypofrontal, making it unlikely that the hypofrontality can be explained as a medication effect (Berman et al., 1992).

In terms of correlations, negative symptoms scores as measured by the Scales for the Assessment of Negative Symptoms (SANS) were found to correlate directly with hypofrontality ($p <. 05$, Goldberg, Torrey, Berman, et al., 1993), as has been described in previous studies. A direct correlation between neurological abnormality score and hypofrontality was also found ($r = .72$, $p = .02$, Spearman rank order correlation coefficient). A correlation between lower functioning at the time of testing (axis V on DSM-III-R) and hypofrontality approached significance ($r = .53$, $p = .11$). No correlation was found between hypofrontality and age of first referral in these twins.

The most interesting correlation that emerged from the study of cerebral blood flow in these twins was between hypofrontality and the size of the anterior hippocampus. As summarized in the report published on this finding: "Specifically, the smaller the hippocampal volume of the affected twin relative to his or her co-twin, the less activation of the dorsolateral prefrontal cortex during performance of the Wisconsin Card Sort Test. . . . The differences within twin pairs on the MRI and rCBF measures were strongly and selectively correlated" (Weinberger, Berman, Suddath, et al., 1992). The correlation between hippocampal volume and prefrontal activation was stronger for the left side ($p < .01$) than for the right side ($p < .40$, Pearson). This is one of the first instances in which a correlation has been demonstrated between brain structure and brain function in schizophrenia.

The cerebral blood flow data were also examined for possible associations with etiological factors. Regarding family history, only 1 of the 10 discordant pairs for which cerebral blood flow data were available had a family history for serious mental illnesses, and the affected twin in that pair had the least hypofrontality of the 10 affected twins. Genetic antecedents of schizophrenia were also examined by comparing cerebral blood flow in the *well* twins in discordant pairs with the 3 pairs of normal control twins. If hypofrontality in schizophrenia is genetically determined, then one would expect that the well twins in pairs discordant for schizophrenia should also have some hypofrontality because they share the same genes as their affected co-twins. However, no such genetic effect was found, since the degree of hypofrontality in the well twins in discordant pairs was virtually identical to that of the normal controls under conditions of frontal lobe activation (Berman et al., 1992).

Other etiological factors were also examined for possible correlations with hypofrontality. No significant correlations were found for total finger ridge counts, obstetrical complications, birth weight, or age of divergence. A trend for hypofrontality to correlate directly with minor physical anomaly scores ($r = .69$, $p = .04$) was not considered to be robust due to the large number of variables tested, but they should be examined with a larger sample of affected individuals.

PET scans, another method used for measuring cerebral blood flow, were done on subgroups of twins at the National Institutes of Health and at the University of Pennsylvania. At the NIH, 0–15 water was used as the isotope, and preliminary data are available on 9 pairs discordant for schizophrenia. Each of the 9 affected twins showed hypofrontality relative to their co-twins during frontal activation with the Wisconsin Card Sorting Test (Figure 7.1). Other cerebral activation tasks were also undertaken, and the initial analysis of the data suggests that changes in blood flow occurred in specific subareas of the frontal and temporal lobes (Weinberger et al., 1993).

The PET scans carried out at the University of Pennsylvania used the isotope 18-fluorodeoxyglucose to measure cerebral glucose metabolism. Preliminary data on 7 discordant twin pairs suggest that glucose metabolism was increased in the affected twins in the basal ganglia, especially the left lenticular nucleus, in relation to the cortex (Resnick et al., 1990); however, it is unclear at this time whether the changes in the basal ganglia are an effect of medication. Because PET scans can localize metabolic function with great precision, it will be possible in the future to pinpoint metabolic abnormalities in schizophrenia to increasingly more specific areas of the brain.

Cognitive Function

It was assumed for many years that cognitive functions such as intelligence, orientation, and memory remain relatively intact in individuals

FIGURE 7.1

PET scan study of 31-year-old identical twins discordant for schizophrenia. Well twin on left shows evidence of more cerebral blood flow in the area of frontal lobe (arrows). Twin with schizophrenia has less cerebral blood flow to the frontal lobe and is thus "hypofrontal."

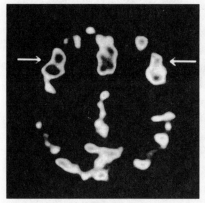 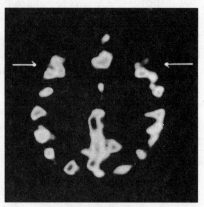

Well twin   **Affected twin**

with schizophrenia except for the most severe cases. Indeed, the purported lack of cognitive dysfunction in schizophrenia was the principal reason it was originally categorized as a "functional" psychosis, to distinguish it from the "organic" psychoses for which there was evidence of cognitive dysfunction. During the intervening years, cognitive dysfunction was noted to occur in some individuals with schizophrenia whose illness was neither severe nor longstanding, but such observations were usually attributed to the effects of medication or hospitalization, or to the individuals' inability to concentrate on the testing.

Past Studies

Doubts regarding the validity of this view began to accrue in the 1960s. Watson and his associates in Minnesota used the Reitan-Halstead battery of neuropsychological tests, which measure a wide variety of cognitive functions, to compare 25 people with chronic schizophrenia and 25 people with "chronic brain syndrome" who "displayed strong clinical and/or laboratory evidence of cerebral lesions" (Watson et al., 1968). The tests could not distinguish the people with schizophrenia from those with a "chronic brain syndrome."

Two years later Klonoff et al. (1970) at the University of British Columbia, also using the Reitan-Halstead battery to test 66 individuals with schizophrenia, reported that "about 80 percent of the chronic schizophrenics examined in this study performed at least at a mildly brain-damaged level on the neuropsychological test battery." Several researchers replicated these findings, including Taylor and Abrams at the University of Chicago, who concluded, after testing 62 individuals with schizophrenia, that "approximately three-quarters of our rigorously defined schizophrenic subjects showed marked to severe cognitive impairment" (Taylor & Abrams, 1984). The idea that schizophrenia does not affect cognitive functions had been permanently discredited.

The cognitive functions most frequently disturbed in schizophrenia are attention, memory, problem solving, and abstract thinking. Attention is a complex phenomenon, with several aspects involving many parts of the brain. One test commonly used to test attention is the Continuous Performance Test, in which the person is asked to watch flashing letters on a screen and press a button whenever a particular sequence is observed (e.g., an "A" followed by an "X"). In order to do this, the person must be continuously alert, must scan the visual displays rapidly, and must distinguish the correct sequence from similar but incorrect sequences (e.g., an "X" followed by an "A").

Another test used to measure attention is the Digit Symbol Test, given as part of the Wechsler Adult Intelligence Scale, in which numbers 1 through 9 are given symbols; the person is then given a long sequence of numbers and asked to code the correct symbol for as many numbers as possible in a 90-second time period. Most people with schizophrenia are impaired in such tests of attention when compared with people who do not have schizophrenia. As summarized by Goldberg, Gold, et al. (1991) in a comprehensive review of neuropsychological deficits in schizophrenia: "Abnormalities in schizophrenic patients have thus been described throughout the various components of attention."

Memory is a second cognitive function that is commonly impaired in schizophrenia. According to Goldberg and his colleagues, "deficits have been reported from a variety of paradigms implicating all stages of memory function from initial encoding, to consolidation, retrieval, and recognition." In general, individuals with schizophrenia have better memory for events preceding the onset of their illness than for events following it. They do relatively well on tests of recognition memory and less well on tests of recall of stories or lists.

Another cognitive task that is often impaired in individuals with schizophrenia is problem solving. The most widely used test for this is the Wisconsin Card Sorting Test, in which the person is asked to match a design of various shapes and colors with one of four other designs of various shapes and colors. After each attempt at matching, the person is told whether the attempt was right or wrong. Initially, the correct match may be based on color (e.g., a yellow triangle with a yellow circle) but then, with no warning, the rule changes and the correct match may be based on shape (e.g., a yellow circle with a red circle). In order to do well on the test, the person must be able to learn from mistakes and rapidly change his or her strategy to coincide with the changing rules. People with schizophrenia usually do poorly on this test, frequently perseverating by continuing to use one strategy despite repeated feedback that it is no longer correct.

An impaired ability to abstract is the fourth, and probably the best-known, cognitive deficit frequently found in individuals with schizophrenia. Considered a subtype of problem solving, it involves the ability to move from concrete images to abstract ideas. Asking someone with schizophrenia to interpret proverbs is a standard part of most psychiatric examinations (e.g., "What does it mean when I say: 'People who live in glass houses shouldn't throw stones'?"). Individuals with schizophrenia commonly interpret such proverbs literally: "It means that the stone may break the glass." They may also exhibit in their replies delusional thinking, loose associations, or other thinking disorders characteristic of the disease.

How frequently are cognitive deficits found in people with schizophrenia? Taylor and Abrams (1984) claimed that they occur in approximately three-quarters of such individuals, although the percentage varies among tests and depending on the cutoff selected to define the deficit. The severity of the cognitive impairment, according to Goldberg, Gold, et al.'s (1991) summary of the literature, "is generally at the level of mild to moderate impairment." Most studies have concluded that the cognitive dysfunction is present at the onset of the illness and is not progressive (Goldberg et al., in press). Antipsychotic medication taken to ameliorate the symptoms of schizophrenia tends to have little effect on cognitive functioning (Medalia et al., 1988).

The only previous study of cognitive function in identical twins with schizophrenia was carried out by Rosenthal and Van Dyke (1970) on the Pollin et al. twin cohort at the National Institute of Mental Health. A wide variety of neuropsychological tests were performed on these twins, but the only results published were on the Wechsler Adult Intelligence Scale. Among 11 twin pairs discordant for schizophrenia, the well twin scored higher than the affected twin on every aspect of the test except for visual spatial ability (block design). The overall IQ of the affected twins was modestly lower than that of the well twins, consistent with other studies of IQ in individuals with schizophrenia.

Present Study

As detailed in Appendix B, each twin in the study was asked to do an exhaustive battery of neuropsychological tests, which took approximately 3 hours. Not surprisingly, "as a group the affected twins scored more poorly than the unaffected twins on every test" and significantly so on some test of attention, memory, or problem solving (Goldberg et al., 1990; Goldberg, Torrey, Gold, et al., 1993). The tests that most clearly differentiated the affected twins from the well twins were those measuring attention (Continuous Performance Test), memory (Wechsler Memory Scale), problem solving (Wisconsin Card Sorting Test), information processing speed (Stroop Color-Word Interference Test and Trails A), and verbal fluency (Verbal Fluency Test). It should be emphasized that on many other tests, the affected twins as a group performed at a level only slightly below their well co-twins.

Regarding the question of what percentage of the affected twins showed some cognitive dysfunction on neuropsychological tests, a composite analysis showed that 3 of the 27 affected discordant twins were severely neuropsychologically impaired, performing significantly below their well co-twin on virtually all tests. An additional 11 affected twins were moderately neuropsychologically impaired, performing significantly below their co-twins on at least 2 of the 5 functions that most clearly differentiated the affected twins (attention, memory, problem solving, information processing, and verbal fluency). The degree of cognitive impairment in these 14 affected twins was clearly sufficient to impair their daily functioning on cognitive tasks. Ten affected twins were less neuropsychologically impaired, and 3 affected twins showed minimal or no neuropsychological impairment. Summarizing the tests as a whole, Goldberg and colleagues noted: "Simply put, the disease appears to prevent the affected twin from reaching his or her genetically and environmentally endowed potential on many cognitive tasks. Most importantly, this was the case even when the performance of the affected twin was considered to be within normal limits" (Goldberg, Torrey, et al., 1991). Some impairment in cognitive function, therefore, is present in almost all the affected twins with schizophrenia and not just a small subgroup of them.

Like all observations in science, however, the exceptions to the rule are often the most interesting cases to study. Among the 27 affected twins, the 3 with minimal or no cognitive impairment on neuropsychological tests were of special interest. One of them was in complete remission at the time of the testing. Another appeared to be intent on proving to the examiners and to his co-twin that there was nothing wrong with him. The third one was the affected twin in pair DS-17 (described in Chapter 5) who had had a severe head injury followed by unconsciousness for a week, decerebrate posturing, and hyperreflexia, suggesting severe brain trauma. Despite the injury and the onset of schizophrenia 9 years later, this twin outperformed his well co-twin on most tests of cognitive function and had an IQ 10 points higher.

In order to ascertain whether cognitive impairment among the affected twins was associated with other clinical or etiological aspects of schizophrenia, the 14 more impaired twins (3 severely, 11 moderately) were compared as a group to the 13 less impaired twins on a variety of measures. The more impaired affected twins were found to have a significantly higher mean score for negative symptoms as measured by the SANS (54.1 vs. 27.9, $p = .004$, Wilcoxon rank sum test). The more impaired affected twins also had a significantly lower mean score on axis V of DSM-III-R, which assesses global functioning (34.4 vs. 46.0, $p = .02$, Wilcoxon rank sum test).

Except for the scores for negative symptoms and overall level of function, neuropsychological impairment in the affected twins was not significantly associated with other clinical measures, including age, sex, age of first referral, acuteness of onset, duration of illness (suggesting that the cognitive impairment is not progressive), total time hospitalized, response to medication, medication dosage at time of testing (suggesting that the cognitive impairment is not an effect of the medication), or lifetime antipsychotic medication intake. The more cognitively impaired twins had a higher mean score for neurological abnormalities (6.0 vs. 4.2, $p = .16$) but this was not statistically significant. Measurements of smooth-pursuit eye movements (gains and saccades) were also not associated with neuropsychological impairment in the small subgroup for which such data were available.

There was also no significant association between neuropsychological impairment and any measures that might pertain to causation, including family history, total finger ridge counts, minor physical anomalies, obstetrical complications, birth weight, non-right-handedness, or early divergence (as defined in Chapter 5). The more neuropsychologically impaired group was also compared with the less neuropsychologically impaired group on measures of brain structure, including left lateral ventricle; third ventricle; and right, left, and total hippocampus-amygdala volume. No significant differences were seen. In an earlier analysis of 15 of the discordant twin pairs, a significant correlation ($p < .05$) was found between reduced size of the left hippocampus and memory for stories (Goldberg et al., in press). There was a trend for the more cognitively impaired group to have more hypofrontality on cerebral blood flow for the 10 pairs for which such data were available (mean within-pair score difference 9.1 vs. 4.6, $p = .09$, Wilcoxon rank sum test), but this was not statistically significant.

One additional measure of cognitive function was carried out as part of the structured diagnostic interview. This was the interpretation of proverbs, which assesses a person's ability to think abstractly. All twins were given two standard proverbs to interpret. Most well twins and the majority of affected twins did reasonably well in interpreting those proverbs. Some of the affected twins, however, were not able to respond abstractly; the following are some representative examples, along with the response given by their well co-twin in each case.

A. A rolling stone gathers no moss.

AFFECTED TWIN	WELL TWIN
"It's like a rock in the ocean which gathers no moss."	"If you keep on moving all the time, you'll never settle down."
"It means you're not in the south, not near water."	"Somebody who just goes through life and doesn't stop anywhere is not going to have much."
"A stone is a stone and a moss is a moss."	"Someone who is always moving and doing things won't get results."

B. He who lives in a glass house shouldn't throw stones.

AFFECTED TWIN	WELL TWIN
"It's fragile."	"You shouldn't be criticizing somebody else when you are open to criticism yourself."
"If you throw a stone you might break a glass house."	"Don't do things which are against your principles."
"If you don't want your house to get ruined you shouldn't throw stones."	"Don't judge someone else when you don't know their situation."

There was one other neuropsychological finding in the present study that bears directly on genetic theories of schizophrenia. When the well twins in the pairs discordant for schizophrenia were compared with the normal control twin pairs in which neither twin was sick, it was found that on almost every test the well twins in the discordant pairs performed less well than the normal control twins. For most tests the differences in scores were slight and did not approach statistical significance. For a few tests, however, such as a memory test of immediate recall of stories ($p = .03$) and a problem-solving test (Tower of Hanoi, 4 disks) ($p = .007$), the well twins in the discordant pairs performed significantly less well than the normal controls (Goldberg et al., 1990; Goldberg, Torrey, Gold, et al., 1993).

What does this mean? One possible interpretation of these data is genetic and argues that the minor cognitive deficiencies in the well twins in discordant pairs compared to normal control twins is a marker for an underlying genetic predisposition to schizophrenia, which these well twins share with their affected co-twins. Another possible interpretation is that the well twins in the discordant pairs are known to have had a slightly lower intelligence than the normal control twins (full-scale mean IQ 103.1 vs. 108.6, as discussed in Chapter 3) and that the lower neuropsychological function is merely a consequence of this IQ difference. In addition, the well twins in the discordant pairs were clearly more anxious than the normal control twins during the testing, some of them consciously fearful that the test would reveal underlying illness in them as well. This anxiety was especially evident on the first day of the overall testing, which was when the neuropsychological testing was carried out. The normal control twins brought with them no such emotional baggage and were much more relaxed for the test procedures.

Neurological Function

Neurological abnormalities in individuals with schizophrenia have been observed for well over a century but have been largely ignored by researchers until the past 20 years. In a recent analysis of the clinical records of patients who had been hospitalized in England's Ticehurst House Asylum between 1850 and 1889, Trevor Turner noted: "A particular feature was the extraordinary prevalence of abnormal movements and postures. Terms like grimaces, fidgets, jerkiness and twitching recur constantly" (Turner, 1989). As mentioned earlier, by the time Kraepelin wrote his classic textbook on schizophrenia in 1919, it had become well accepted by clinicians that neurological abnormalities were a common concomitant to this syndrome.

For half a century after Kraepelin, however, little attention was directed to these neurological abnormalities. During those years the prevailing wisdom among psychiatrists was that schizophrenia was a "functional" psychosis caused by psychological experiences in childhood, in contrast to psychoses caused by syphilis or brain tumors, which were said to be "organic" psychoses. As Freudian doctrines became more solidly established in American psychiatry, the causes of schizophrenia were increasingly assumed to originate in early childhood experiences, especially in the child's relationship with its mother. Within such a milieu, the putative functional-organic dichotomy became even more firmly entrenched. Neurological abnormalities, which imply an organic etiology, did not fit with the "functional" hypothesis, so most researchers simply ignored them. As recently as 1974 Jonathan Pincus and Gary Tucker noted: "Minor neurologic abnormalities are commonly found in schizophrenia. This is not what one would expect in a 'functional' disease and for this reason the presence of such signs is often overlooked or they are considered epiphenomena" (Pincus & Tucker, 1974, pp. 75–76).

A more recent reason for ignoring neurological abnormalities in patients with schizophrenia is that the antipsychotic drugs used to treat the disease can also cause such abnormalities. It is therefore assumed by many clinicians that any neurological abnormality seen in patients with schizophrenia must be due to the antipsychotic medication they are taking or have taken in the past. This is especially true for involuntary movements, virtually all of which are said to be caused by the tardive dyskinesia syndrome secondary to medications. In fact, studies have shown that similar involuntary movements occur in approximately 6% of patients with schizophrenia who have never been treated with medication (Gerlach & Casey, 1988; Khot & Wyatt, 1991).

Past Studies

"Neurological abnormalities" imply that there is some dysfunction of the areas of the brain that control the cranial nerves coming directly from the brainstem, or of the nerves that emanate from the spinal cord. Traditionally, such neurological abnormalities have been divided into "hard signs," in which it is possible to specify with some precision which part of the brain is affected, and "soft signs," which involve more complex behaviors for which it is not yet possible to specify which part of the brain is affected. This is clearly an artificial division, reflective more of our ignorance than of any meaningful dichotomy of neurological function.

Examples of hard neurological signs include the patellar tendon reflex (person's leg jumps when knee tendon is hit with a reflex hammer) and the continuing grasp reflex (person automatically grasps any object put in the hand, as infants normally do). Examples of soft neurological signs include astereognosis (being unable to identify the type of coin in one's hand without looking at it) and constructional apraxia (being unable to draw two intersecting pentagons without mistakes). Douglas Heinrichs and Robert Buchanan

(1988), in a lucid discussion of the soft signs found most frequently in people with schizophrenia, claim that soft signs suggest impairments in "three higher-order functional areas: the integration of more complex sensory units, the coordination of motor activity, and the sequencing of motor patterns."

What is defined as a "neurological abnormality" in schizophrenia is, in fact, quite arbitrary. Research on individuals with this disease has shown abnormalities in vestibular function, dichotic listening, eye movements, and skin conductance patterns. All of these also imply neurological abnormalities, but they are usually not categorized as such.

It should be emphasized that neither hard nor soft neurological signs are unique to schizophrenia and may be found in virtually any neurological disorder. Soft signs are found in people with dyslexia and attention deficit disorders, and have also been reported in bipolar disorder, although with less frequency than in schizophrenia. The findings of prominent hard or soft neurological signs, then, cannot be used to diagnose a person with schizophrenia but merely as evidence of a nonspecific neurological dysfunction.

Although there have been reports of hard sign abnormalities in schizophrenia, such as a persistent grasp reflex (Lohr, 1985) and an impaired gag reflex (Craig et al., 1983), soft signs have been the major focus of interest. The modern era of interest in neurological signs in schizophrenia began in 1960 with Margaret Kennard's report of widespread neurological abnormalities in 42 teenage children with schizophrenia (Kennard, 1960). Over the next 20 years seven other studies were published. These were summarized in 1983 by Larry Seidman, who concluded:

> The frequency of abnormal neurological examinations using soft signs is consistently between 36 percent and 75 percent for those studies providing frequency data. . . . A second clear-cut finding is that schizophrenics have more frequent neurologic abnormalities than other psychiatric patients (e.g., affective disorder) and normal controls. . . . The data are very consistent from study to study and consequently are rather convincing.

Since Seidman's review, at least 15 additional studies have been published showing that neurological soft-sign abnormalities occur more frequently in individuals with schizophrenia than in normal control populations. A 1988 review of such studies estimated the prevalence rate of neurological abnormalities in schizophrenia to be between 50 and 60% and said that "the results of these studies demonstrate, without exception, a higher prevalence of neurological signs in schizophrenic patients than in nonpsychiatric control subjects" (Heinrichs & Buchanan, 1988).

A recurring question in all of these studies is what role medications play. It is known that medications used to treat schizophrenia can also cause neurological symptoms; for example, chlorpromazine can cause a shuffling gait, haloperidol can cause involuntary movements, and lithium can cause a tremor. It is therefore important to ascertain which neurological abnormalities are inherent in the disease process and which are simply side effects of the medication.

Several studies have provided data that help to clarify this question. Two studies (Kolakowska et al., 1985; Rossi et al., 1990) compared the antipsychotic medication dose being taken by people with neurological abnormalities against the dose being taken by people without abnormalities and found no relationship between dose and abnormalities. In one of these studies, in fact, the individuals with neurological abnormalities were taking a 50% *lower* average dose of medication than those without abnormalities (Kolakowska et al., 1985). At least nine additional studies have included people who were not receiving any medication at the time of the study, and all reported that individuals off medications had as many neurological abnormalities as those taking medications (Heinrichs & Buchanan, 1988; Torrey, 1980a). In one of these studies the ones taking medications had substantially *fewer* neurological abnormalities than those not taking medications (Manschreck et al., 1982).

The most important study that has been done for assessing the possible effects of antipsychotic medication on neurological abnormalities was a study in which 17 never-treated (drug-naive) individuals with schizophrenia were included among the patients being tested. The study found that the neurological soft-sign score for never-treated patients "did not differ from that of the remaining patients" (Schroder et al., 1992). Considering all these studies, it seems highly unlikely that neurological abnormalities in individuals with schizophrenia are primarily side effects of the medications used to treat the disease; rather, the abnormalities are inherent in the disease process itself.

The only previous study of neurological abnormalities in twins with schizophrenia was the National Institute of Mental Health study carried out in the 1960s. The neurological abnormalities found in the twins with schizophrenia were, in fact, the single most important finding from that study. The neurological data were carefully collected with consensus ratings following two independent neurological examinations. Among the 15 identical twin pairs discordant for schizophrenia in the initial report, 11 of the affected twins had definite neurological abnormalities compared with just 2 of the well co-twins (Mosher et al., 1971).

Follow-up of the twins in this study several years later revealed that 3 of the 15 originally discordant twin pairs had become, or were suspected of becoming, concordant for schizophrenia (Belmaker et al., 1974). When these twins were deleted from the analysis, the frequency of neurological abnormalities among the twins was still impressive and can be summa-rized as follows: In 8 pairs the affected twin was found to have markedly more neurological impairment; in 2 pairs the affected twin was found to have slightly more neurological impairment; in 1 pair there was no differ-ence neurologically; and in 1 pair the well twin was found to have slightly more neurological impairment.

Present Study

All twins who participated in the study underwent a detailed neuro-logical examination. In all except three pairs, the examination was done by Kenneth Rickler, a senior neurologist with extensive experience in working with the mentally ill; the other three exams were carried out by Thomas Hyde, a neurologist working with Dr. Rickler. The neurologists were not told the clinical status of the twins prior to examination in order to remain blind; in approximately half of the affected twins, how-ever, the individual's psychiatric symptoms were sufficiently marked so that the diagnosis was obvious.

The neurological examination included testing of the motor and sen-sory systems, cranial nerves, cerebellar function, neurological soft signs, and an abbreviated mental state exam. The person being examined was scored 0 (normal or absent), 1 (questionable, equivocal, or minor abnor-mality), or 2 (definite abnormality) on 8 hard signs and 11 soft signs. The soft signs were selected for inclusion based on previous studies. The items scored were as follows:

HARD SIGNS
1. speech
2. cranial nerves
3. motor tone and strength
4. gait
5. coordination
6. reflexes
7. clonus
8. sensory system (touch, pain)

SOFT SIGNS
1. gaze persistence
2. finger-thumb mirror movements
3. pronation-supination
4. frontal release signs (grasp, glabellar, suck, snout, and pal-momental reflexes)
5. face-hand test
6. graphesthesia
7. stereognosis
8. constructional apraxia
9. ideational apraxia
10. right-left disorientation
11. finger and visual agnosia

Details of these tests are provided in Appendix C.

After testing was completed, the neurologist was told which medications the person was taking. Any neurological abnormalities that coincided with documented side effects of the medications (e.g., hand tremor in a person taking lithium) were subtracted from the score and deleted from further analysis. The minimum possible score for the neurological examination was 0, which was achieved by one discordant affected twin, two discordant well twins, and three normal control twins. The maximum score achieved by any individual was 14 by one of the concordant twins.

The following twin pairs were among those in which the affected twin was clearly more neurologically impaired than the well twin:

DS-15: 26-year-old females in which the affected member had been sick for 6 years. Both twins had problems with stereognosis. The well twin also had a problem with graphesthesia. The affected twin had abnormalities on speech, reflexes, gait, finger-thumb mirror movements, and the face-hand test.

DS-22: 39-year-old males in which the affected member had been sick for 16 years. The well twin had an abnormality on graphesthesia. The affected twin had abnormalities on facial asymmetry (7th cranial nerve), gait, finger-thumb mirror movements, the face-hand test, stereognosis, and constructional apraxia.

Several neurological findings from this study are noteworthy. First, as seen in Table 7.1, the affected twins in the discordant pairs had a significantly higher mean neurological abnormality score than their well co-

TABLE 7.1
Mean Neurological Abnormality Score by Groups

	Number of Individuals	Mean Neurological Score
Schizophrenia		
discordant	27	5.1[†*]
concordant	26	4.9 *
Discordant well	27	3.5
Normal controls	16	1.6

[†]Significantly different from discordant well; $p = .01$, paired t test.
* Significantly different from normal controls; $p < .05$, studentized range test.
ANOVA F = 7.5, $p = .0002$, degrees of freedom = 3.

twins (p = .01, paired t test). The mean total scores for neurological abnormalities in the twins with schizophrenia (both discordant and concordant) were also significantly higher than the mean total scores for the normal control twins ($p < .05$, Tukey's studentized range test); this is in agreement with previous studies of neurological abnormalities in schizophrenia.

The answer to the question of what *percentage* of schizophrenic twins were neurologically impaired depends on what neurological score is selected as the cutoff. The highest score for any of the 16 normal control twins was 4. If this is used as the upper limit of normal, then 29 out of 53 (55%) twins with schizophrenia were neurologically impaired, a percentage that falls squarely into the 50 to 60% range estimated by prior neurological studies of schizophrenia (Heinrichs & Buchanan, 1988).

The results of the present study can also be compared to the Mosher et al. (1971) study of neurological abnormalities in identical twins. Although the scoring systems used in the two studies are not directly comparable, the neurological data for the discordant twins with schizophrenia are summarized in Table 7.2.

TABLE 7.2

A Comparison of Neurological Findings in Previous NIMH Twin Study with Present Study

	Pollin et al. Study		Present Study	
	No.	(%)	No.	(%)
Affected twin markedly more neurologically impaired than well twin	8	(67)	10	(37)
Affected twin slightly more neurologically impaired than well twin	2	(17)	6	(22)
No difference between affected and well twins	1	(10)	4	(15)
Well twin slightly more neurologically impaired than affected twin	1	(10)	4	(15)
Well twin markedly more neurologically impaired than affected twin	0	—	3	(11)
	12		27	

FIGURE 7.2
Total scores for neurological abnormalities.

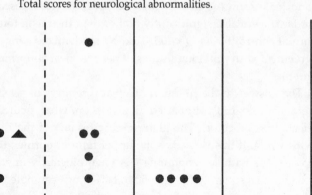

▲ indicates off medication at time of testing.

It appears that the affected twins in the Mosher et al. study were, as a group, more neurologically impaired than were the affected twins in the present study.

Another finding of interest is that medications do not appear to be the cause of the neurological abnormalities. In our study 5 of the twins with schizophrenia were medication-free (one for 7 months, the others for 2 years or longer) at the time of the testing. Figure 7.2 illustrates the neurological abnormality scores of these twins in comparison to the twins who were taking medication. The mean score for the 5 twins off medication (5.00) was virtually the same as the mean score for the twins who were taking medication at the time of testing (5.02). This agrees with previous studies, which have not found medications to be an important contributor to the neurological abnormalities that occur in individuals with schizophrenia.

Another interesting finding is that there is no single hard or soft neurological sign that is found regularly in schizophrenia and that can therefore be said to be typical of the disease. In this study, as in previous studies of neurological abnormalities in schizophrenia, soft-sign abnormalities occurred more frequently than hard-sign abnormalities. Several neurological abnormalities occurred at a substantially higher frequency in the affected individuals (e.g., impaired coordination, right-left disorientation, constructional apraxia, and gaze impersistence). However, no single neurological sign predominated. The overall neurological picture suggests a diffuse disease process that does not affect precisely the same part of the brain in each patient.

Also of interest is the question of whether neurological abnormalities in the twins with schizophrenia correlate with any other aspects of the disease. In other words, did the twins who are more neurologically impaired have more family history of serious mental illnesses, more obstetrical problems, lower birth weights, more problems in school, an earlier age of onset of disease, more negative symptoms, more neuropsychological impairment, more non-right-handedness, more brain changes as measured by MRI, or more impairment in function as adults?

In order to answer these questions, the discordant twin pairs were divided into two groups based on the intrapair difference in their neurological abnormality scores. In 10 pairs, the affected twin had a score equal to or greater than 3 points higher than the well twin, and these were designated as the more neurologically impaired group. This group was compared with the other 17 pairs, designated as the less neurologically impaired group, in which the affected twins had neurological abnormality scores only slightly greater (2 or 1 more) than the well twins, or the scores were the same, or the well twins had slightly greater scores.

When the more neurologically impaired affected twins were compared to those less neurologically impaired, no significant differences were found in age at time of testing, age of first referral, duration of illness, sex, family history for serious mental illnesses, birth order, or birth weight. The failure to find an association between neurological abnormalities and lower birth weight contrasts to the findings of the Pollin et al. twin study, in which there was such a finding. There were also no significant associations between neurological impairment and minor physical anomaly scores, total finger ridge counts, obstetrical complication scores, age of divergence (as defined in Chapter 5), or having had more problems in school, even though neurological abnormalities had been noted in some of these children during the school years.

Significant associations were found, however, between greater neurological impairment and clinical dysfunction. Two measurements of dysfunction were used. On the Scales for the Assessment of Negative Symptoms (SANS), the neurologically impaired affected group had significantly higher scores (means 55.3 vs. 33.3, $p = .01$, Wilcoxon rank sum test). The other consideration was the person's level of overall function within the past year as measured on the axis V scale of the DSM-III-R diagnostic scheme (means 32.2 vs. 44.6, $p = .02$, Wilcoxon rank sum test).

In addition, the person's general level of neuropsychological function tended to correlate with neurological abnormalities in the expected direction (more neuropsychological dysfunction with more neurological dysfunction), although this relationship was not statistically significant ($p = .17$, t test, for a grand Z score obtained by summing performances on seven separate neuropsychological tests). The fact that the more neurologically impaired twins are, in general, more clinically dysfunctional than the less impaired ones is consistent with previous studies, which found an association between neurological impairment in schizophrenia and a more chronic course, greater severity of symptoms, and longer duration of hospitalization. Our study showed that the neurologically impaired twins had a mean time of total hospitalization more than three times greater than the less impaired ones, although this difference was not statistically significant ($p = .06$, Wilcoxon rank sum test).

Given the fact that the more neurologically impaired twins are also more clinically dysfunctional, it is reasonable to ask whether greater neurological impairment might also correlate with structural changes in the brain. Four previous studies of neurological abnormalities in schizophrenia attempted to answer this question using CT scans and measuring the size of the lateral ventricles in the brain. When neurological abnormalities were compared with cerebral ventricular size, one study (Weinberger & Wyatt, 1982) found that there was a correlation, but three other studies (Torrey, 1980a; Kolakowska et al., 1985; King et al., 1991) did not.

We used MRI scans to measure brain structures considered to be likely candidates to be involved in the etiology of schizophrenia. When the more neurologically impaired twins were compared with the less neurologically impaired twins among the 27 affected twins, no association was found between the size of the cerebral ventricles (left lateral, right lateral, or third ventricle) and neurological impairment. Similarly, no association was found between the size of brain structures thought to be involved in schizophrenia (hippocampus-amygdala complex, left superior temporal gyrus, and whole temporal lobe) and neurological impairment.

Overall, our attempts to identify specific structural changes in the brain that are associated with neurological dysfunction were not successful. This may be due to the lack of specificity in the measures of neurological functioning, the lack of precision in measures of brain structures, or the possibility that the wrong structures are being measured. Alternatively, the lack of association may be because brain pathology in schizophrenia is not localized to a few structures but rather is more widespread, with small, scattered areas of involvement distributed in such a way as to produce neurological abnormalities, which do not necessarily correlate with measurable structural change. We believe this to be the more likely explanation.

Perhaps the most interesting neurological finding from the study was the number of neurological abnormalities found in the discordant well twins. Although these twins have shown no signs of schizophrenia or related spectrum disorders, the mean score for neurological abnormalities for this group fell midway between the twins with schizophrenia and the normal controls (Table 7.1 and Figure 7.2).

Two studies of the relatives of individuals with schizophrenia suggest that this finding is not idiosyncratic. In one of the studies, neurological abnormalities were assessed in 12 siblings and 9 parents; the reported prevalence of hard signs (38%) was not as high as the prevalence among the individuals with schizophrenia (50%) but higher than the prevalence among normal controls (13%) (Kinney et al., 1986). In a similar study, 28 siblings and 3 parents of individuals with schizophrenia were examined; the mean neurological score for soft-sign abnormalities was 9.8 for the relatives compared with 12.6 for the affected individuals and 4.1 for normal controls (Rossi et al., 1990). Thus the finding of neurological abnormalities in the well co-twins in the present study is in agreement with the findings among close relatives in other studies.

What does this mean? One possible interpretation is a genetic one, in which the neurological abnormalities in the well twins might represent manifestations of a genetic defect that affects both of the twins. As such, the neurological abnormalities would be trait markers. The theoretical reason one of the twins might have developed schizophrenia but the other not (even though they both share a genetic defect) might be that only one of them was exposed to a precipitating factor. An example of such a model is the "two-factor model" of schizophrenia developed by Dennis Kinney and his colleagues, in which both "neuropathogenic" and "psychopathogenic" factors must occur in the same individual to produce the schizophrenia disease state (Kinney, Yurgelun-Todd, et al., 1991).

Another possible interpretation is a nongenetic biological one. In this model both twins would have been exposed to a similar insult to their brains, such as anoxia or a virus, but their exposure differed in severity or by the part of the brain affected. At least three studies of neurological abnormalities in individuals with schizophrenia have described changes in the abnormalities coinciding with changes in the clinical state; in other words, as the person improved clinically, the neurological abnormalities became less marked (Torrey, 1980a; Lohr, 1985; Schroder et al., 1992). In research parlance, such changes argue for the neurological abnormalities being state markers (due to the disease itself), rather than trait markers (due to genes that are thought to cause the disease). Of course, the genetic and the nongenetic biological explanations are not mutually exclusive, as will be discussed in Chapter 12.

Eye-Tracking Function

Eye tracking, a measure of the movements of the eyes as they follow a moving target on a screen, is another function of the brain that has been studied extensively in schizophrenia. Although abnormalities in eye movements were noted to occur in people with schizophrenia in the early years of this century, the modern era in eye-tracking research began with a 1973 publication by Philip Holzman and his colleagues (Holzman et al., 1973). In the intervening years, abnormal eye tracking has been shown to occur in individuals with schizophrenia in approximately 20 studies, with the abnormality varying from 50 to 85%. It has also been shown to occur in 40% of individuals with bipolar disorder, in some people with other central nervous system diseases such as multiple sclerosis and Parkinson's disease, and in 8% of normal people.

The precise relationship of eye-tracking dysfunction to schizophrenia is unknown. Holzman and his colleagues have postulated that it is a genetic marker for the disease and suggested that both eye-tracking dysfunction and schizophrenia may be carried on a single dominant gene (Holzman et al., 1988). They reported that 45% of parents and siblings of individuals with schizophrenia also have eye-tracking dysfunction, including relatives of some individuals with schizophrenia whose own eye tracking was normal. They therefore suggested that a single latent genetic trait may manifest itself as schizophrenia, as deviant eye tracking, or as both (Holzman et al., 1984) and that "bad eye tracking indicates a genetic predisposition for schizophrenia in the absence of a clinical diagnosis of this disorder" (Holzman et al., 1977). Other researchers have questioned these conclusions (Iacono & Clementz, 1993).

Eye tracking is a composite measurement of two separate eye functions that are phylogenetically and neuroanatomically very different. One function is smooth-pursuit eye movements, which are coordinated by many parts of the brain, but especially by the parietal lobe. The other function is saccadic (jerky) eye movements, which are thought to be coordinated primarily by the basal ganglia and thalamus. The quality of an individual's eye tracking decreases with age and may also be altered by some drugs such as lithium. Past attempts to associate eye-tracking dysfunction with cerebral ventricular size in schizophrenia have had mixed results. A recent study that included MRI analysis of the lateral ventricles, third ventricle, frontal-parietal cortex, and medial temporal cortex (encompassing the hippocampus) "found *no* relation between abnormal eye tracking and any single feature of abnormal brain morphology" (Levy et al., 1992).

Past Studies

Two studies of eye tracking in twins with schizophrenia have been carried out by Holzman et al. In 1977 they reported the results of eye tracking in 11 identical and 15 fraternal twin pairs; 7 of the 11 identical pairs were discordant for schizophrenia and 4 were concordant. They found a correlation of .77 ($p < .005$) for smooth-pursuit eye movement among the identical twins and .40 among the fraternal twins, which they said supported eye tracking as a genetic marker for schizophrenia (Holzman et al., 1977). They also examined the eye-tracking tracings qualitatively, categorizing individuals as having either "good tracking" or "bad tracking" and found that in 9 of the 11 identical twin pairs, both twins had the same type.

In 1980 Holzman et al. published data on 10 additional identical twins (including 3 discordant for schizophrenia) and 15 fraternal twins. They found a correlation of .80 ($p = .005$) for pursuit accuracy among the identical twins and .39 among the fraternal twins, virtually identical to the results in their earlier study. A qualitative assessment of eye-tracking tracings showed 100% concordance among the identical twin pairs and 67% concordance among the fraternal twins. The two twin studies together were said to show "that MZ [identical] twins were almost perfectly concordant for smooth pursuit dysfunctions and that DZ [fraternal] twins were almost 50 percent concordant" (Matthysse & Holzman, 1987). In other words, the identical twins tended to have qualitatively identical eye tracking regardless of whether they were discordant or concordant for schizophrenia. Table 7.3 lists the pursuit arrest scores for the 7 identical twins discordant for schizophrenia in the Holzman et al. 1977 twin study and the pursuit accuracy scores for the 3 identical twins discordant for schizophrenia in their 1980 study.

TABLE 7.3

Eye-Tracking Measurements for 10 Identical Twins Discordant for Schizophrenia from the Holzman et al. Studies

Holzman et al. 1977 Study

Twin Pair	Pursuit Arrest Scores	
	Well Twin	Affected Twin
5	1.24	1.30
6	1.74	1.57
7	1.74	1.77
8	1.47	1.43
9	1.70	2.01
10	1.60	1.52
11	1.73	1.80

Holzman et al. 1980 Study

Twin Pair	Pursuit Arrest Scores	
	Well Twin	Affected Twin
1	2.68	2.33
4	2.71	2.26
6	2.47	2.54

In addition to these two studies of twins with schizophrenia, a study of eye tracking was also carried out on 32 normal identical twins (Iacono & Lykken, 1979). Quantitatively, they found high correlations for smooth-pursuit eye tracking and for saccadic eye tracking. They also found a striking qualitative correlation within pairs; in other words, the eye tracking tracings of normal identical twins tend to be very similar.

Present Study

Eye-tracking testing was completed on 4 normal control pairs, 11 pairs discordant for schizophrenia, and 5 pairs concordant for schizophrenia; the last group has not yet been analyzed. They were rated on smooth-pursuit eye movement gain, which is the ratio of eye velocity to target velocity as the eye follows the target, and also on the number of saccades, or rapid shifts of the eye. People with schizophrenia have been found to have lower gain and more saccades compared to normal controls.

The results of the present study are shown in Table 7.4. Compared to their well co-twins, the twins with schizophrenia were found to have lower gain (means .765 vs. .895, p = .005, paired t test) and more saccades (means 47.0 vs. 40.9, p = .008, paired t test). Within twin pairs, the affected twin had a lower gain in 10 of the 11 pairs and more saccades in 8 of the 11 pairs. Thus the results of this study support previous reports that eye-tracking dysfunction is commonly found in people with schizophrenia.

Comparison of the well twins in the discordant pairs with the normal control twins yielded surprising findings. The well twins in the discordant pairs had a slightly higher mean gain (.895 vs. .872) and fewer mean saccades (40.9 vs. 43.8) than the normal controls. This is not what would be expected if the well twins in the discordant pairs were carrying a "bad tracking" genetic trait. Since the affected twins in the discordant pairs differ significantly from the well co-twins, but the well co-twins do not differ from normal controls, there appears to be no evidence in the present study to support eye-tracking dysfunction as a genetic marker for schizophrenia.

In order to ascertain whether eye-tracking dysfunction in the affected twins is associated with other aspects of schizophrenia, the scores for smooth-pursuit eye movement gain were compared with several clinical and etiological indicators. No significant correlation was found with the duration of illness; antipsychotic medication dose at the time of testing; total lifetime antipsychotic medication intake; score for neurological abnormalities; negative symptom score (SANS); level of function (axis V of DSM-III-R); family history for serious mental illnesses; minor physical anomalies; total finger ridge counts; obstetrical complications; birth weight; and the volumes of the right or left hippocampus, the right and left lateral ventricles, or the third ventricle. The failure to find any association between eye-tracking dysfunction and structural changes in the brain replicates the recent study by Levy et al. (1992).

We did not carry out a qualitative assessment of the eye-tracking records and divide individual records into "good tracking" and "bad tracking" because the study done by Iacono and Lykken (1979) showed that there is high within-pair similarity in normal identical twins, presumably genetic in origin. In that respect, the qualitative eye-tracking patterns of identical twins are comparable to the qualitative EEG patterns of brain waves, which are also known to show a high degree of visual similarity within identical twin pairs.

TABLE 7.4

Eye-Tracking Measurements for 11 Identical Twins Discordant for Schizophrenia from this Study

	Normal Control Twins (N = 4)				
	Gain Score			Saccade Score	
Twin Pair	Twin A	Twin B		Twin A	Twin B
N-5	.85	.91		55	59
N-6	.75	.84		50	41
N-7	.90	.89		35	39
N-8	.91	.82		45	26
means	.853	.890		46.3	41.3
	.872			43.8	

	Twins Discordant for Schizophrenia (N = 11)				
	Gain Score			Saccade Score	
Twin Pair	Well Twin	Affected Twin		Well Twin	Affected Twin
DS-1	.92	.81		31	48
DS-6	.92	.84		38	50
DS-7	.75	.44		55	64
DS-16	.83	.50		47	70
DS-17	.85	.60		55	66
DS-18	.91	.86		55	41
DS-21	.97	.91		21	36
DS-22	.98	.96		13	26
DS-24	.98	.92		57	43
DS-25	.87	.89		38	31
DS-27	.87	.69		40	42
means	.895	.765		40.9	47.0

What Do Twins Tell Us About Brain Function in Schizophrenia?

What do the tests of metabolic, cognitive, neurological, and eye-tracking functions in these identical twins tell us about brain function in schizophrenia? First, they confirm that there *is* brain dysfunction in this disease and that it is found in most affected individuals to one degree or another. As such, brain dysfunction in schizophrenia appears to exist along a continuum rather than being dichotomous, with one subgroup showing impairment but other subgroups not showing it. There is also evidence that the brain dysfunction found in schizophrenia is not an effect of antipsychotic medication; in each of these areas, dysfunction was well described before the introduction of such medication, and no association was found in the present study between medication intake and measures of dysfunction.

There was also no association in the present study between measures of brain dysfunction and having a family history for serious mental illnesses. It was especially surprising to find no support for eye-tracking dysfunction as a genetic marker, because this possibility has been widely accepted. Our results suggest that eye-tracking dysfunction, rather than being a genetic marker, may be a neurological abnormality, which, like other neurological abnormalities, occurs with increased frequency in schizophrenia. As such, it may be analogous to a soft neurological sign that involves complex functions in many parts of the brain.

Neuropsychological dysfunction and neurological dysfunction both show significant direct correlations with negative symptoms and inverse correlations with global assessment of functioning (axis V of DSM-III-R). These four aspects of schizophrenia appear to be related and may simply be different parts of a larger whole. The similarities of the neuropsychological and neurological findings are especially striking. Most affected individuals have some abnormal findings for each, but no single test elicits abnormalities in most of these people, although some tests (e.g., the Wisconsin Card Sorting Test for cognitive function and some soft signs for neurological function) are better discriminators than others. The well twins in the discordant pairs show some neuropsychological and neurological dysfunction compared with normal control twins but less dysfunction than the affected twins.

At the same time, there is a striking absence of correlations between metabolic, cognitive, neurological, or eye-tracking dysfunction and any other clinical or etiological measure of schizophrenia. This is also consistent with the idea of brain dysfunction in schizophrenia as being a continuum rather than a marker of a particular clinical or etiological subgroup.

CHAPTER 8

Does Schizophrenia Change the Underlying Personality?

D OES SCHIZOPHRENIA change a person's underlying personality? Emil Kraepelin thought it did. In fact, his 1919 treatise claimed that, for a person with schizophrenia, "the essence of personality is thereby destroyed, the best and most precious part of its being" (Kraepelin, 1919, p. 74). Some patients, said Kraepelin, "have lost the unity and especially that permanent inner dependence on the essence of the psychic personality," which "indicates a complete destruction of the personality" (ibid., p. 53). The popular but incorrect image of schizophrenia as a "split personality" also reflects a belief that schizophrenia changes the personality, even splitting it into separate parts.

One looks in vain for research data to support Kraepelin's conclusion. Despite almost 100 years of research on schizophrenia, virtually nothing has been done to assess the effects of the disease on the person's underlying personality. The main reason for this lack of research is that there is no way to measure a person's premorbid personality—what the person was like before he or she got sick—once the illness has begun. The exception to this is identical twins, in which one develops schizophrenia and the other remains well. In such cases the well twin can be used as a baseline for personality traits against which the affected twin can be compared. Using our discordant twins to answer this question was one of the goals of the project from its inception.

Contributing to research discussed in this chapter were Drs. Irving I. Gottesman and David L. DiLalla.

The Personalities of Twins

Personality is that ineffable combination of beliefs, attitudes, temperament, and behavior that makes each individual unique. Research on infants suggests that one's personality stabilizes by the end of the first year of life (Green, Bax, et al., 1989), although some changes may continue to take place until early adulthood. Longitudinal studies "consistently show remarkable stability of personality over intervals of up to 30 years, despite biological aging, the acquisition and loss of social roles, and the occurrence of major life events" (Costa & McCrae, 1987).

The single most important determinants of personality are genetic factors (Eaves et al., 1989). For example, a study of 850 high school twin pairs found that approximately 50% of the variation in their personality traits, as measured by questionnaires, was inherited (Loehlin & Nichols, 1976). Another twin study of personality traits reported that the "rough estimate of broad heritability" for altruism was 56%, for empathy 68%, and for nurturance 72% (Rushton et al., 1984).

Studies of twins reared apart and those reared together have convincingly demonstrated the importance of genetic determinants of personality. James Shields, in his study of 44 British twin pairs reared apart, estimated that 61% of the personality trait labeled as "extraversion" was inherited (Shields, 1962). The recent and highly publicized Minnesota study of twins reared apart has concluded that "genetic factors exert a pronounced and pervasive influence on behavioral variability" (Bouchard et al., 1990). Examining specific personality traits, this study found that "on the average, about 50 percent of measured personality diversity . . . can be attributed to genetic diversity" (Tellegen et al., 1988).

If an average of 50% of personality traits are genetic in origin, then where does the other 50% come from? Nongenetic determinants of personality emanate from a wide variety of sources, including biological influences on the brain prior to birth (such as are described in Chapter 4), birth trauma, parental and familial influences, school experiences, peer pressure, cultural mores, media, advertising, accidents, and illnesses. No single one of these factors appears to exert the influence on personality traits comparable to the influence of genes, however, and for this reason identical twins—with their identical genes—provide an optimal paradigm for examining the effects of schizophrenia or other nongenetic influences on personality.

Before doing so, however, it should be noted that being a twin itself may also influence one's personality. This may happen in three ways. First, parents may treat twins differently than they do singletons, and twins who appear physically to be more identical may be treated more similarly than twins who appear physically to be less identical. Kenneth Kendler reviewed studies bearing on the influence of parental treatment of identical twins and concluded that there were no significant correlations between "the degree of physical similarity and [the twins] similarity of IQ, personality, perceptual and reading performance" (Kendler, 1983). In other words, just because parents treated the twins more similarly did not make their personality more alike.

A second possible way in which being a twin may affect personality is when twins consciously try to be different from each other in order to achieve separate identities. The relative influence of this factor on personality can be assessed by comparing twins reared together, who have a reason to achieve separate identities, with twins reared apart, who have no such reason. Two studies of twins reared together and reared apart have examined this issue. Newman et al. (1937) reported that twins who had been reared apart were slightly more similar than those reared together, suggesting that the latter had made efforts to differentiate themselves. Shields (1962), on the other hand, found that the twins reared apart were slightly less similar than those reared together. In neither study were the differences statistically significant, suggesting that even when twins purposefully act differently in order to establish their own identities, such differences are overridden by their genetic similarity.

The third twin factor that may influence the personality of twins is the effects of "twinness." This is especially true for twins who are identical and who as infants must differentiate themselves not only from other people but also from each other. "I" and "we" are often confused for such twins because their identity is primarily as a pair and only secondarily as individuals. Since identical twins have brains that are virtually identical, they may have similar thinking, tastes, and interests, as well as similar personalities. It is this fusion of thinking and personality that is at the heart of "twinness" and that probably accounts for incidents in which identical twins anticipate what the other is thinking or report telepathy-like experiences. There is no analogue to the "twinness" personality factor in individuals who are not identical twins.

Present Study

Personality traits were noted both informally and formally for all 64 identical twin pairs in the study. The predominant informal impression from the examiners' point of view was how alike most twins were within each twin pair, despite the presence of symptoms of schizophrenia. Diagnostic interviews of the twins were done in the morning and afternoon of the same day, and the examiners experienced frequent flashes of déjà vu as the second twin of the day responded to an interview question with the same posture, gesture, intonation, expressive style, and response as had the earlier twin.

The "twinness" personality factor was also seen in several twin pairs despite the symptoms of schizophrenia in one or both of them. One discordant twin pair, traveling from different parts of the country, independently brought the same book to read on the plane. When these same twins visited an art museum during the week of testing, they went to the gift shop separately and chose the same two boxes of notecards out of 64 possible selections; one of the twins also chose a third box.

There were exceptions to the predominant impression of similarity, however. Differences in personality within discordant twin pairs seemed most marked in twins in which the affected twin had prominent negative symptoms or when the sick twin had shown signs of impending illness early in life (see Chapter 5). In one pair, for example, the affected twin had bullied the well twin throughout childhood, leading the latter to consciously act as differently as he could in order to establish his separate identity.

A formal personality assessment was carried out by having all twins complete a Multidimensional Personality Questionnaire (MPQ), a 300-item self-report questionnaire developed by Auke Tellegen and his colleagues at the University of Minnesota and used in the Minnesota study of normal twins reared apart (Tellegen, 1982; Tellegen & Waller, in press). The MPQ has 11 primary-factor scales as well as 3 secondary scales (which combine elements of the primary scales) and 6 validity scales. MPQ data analysis has been completed for 22 twin pairs discordant for schizophrenia and 12 pairs concordant for schizophrenia.

The first question we addressed using the MPQ data was, How similar or dissimilar are the within-pair personalities of the twins who are discordant for schizophrenia? As expected, there was a statistically significant effect of the schizophrenia on personality characteristics of the affected twin on 8 of the 11 primary scales (DiLalla & Gottesman, 1993). These within-pair differences were most marked on the following 4 scales:

1)   Well being: Measures feelings of happiness and joyfulness; low scorers report few experiences of joy or enthusiasm.

2)   Stress reaction: Measures feelings of anxiety, guilt, and emotional lability; high scorers report being tense, nervous, worried, and miserable.

3)   Aggression: Measures tendency to be physically aggressive and to seek revenge when the person feels wronged.

4)   Social potency: Measures satisfaction with social relationships; low scorers avoid social situations.

Personality differences between the affected and well twins in the discordant pairs were also visible on 3 other scales, but the differences were less marked than those described.

1)   Control: Measures feelings of behavioral control and flexibility; low scorers tend to be impulsive.

2)   Achievement: Measures attitudes about achievement and goal-directed activity; low scorers are doubtful that hard work on their part will accomplish much.

3)   Social closeness: Measures feelings about interpersonal relationships; low scorers are aloof and emotionally distant.

On 4 other primary MPQ scales, the scores of the affected and well twins were much more similar.

1)   Alienation: Measures feelings about the quality of relationships, one's view of his or her place in the world, and whether others can be trusted.

2)   Absorption: Measures emotional responsivity and openness to sensory experiences.

3)   Harm avoidance: Measures interest in exciting and risk-taking endeavors as opposed to avoiding such situations.

4)   Traditionalism: Measures adherence to traditional values and moral beliefs as opposed to nonconformity and rebelliousness.

Summarizing the essential differences in personality traits, as measured by the MPQ, between the affected and well twins, the affected twins did not feel as good (they were more anxious) and they had some personality traits that were directly attributable to the symptoms of their disease (they were more emotionally labile, less interested in social closeness, and less happy). Such traits are predictable consequences of having schizophrenia, and it is not surprising that they were present.

What *is* surprising is that, beyond these disease-related traits, there appeared to be great similarities in the personalities of the twins within each pair despite the fact that one had schizophrenia. This is seen, for example, in correlations for traits such as risk taking and harm avoidance ($r = .49$) and traditionalism ($r = .54$). Such within-pair similarity of personalities were informally demonstrated to the examiners on a regular basis. In one female pair, for example, both twins had been risk-taking, drug-using, hell-raising teenagers before one got sick; at the time of the testing, both twins conveyed these same personality characteristics and were remarkably alike, although one had been severely ill with schizophrenia and intermittently hospitalized for 10 years. Conversely, another female twin pair had been very conservative and religious as teenagers and remained almost identically so at the time of testing, even though one had been sick for 15 years. Putting these two twin pairs side by side, one would find almost no personality traits in common between the two affected twins or the two well twins; rather, the similarities in personality traits would be almost completely within each twin pair.

The second question we asked was, How similar or dissimilar are the within-pair personalities of pairs who are concordant for schizophrenia? Statistically, there were no significant within-pair differences on any of the MPQ scales (DiLalla & Gottesman, 1993) despite the often different clinical symptoms of the twins (see Chapter 9). This striking within-pair similarity was informally demonstrated to the examiners during the course of testing on such personality measures as extrovert-introvert, altruistic-selfish, optimist-pessimist, and stoic-complaining.

Finally, we asked, Do the well twins in the pairs discordant for schizophrenia show personality traits that differ from those of the normal controls? If they do, that might suggest that the well twins are part of a spectrum of disability wherein they have a subthreshold variety of their co-twin's illness. Such a finding would support some genetic theories of schizophrenia.

In fact, the well twins in the discordant pairs did *not* differ significantly from the expected normative values on any of the MPQ scales (DiLalla & Gottesman, 1993). Thus no evidence was found on the MPQ personality test that the well twins have a subthreshold variety of schizophrenia or that they have an increased liability for developing schizophrenia in the future.

In summary, schizophrenia brings about some changes in the personality traits of those affected, but the changes are connected to the fact of having an illness in general (they are more anxious) and to the symptoms of schizophrenia in particular (they are less interested in social closeness). Beneath this overlay, there is evidence that the core personality of people with schizophrenia is changed remarkably little by the disease. This is seen in both discordant as well as concordant twin pairs. In addition, no evidence was found on the MPQ personality test in support of theories postulating that the well twins in discordant pairs have a subthreshold form of schizophrenia.

CHAPTER 9

When Both Twins Get Schizophrenia,
Are Their Diseases Similar?

IDENTICAL TWINS who both develop schizophrenia are said to be concordant for the disease. Over the years, researchers have been intrigued by the question of how similar or dissimilar the clinical manifestations of schizophrenia are in identical twins who are concordant for the disease, and many twin studies have addressed this issue. Equally intriguing is the question of how similar or dissimilar the manifestations are in concordant twins compared to the affected twins in discordant pairs, although less attention has been given to this question despite its implications for etiology. This chapter addresses both of these questions.

Regarding the question of clinical similarity or dissimilarity within concordant twin pairs, different studies have arrived at different conclusions. The first researcher to study this question was Luxenburger, "who was impressed by the comparative rarity of the photographic similarity in concordant MZ [monozygotic] pairs, which the reports of single cases led him to expect" (Gottesman & Shields, 1972, p. 240). What Luxenburger had encountered was the well-known phenomenon that identical twins, in whom the manifestations of a disease are remarkably similar, are more likely to be reported as case studies than twins in whom the manifestations of a disease are very different. In another study, Rosanoff et al. (1934) also noted that "in the medical literature of twin pathology great stress has

Contributing to research in this chapter were Drs. Llewellyn B. Bigelow, Kenneth C. Rickler, Thomas M. Hyde, H. Stefan Bracha, Patricia O. Quinn, Thomas F. McNeil, Terry E. Goldberg, and James M. Gold, and Ms. Elizabeth Cantor-Graae.

been laid on the close similarity or even identicalness of manifestations, particularly in monozygotic twins." After examining the twins in their own study, Rosanoff et al. concluded that "as regards the so-called schizophrenic psychoses, close similarity or identicalness of manifestations is the exception rather than the rule." Slater and Shields (1953), Essen-Moller (1970), and Fischer (1973) were also impressed by the clinical differences between identical twins concordant for schizophrenia. On the other hand, Kringlen (1967), Gottesman and Shields (1972), and, more recently, Onstad et al. (1991b) have been impressed by the clinical similarities rather than the differences in such twins.

Clinical Comparisons of Concordant Twins

As described in Chapter 3, our concordant for schizophrenia (CS) group, as recruited through the National Alliance for the Mentally Ill, consisted of 13 twin pairs, including 3 pairs in which one twin was technically diagnosed with schizotypal personality disorder at the time of testing but was strongly suspected of having schizophrenia. The first clinical variable examined was the age of onset. Data were collected on the age at which the twins' family first became concerned about their symptoms, the age at which they were first referred to a mental health professional, and their age of first psychiatric hospitalization. The age of first referral was used for purposes of comparison. Table 9.1 shows the age of first referral for each twin, listing the twins by increasing intrapair intervals for ages of first referral.

As can be seen, there was some within-pair similarity on ages of first referral ($F = .45$, $p = .08$, intraclass correlation). First referral occurred simultaneously in 2 pairs (the same day in pair CS-9, triplets, as described in Chapter 11; 2 days apart in pair CS-6) and within 2 years of each other in 6 other pairs. In 2 pairs there was a 4-year interval between first referrals. In the 3 twin pairs with the longest intervals between ages of first referral, the intervals were 8, 11, and 15 years. Figure 9.1 shows these intervals graphically.

The findings in the present study are consistent with intervals between ages of onset reported in previous studies of identical twins concordant for schizophrenia (Table 9.2) and are virtually identical to the findings of Gottesman and Shields (1972). These findings suggest that if identical twins are going to become concordant for schizophrenia, they will do so within 5 years following the onset of illness in the first twin in approximately three-quarters of cases. This is also consistent with older twin studies such as that by Kallmann, who reported an interval between onsets of 4

TABLE 9.1 (continued)
Clinical Comparisons of Concordant Twins

Concordant Twin Number	Sex	Age of First Referral	Diagnosis Subtype	Negative Symptom Score (SANS)	Neurological Abnormalities Score	Total Years Hospitalized	Lifetime Antipsychotic Medication Intake*	Level of Function (axis V)	Current Living Situation
CS-8	M	17	Undifferentiated	47	5	0.1	13.8	33	Lives w/family on SSI
		21	Undifferentiated	50	1	0	3.4	55	Lives w/family, full-time blue-collar job
CS-2	M	21	Undifferentiated	72	2	0.6	35.0	35	Lives alone, attends day program
		29	Residual	31	3	0.3	5.0	53	Lives w/wife, full-time blue-collar job
CS-7	M	9	Undifferentiated	36	6	0.1	21.0	49	Lives w/family, occ. entry-level jobs, on SSI
		20	Undifferentiated	33	2	0.1	1.4	60	Lives w/wife, intermittent entry-level jobs
CS-10	F	20	Undifferentiated	51	14	12.0	103.0	25	Continuously hospitalized
		35	Schizoaffective	15	2	0.4	12.0	55	Part-time clerical job

Note: Pairs are listed in order of increasing intrapair interval of first referral. The twin who became ill first is listed first.
*fluphenazine equivalent units in 1000s

TABLE 9.1 (continued)
Clinical Comparisons of Concordant Twins

Concordant Twin Number	Sex	Age of First Referral	Diagnosis Subtype	Negative Symptom Score (SANS)	Neurological Abnormalities Score	Total Years Hospitalized	Lifetime Antipsychotic Medication Intake*	Level of Function (axis V)	Current Living Situation
CS-11	M	17	Undifferentiated	41	10	0.2	39.0	45	Lives w/twin, attends day program, on SSI
		19	Schizotypal	24	2	0.2	22.0	55	Lives w/twin, occ. jobs, on SSI
CS-12	M	18	Undifferentiated	49	2	0.6	101.0	33	Lives w/twin, on SSI
		20	Schizotypal	64	4	0	0.4	37	Lives w/twin, had not worked for 4 yrs, watches TV
CS-13	M	21	Undifferentiated	56	4	0.5	3.6	31	Lives w/family, on SSI, very occ. job
		23	Schizotypal	36	5	0.1	0.1	44	Lives w/wife and child, on SSI, occ. jobs
CS-4	F	13	Undifferentiated	46	9	3.7	156.0	38	Lives w/family, on SSI
		17	Disorganized	72	10	3.8	223.0	28	Lives w/family, on SSI

Note: Pairs are listed in order of increasing intrapair interval of first referral. The twin who became ill first is listed first.

*fluphenazine equivalent units in 1000s

TABLE 9.1

Clinical Comparisons of Concordant Twins

Concordant Twin Number	Sex	Age of First Referral	Diagnosis Subtype	Negative Symptom Score (SANS)	Neurological Abnormalities Score	Total Years Hospitalized	Lifetime Antipsychotic Medication Intake*	Level of Function (axis V)	Current Living Situation
CS-9	F	12	Undifferentiated	32	1	8.0	41.4	32	Intermittently hospitalized
		12	Disorganized	56	7	7.5	76.0	24	Intermittently hospitalized
CS-6	M	17	Paranoid	32	6	1.3	42.0	42	Lives w/wife, on SSI
		17	Paranoid	24	5	1.4	32.0	45	Lives w/girlfriend, on SSI
CS-1	M	24	Schizoaffective	9	5	0.3	9.0	34	Lives w/family, on SSI
		25	Undifferentiated	35	2	0.2	14.0	30	Lives w/family, on SSI
CS-5	M	17	Undifferentiated	46	3	2.6	29.0	32	Intermittently hospitalized
		19	Undifferentiated	52	8	5.5	80.5	25	Intermittently hospitalized
CS-3	M	18	Schizoaffective	56	4	0.5	11.0	47	Lives in apt., occ. entry-level jobs, on SSI
		20	Undifferentiated	53	5	0.1	28.0	35	Lives w/family, attends day program

Note: Pairs are listed in order of increasing intrapair interval of first referral. The twin who became ill first is listed first.

*fluphenazine equivalent units in 1000s

FIGURE 9.1

Age of first referral for identical twins concordant for schizophrenia.

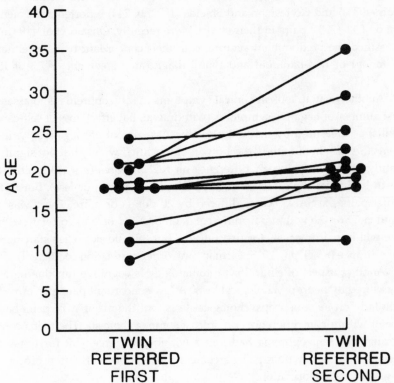

years or less in 71% of cases (Slater & Shields, 1953, p. 191). Exceptions to this rule, however, are often dramatic: two of our concordant twin pairs had onset intervals of 11 and 15 years, Gottesman and Shields's twins included pairs with intervals of 10 and 16 years, Fischer's twins included intervals of 17 and 29 years, Essen-Moller's study included pairs with intervals of 11 and 23 years, and Slater's twins included pairs with intervals of 20, 22, and 31 years.

Another aspect of clinical comparisons between identical twins concordant for schizophrenia is the predominant symptoms of their illnesses. Unfortunately, psychiatry has not yet developed an accurate method for describing such symptoms, and subtyping people into categories such as paranoid, disorganized, and undifferentiated is largely discredited. We nevertheless undertook such subtyping in order to compare our findings with previous studies. As seen in Table 9.1, there was agreement on subtype in only 4 of the 13 pairs (31%). This is lower than the agreement on schizophrenia subtypes reported by other twin researchers. Kringlen (1967, p. 100) reported agreement on subtype in 13 of 14 concordant twin pairs (93%) and Gottesman and Shields (1972, p. 244) reported agreement on 8 of 11 (73%) pairs in their study. More recently, Onstad et al. (1991a) classified the predominant symptoms in their concordant twins as either paranoid or non-paranoid and found diagnostic agreement on 13 of 15 pairs (87%).

Another way to look at clinical symptoms in schizophrenia is to assess the number of negative symptoms (withdrawal, flat affect, loss of self-care skills) as measured by the Scales for the Assessment of Negative Symptoms (SANS). In our study the 13 twin pairs varied widely but not significantly in their within-pair difference on SANS scores ($p = .14$, paired t test). In 5 pairs the scores were quite similar (8 points or less), but in 6 other pairs the SANS scores differed by 20 points or more. There was a tendency for the within-pair differences on SANS scores to correlate with the within-pair intervals for first referral, but this did not reach statistical significance ($r = .4, p = .20$, Spearman rank order correlation coefficient).

Another aspect of clinical symptomatology is cognitive functioning as measured by neuropsychological tests. A few concordant pairs performed similarly on most neuropsychological tests, but the majority of pairs had major within-pair differences on at least some of the tests. The twins concordant for schizophrenia had better within-pair agreement for tests of memory and less within-pair agreement for tests of information processing and concept formation.

Neurological functioning can also be used to compare twins in concordant pairs. In this study there were 5 pairs with virtually the same degree of neurological dysfunction (1 point), although not necessarily the same specific neurological abnormalities. On the other side of the ledger, there were also 3 pairs who were widely discrepant in their degree of neurological dysfunction (a difference of 6 points or more). The wide range of

TABLE 9.2
Interval Between Ages of Onset of Illness in Concordant Twins

	Total No. of Twin Pairs	Less Than 2 Years	2 to 5 Years	More Than 5 Years
Present study	13	62%	15%	23%
Fischer (1973)	10	20%	40%	40%
Kringlen (1967)	13	46%	23%	31%
Gottesman & Shields (1972)	11	64%	18%	18%

within-pair scores for neurological function produced a nonsignificant statistical result for within-pair differences ($p = .87$, paired t test). Except for twin pair CS-10, which was the most discrepant pair on age of first referral (15 years), SANS score (36 points), and neurological dysfunction (12 points), there appears to be little relationship among these three measures in the other 12 twin pairs.

Severity of illness is another clinical variable that can be used to compare the twins in the concordant pairs. One measure of severity is the total time spent in psychiatric hospitals. As seen in Table 9.1, with the exception of twins CS-10, there is a noticeable within-pair similarity on total hospital time ($p = .44$, paired t test). Another measure of severity of illness is the cumulative lifetime intake of antipsychotic medication (calculated by converting all antipsychotic medication to fluphenazine equivalents). Table 9.1 shows a within-pair correlation on this measure ($F = .23, p = .008$, intraclass correlation), with a few exceptions such as twin pair CS-12, in which one twin had been virtually untreated for his illness.

A third measure of severity of illness is the Global Assessment of Functioning Scale, incorporated as axis V on DSM-III-R. This is a scale from 0 to 90 on which the person is rated on overall psychological, social, and occupational functioning. In the present study the person was rated on level of function for the 3-month period immediately preceding the testing. The mean within-pair difference was not significantly different from 0 ($p = .54$, paired t test). There was, however, a significant correlation between the within-pair difference for level of function and age of onset ($r = .6, p = .03$, Spearman rank order correlation coefficient); in other words, the level of function among the twins was closer in those twin pairs who had a similar age of onset and not as close in those twins whose age of onset was less similar.

Axis V can also be considered as a measure of the outcome of the person's illness. Another way to look at outcome is by assessing the person's living situation, as shown in Table 9.1. Even allowing for the tendency of families to treat two affected members in the same manner, there was a noticeable within-pair agreement on the twins' living situation at the time of testing. The examiners were impressed by the similarity of activities and lifestyle for most concordant pairs. Even pairs who appeared to be superficially different were found to be more similar on close questioning; for example, one twin in pair CS-8 was working full-time in a factory, but like his sicker co-twin, he also lived at home and had virtually no social life. The agreement on living situations is most impressive for twins with a similar age of onset and less impressive for those with a dissimilar age of onset. It is also noteworthy that in two of the pairs with the widest discrepancy in age of onset (CS-2, 8 years, and CS-10, 15 years), it is the twin who became sick later who is functioning at a higher level; this is consistent with other studies of adult onset schizophrenia, which have shown that the later the onset of the disease, the more favorable the outcome is likely to be.

In summary, comparisons of identical twins who are concordant for schizophrenia show relatively good agreement between the twins on clinical measures such as age of first referral, neurological function, and measures of severity and outcome. On the other hand, there was found to be lower within-pair agreement on other clinical measures, including subtypes of schizophrenia and negative symptom scores. Insofar as genes or perinatal complications determine the clinical symptoms and course of schizophrenia, these findings suggest that genes or perinatal complications are more important in determining the onset, severity, and outcome of the disease and less important in determining its specific clinical manifestations.

Etiological Comparisons of Concordant Twins

It is assumed by some schizophrenia researchers that identical twins who are concordant for the disease have a heavier genetic loading, and therefore a greater frequency of family history for schizophrenia, than do identical twins who are discordant for the disease. The evidence usually cited for this belief is David Rosenthal's reanalysis of Slater's twins, in which a positive family history for serious psychiatric illnesses was reported as having occurred in 69% (9 of 13) of twins concordant for schizophrenia compared to only 8% (1 of 12) of twins discordant for this disease (Rosenthal, 1959). Kringlen reported a nonsignificant trend in this same direction; 47% of concordant twins versus 35% of discordant twins had a history of "schizophrenia and schizophreniform psychosis in the immediate family" (Kringlen, 1967, p. 129). However, Gottesman and Shields in their twin study reported that "none of the first-degree relatives of our MZ [monozygotic] pairs, concordant or discordant, has been diagnosed as schizophrenic" (Gottesman & Shields, 1982, p. 122). Furthermore, Luxenburger "found that the siblings of his discordant twins had in fact a slightly higher incidence of schizophrenia than did the siblings of his concordant pairs" (Wahl, 1976), a finding that is opposite to that of Rosenthal.

As discussed in Chapter 4, only 15% (2 of 13) of our concordant twin pairs were found to have a history of psychosis (schizophrenia, bipolar disorder, or severe depression with psychosis) in a first-degree (mother, father, brother, or sister) or second-degree (aunts, uncles, or grandparents) relative (Table 9.3). One reason for this difference is that the concordant twin pairs had fewer brothers and sisters (mean of 1.5) than the discordant twin pairs (mean of 2.4). In one of the concordant pairs (CS-10), a grandmother had been diagnosed with schizophrenia and an aunt with bipolar disorder; in the other (CS-13), the history was vague, with a grandmother who is said to possibly have had bipolar disorder but who was never evaluated or treated psychiatrically. By contrast, 27% (7 of 26; family history was not available for the other twin pair) of identical twins discordant for schizophrenia had a family history of psychosis in a first- or second-degree relative, including two pairs in which the father had been definitely diagnosed with schizophrenia. These findings, like those of Luxenberger, are at odds with those of Rosenthal.

Minor physical anomalies and fingerprint patterns are other measures that may provide clues to etiology. As noted in Chapter 4, both are thought to have strong genetic antecedents but also to be influenced by conditions *in utero* in the early months of pregnancy. If identical twins concordant for schizophrenia have a genetically determined disease, one might expect that within-pair minor physical anomalies and fingerprint patterns would be very similar. On the other hand, if these twins have a disease caused by *in utero* conditions that are not genetically determined, one might expect that the within-pair minor physical anomalies and fingerprint patterns would be more dissimilar.

There are substantial within-pair differences for both minor physical anomalies ($p = .02$, paired t test) and total finger ridge counts ($p = .10$, paired t test) for the twins concordant for schizophrenia. For minor physical anomalies, 31% (4 of 14) of the pairs have within-pair differences of 2 or more points. The differences in minor physical anomalies within a single twin pair were both quantitative and qualitative. For example, in twin pair CS-3 both twins had large gaps between their first and second toes and malformed ears. Both also had adherent ear lobes, but in one twin these were much more pronounced than in the other. One of these twins also had a pronounced high arched palate, which the other twin did not have. In twin pair CS-1 their minor physical anomalies were completely different; one had low-seated ears, while the other had adherent ear lobes, tongue furrows, and a curved fifth finger.

In examining birth weights of the 13 twin pairs concordant for schizophrenia, there were (as noted in Chapter 4) 2 pairs in which the weight differences were greater than 20%, presumptive evidence of a twin transfusion syndrome. These included twin pair CS-1 (23% birth weight difference), whose age of first referral and outcome of their disease were quite similar, and also twin pair CS-10 (28% birth weight difference), who were clinically the most different of any of the concordant twin pairs.

TABLE 9.3 (continued)
Etiological Comparisons of Concordant Twins

Concordant Twin Number	Family History for Psychosis in 1st- & 2nd- Degree Relatives	Firstborn	Minor Physical Anomaly Score	Total Finger Ridge Count	Birth Weight (g)	Obstetrical Complication Score
CS-8	None	*	3	142	2,694	0
			2	142	2,635	2
CS-2	None		4	77	3,035	3
		*	3	80	2,862	3
CS-7	None	*	3	157	2,495	14
			3	151	2,495	6
CS-10	Schizophrenia in grandmother and bipolar disorder in aunt		4	127	1,760	1
		*	5	135	1,275	2

Note: Pairs are listed in order of intrapair interval of first referral. The twin who became ill first is listed first.

TABLE 9.3 (continued)
Etiological Comparisons of Concordant Twins

Concordant Twin Number	Family History for Psychosis in 1st- & 2nd-Degree Relatives	Firstborn	Minor Physical Anomaly Score	Total Finger Ridge Count	Birth Weight (g)	Obstetrical Complication Score
CS-11	None	*	3	185	2,694	1
			5	181	3,035	1
CS-12	None	*	4	165	2,808	0
			5	145	2,722	8
CS-13	Possible bipolar disorder in grandmother but never treated		4	71	2,894	3
		*	4	81	2,776	1
CS-4	None		6	20	2,295	2
		*	5	30	2,635	0

Note: Pairs are listed in order of intrapair interval of first referral. The twin who became ill first is listed first.

TABLE 9.3
Etiological Comparisons of Concordant Twins

Concordant Twin Number	Family History for Psychosis in 1st- & 2nd-Degree Relatives	Firstborn	Minor Physical Anomaly Score	Total Finger Ridge Count	Birth Weight (g)	Obstetrical Complication Score
CS-9	None	*	7	NA	2,068	1
			8	NA	2,440	1
CS-6	None	*	6	161	2,749	9
			8	165	2,835	5
CS-1	None	*	2	126	2,522	0
			4	83	1,955	6
CS-5	None	*	9	130	2,894	0
			10	140	2,776	2
CS-3	None	*	3	171	1,955	2
			6	175	2,354	5

Note: Pairs are listed in order of intrapair interval of first referral. The twin who became ill first is listed first.

Analysis of the obstetrical complication scores among the concordant twin pairs also showed that, statistically, the within-pair differences were not significantly different from 0 ($p = .48$, paired t test). There were some concordant pairs with uneventful pregnancies and no complications in either delivery. There were, however, other concordant pairs in which there were major differences in their obstetrical histories, and yet both twins developed schizophrenia; for example, in twin pair CS-12 the first twin was born uneventfully but the second twin was said to be "blue-black" at birth, was resuscitated, and then kept under special observation for two days before being brought to his mother.

Comparison of Concordant and Discordant Twins

If major clinical differences exist between identical twins concordant and those discordant for schizophrenia, such differences would suggest that there may be different etiological factors involved in causing the disease in the two groups. Rosenthal (1959), in his reanalysis of twins in Slater's twin study, reported clinical differences between concordant and discordant twins in addition to the differences in family history discussed earlier. According to Rosenthal, the concordant twins had an earlier age of first hospitalization (24.2 years compared to 37.7 years; $p < .001$) and also to have had a more severe course and a worse outcome. Neither Kringlen (1967, p. 130) nor Gottesman and Shields (1982, p. 122) were able to replicate Rosenthal's finding of an earlier age of onset for concordant twins. For severity of disease outcome, both Kringlen and Gottesman and Shields (1972, p. 245) reported nonsignificant trends for concordant twins to have worse outcomes, and thus were in agreement with Rosenthal. However, Fischer (1973, p. 39) in her twin study found no such trend.

Another comparison of twins concordant and discordant for schizophrenia was carried out by Dworkin and Lenzenweger (1984). They rated negative symptoms, using case records from five previous twin studies, and reported that twins concordant for schizophrenia had more negative symptoms than the affected twins in pairs discordant for schizophrenia. In two of the five studies (Fischer and Tienari), the differences achieved statistical significance ($p < .05$); in two others (Slater and Gottesman & Shields), there was a trend in the same direction; and in the final study (Kringlen), there was a trend in the opposite direction. Clearly, these clinical comparisons of concordant and discordant twins have yielded conflicting results. Otto Wahl (1976) aptly summarized this literature by commenting that "the evidence for the coexistence of an environmental and a genetic type of schizophrenia, as explored through comparisons of concordant and discordant cases, is equivocal."

We compared the 26 twins with schizophrenia in the concordant pairs with the 27 affected twins in the discordant pairs. The results are summarized in Table 9.4. Among the findings, there is—in agreement with Rosenthal—a nonsignificant trend for the concordant twins to have been younger when first referred to a mental health professional ($p = .20$). There is also a trend for the concordant twins to have spent more total years hospitalized ($p = .20$), suggesting that their disease course may have been more severe, as Rosenthal reported. This finding, however, is not supported by the fact that the concordant twins had a mean lifetime intake of antipsychotic medication almost equal to the discordant affected twins, and that the mean scores for current level of function, as measured by axis V of DSM-III-R, were virtually identical.

There are nonsignificant trends for the affected discordant twins to have a higher mean score for both minor physical anomalies ($p = .17$) and for obstetrical complications ($p = .28$); these would be consistent with a hypothesis that identical twins discordant for schizophrenia, compared with twins concordant for schizophrenia, have more harmful events occurring during the perinatal period. Despite such trends, however, there were no statistically significant differences between the concordant and the affected discordant twins. The overall impression is one of similarity rather than differences.

The impression of similarity rather than differences between the concordant twins with schizophrenia and the affected discordant twins with schizophrenia was strengthened by the results of neuropsychological and MRI tests. On neuropsychological tests, there were no significant differences between the two groups. On MRI scans, there were also no significant differences for mean measurements of the lateral or third ventricles, and for the hippocampus-amygdala complex (Zigun et al., 1992). When correlations were examined between MRI findings and clinical and etiological variables in the concordant pairs, a within-pair difference in the left hippocampus-amygdala size correlated directly with within-pair differences in obstetrical complications ($r = .60$, $p = .05$, Spearman rank order correlation coefficient); however, because of the large number of correlations tested, the Bonferroni correction casts doubt on the significance of this finding.

Peter and Vincent: A Very Similar Illness

Peter and Vincent (CS-6) took part in the study at age 27. They came from a family of modest means in a small town in New England. There was no

TABLE 9.4

Comparison of Concordant Twins with Affected Discordant Twins

	Concordant Twins ($n = 26$)	Discordant Affected Twins ($n = 27$)	*p value
Male:female ratio	20:6	16:11	0.32
Family history of psychosis	15%	27%	0.69
Mean age of testing	30 (range 22–41)	31 (range 17–44)	0.70
Mean age of first referral	19.3 (range 9–35)	21.1 (range 11–31)	0.20
Mean negative symptom score	43.0	41.5	0.42
Mean score for neurological abnormalities	4.9	5.2	0.43
Mean total years hospitalized	2.1	1.1	0.20
Mean lifetime intake of antipsychotic medication (fluphenazine equivalents)	42,000	48,000	0.79
Mean score on axis V (level of function at time of testing)	40.1	40.0	0.91
Mean score for minor physical anomalies	4.9	5.7	0.17
Mean total finger ridge count	123.5	128.8	0.70
Mean birth weight (g)	2,525	2,467	0.63
Number of twin pairs with >20% difference in birth weight	2/13	4/26	1.00
Mean score for pregnancy and birth complications	3.0	4.7	0.28

*Statistical analysis used chi-square for dichotomous variables (e.g., sex, family history, and number of twins more than 20% different in birth weight) and Wilcoxon rank sum tests for the remaining (continuous) variables.

family history of severe mental illness. Peter, the firstborn, had been a breech birth and weighed 2,749 g (6 lbs 1 oz), while Vincent had weighed 2,835 g (6 lbs 4 oz); forceps had been used for both deliveries.

As children, Peter and Vincent were regarded by their family and teachers as very similar, with Peter being somewhat more shy and Vincent being more assertive and the leader of the two. Academically their grades were low average, but athletically and socially they excelled. Standardized testing in the eighth grade, for example, showed virtually identical scores in spelling, verbal reasoning, and numerical ability but a difference in spatial relationships. In junior high school both twins used marijuana regularly, as did most of their peers, but not other drugs.

Both of their illnesses began at age 17 following respiratory infections. Peter initially had a cold, after which Vincent developed a severe flulike syndrome that progressed to viral pneumonia. While recovering from the pneumonia, Vincent recalled that at that time he had first heard voices and had begun feeling that people were out to get him, although he did not tell anybody about these experiences. Two months later both twins again had upper respiratory infections, and shortly thereafter Peter complained to his family that he was "confused and mixed up" and that he was having trouble concentrating in school. Family members recalled that Peter was complaining of "a plot" against him and that he was also walking with a strange gait. When asked about his walking, Peter explained that he did not know "which part of my foot to put down first, like I had forgotten how to walk." Peter's problems continued to get worse and, two months later, he was hospitalized at his own request and diagnosed with schizophrenia.

Meanwhile, Vincent's problems were also becoming more prominent, but because of his brother's illness they were not noticed by his family. When Peter was finally hospitalized, Vincent was described as "very upset," confused, having "blank spells" and headaches, complaining of being psychic, and having strange sensations in his body. Two days after Peter's hospitalization, Vincent was evaluated by Peter's psychiatrist, who recommended hospitalization for Vincent as well. This hospitalization was delayed for 5 weeks, during which time Vincent's condition slowly deteriorated. When finally hospitalized, Vincent was also diagnosed with schizophrenia.

During the 10 years between their initial hospitalizations and participation in the study, Peter's and Vincent's clinical courses were remarkably similar. Peter was hospitalized 11 more times and Vincent 15 more times, mostly for brief periods, totaling 1.3 and 1.4 years of total hospitalization, respectively. The hospital records of both twins noted prominent ideas of reference and paranoid delusions, feelings of thought insertion and thought broadcasting, and hearing voices. Less prominent, but occasionally present in both histories, were delusions of grandeur and somatic dysfunction, olfactory hallucinations, visual hallucinations, and visual illusions (Peter: "bright lights which blur faces"; Vincent: "distortions of colors"). The only significant differences in symptoms were Vincent's two episodes of severe depression, accompanied by suicide attempts and his single episode of mania (all concurrent with psychotic symptoms), whereas Peter had had only a single episode of depression. Both responded very well to antipsychotic medications but took them only intermittently.

When they participated in the study, both Peter and Vincent were on medication and in good remissions. On separate structured interviews, they were noted to be remarkably similar and frequently gave answers that echoed each other. For example, when asked to interpret the proverb "People who live in glass houses shouldn't throw stones," Peter replied, "It will break the house"; Vincent answered, "Because the glass house might break." In response to the proverb "A rolling stone gathers no moss" Peter said, "If it rolls too fast it won't get any moss," while Vincent replied, "Because it's rolling it can't gather moss." Both had relatively few negative symptoms as measured by the SANS (Peter, 32; Vincent, 24); both were diagnosed with chronic paranoid schizophrenia; and both were functioning at approximately the same level (axis V scores 42 and 45, respectively). Peter had married and Vincent was living with his girlfriend; both twins were supported by Supplemental Security Income.

On tests of brain function there were relatively few differences between them. Neuropsychologically, their test results were the most similar of any of the concordant pairs. On neurological examination both twins had moderate dysfunction, with Peter exhibiting more "soft" signs and Vincent having more "hard" signs. On mental status exam Vincent performed better (27 out of 28) than Peter (22 out of 28).

On testing for minor physical anomalies, both twins had anomalies of their eyes, mouth, ears, and head circumference; in addition, Vincent had an anomaly of his toes. Their fingerprint patterns, including their total finger ridge counts, were virtually identical.

On MRI scans more differences were found between them. There was a 32% difference in the size of their right lateral ventricle, a 14% difference in the left lateral ventricle, a 19% difference in the third ventricle, a 22% difference in the size of the left hippocampus-amygdala, and only a 3% difference in the right hippocampus-amygdala.

Celeste and Celine: A Very Different Illness

Celeste and Celine (CS-10) came from an urban middle-class Hispanic family in the Southwest; an aunt and a grandmother had been diagnosed with bipolar disorder and schizophrenia, respectively. They were born prematurely following a 7½-month pregnancy, with Celeste, the first-born, weighing 1,275 g (2 lbs 13 oz) and Celine weighing 1,760 g (3 lbs 14 oz). Despite their prematurity, their development was within normal limits and their personalities and academic achievements were said to be similar.

Following graduation from high school, the girls enrolled at different colleges. Celine initially did well until her third year, at which time she began exhibiting odd behavior. She believed that the words on a record referred to her, and during one telephone call home, she told her mother that she could see her through the telephone. College officials became alarmed and had Celine hospitalized. She was diagnosed with schizophrenia and initially responded to antipsychotic medication and electroconvulsant therapy (ECT) but then relapsed quickly. Her condition deteriorated as she exhibited severely disorganized thinking (including word salad), bizarre behavior (walking naked outside), bizarre delusions (a belief that she was from another planet), confusion, and self-destructive behavior. She became increasingly unresponsive to antipsychotic medications and, at the time of the study, had been hospitalized almost continuously for 14 years. Despite massive amounts of many different antipsychotic medications during those years, she showed no evidence of tardive dyskinesia. A recent trial of clozapine had produced only modest improvement.

Celeste, meanwhile, graduated from college and embarked on a career in the performing arts. She married but was divorced after 5 years and supported her performing arts career by working at entry-level jobs. She showed no signs or symptoms of mental illness until age 33, 13 years following the onset of illness in her sister, at which time she began having extrasensory experiences and the insertion of thoughts into her head; she gradually became convinced that she was a psychic. These experiences increased in intensity until she was psychiatrically hospitalized by her friends because of their concern.

Three more brief hospitalizations followed within the next 2 years. Her thinking became increasingly confused and bizarre (she believed that she was hundreds of years old) and she began hearing voices. During one hospitalization, she exhibited signs and symptoms of major depression with relatively few symptoms of psychosis, so she was diagnosed as having schizoaffective disorder.

The most striking aspect of Celeste's illness was her response to medications. She responded rapidly to low-dose antipsychotics and lithium and, on these medications, went into almost complete remissions. Each time she discontinued the medications, she quickly relapsed and had to be rehospitalized for stabilization. Approximately 6 months after beginning antipsychotic medication, however, she began exhibiting neurological side effects of tardive dystonia and dyskinesia. These side effects rapidly progressed, necessitating the discontinuation of antipsychotic medication and a subsequent relapse of her psychosis. An attempt to treat her with lithium alone failed. Finally, clozapine was instituted and she had an excellent response, with a remission of her illness. Her neurological side effects continued to be prominent even after all antipsychotic medication except clozapine had been stopped; the side effects slowly abated over a period of 18 months.

At the time of the study, Celeste was in good remission and able to work part-time. The contrast in mental state between Celine and Celeste was striking and was reflected by their response to proverbs. When asked to interpret "A rolling stone gathers no moss," Celine replied, "Little kids don't date little kids, they date big people." Celeste, by contrast, replied, "Someone who moves around a great deal cannot form attachments."

Celine presented clinically with the symptoms of classic chronic undifferentiated schizophrenia with many negative symptoms (SANS score of 51), required continuous psychiatric hospitalization, scored very low (25) on axis V level of function, responded very poorly to medication, and had no symptoms of tardive dyskinesia but many other signs of neurological dysfunction (score of 14 for neurological abnormalities). Celeste, by contrast, had schizoaffective disorder with very few negative symptoms (SANS score of 15), was working part-time, scored much higher (55) on axis V level of function, responded very well to medications, and had had severe symptoms of tardive dyskinesia but very few other signs of neurological dysfunction (score of 2 for neurological abnormalities). The widely varying response to antipsychotic medications and the development of symptoms of tardive dyskinesia in only one of these identical twins is especially surprising, since it is generally assumed that genes play an important role in both of these (Yassa & Ananth, 1981).

On neuropsychological testing Celeste and Celine had markedly different scores on most tests. On MRI scans the size of their right lateral ventricle differed by 57%, their left lateral ventricle by 53%, their third ventricle by 15%, their left hippocampus-amygdala by 22%, and their right hippocampus-amygdala by only 3%. Interestingly, although Peter and Vincent differed from Celeste and Celine in almost every within-pair measure, the differences in sizes of their hippocampus-amygdala on both sides were virtually identical.

These two case studies represent the two ends of the spectrum. A few twins concordant for schizophrenia are, like Peter and Vincent, very much alike. A few others, like Celeste and Celine, are very different. The majority fall somewhere between these extremes, but more toward the different end of the spectrum and fewer toward the similar end.

CHAPTER 10

How Different Are Twins with Bipolar Disorder from Twins with Schizophrenia?

W HEN THE present study was originally planned, it included twins discordant and concordant for schizophrenia as well as normal control twins. As the project evolved and data from the initial twin pairs were analyzed, questions were increasingly raised among the researchers regarding the specificity of the findings. Were the differences being observed in the twins with schizophrenia specific to schizophrenia, or could these same findings be found in twins with bipolar disorder? The only way to answer such a question was to recruit identical twins with bipolar disorder and compare them to the identical twins with schizophrenia. With the approval of and supplemental funding from the National Institute of Mental Health, this was accomplished.

Recruitment of identical twins in which one has bipolar disorder and the other is well is not an easy task. Kallmann (1946) claimed that the pairwise concordance rate for bipolar disorder among identical twins was 93%. More recent studies, using twins in which zygosity and diagnoses were carefully ascertained, have suggested that the pairwise concordance rate among identical bipolar twins is approximately 58% (Bertelsen et al., 1977). This is twice the pairwise concordance rate for identical twins with

Contributing to the research discussed in this chapter were Drs. Llewellyn B. Bigelow, Patricia O. Quinn, H. Stefan Bracha, Thomas F. McNeil, Karin Sjostrom, Ned Higgins, Kenneth C. Rickler, Terry E. Goldberg, James M. Gold, Monica Gourvitch, Daniel R. Weinberger, Katalin Vladar, and J. Thomas Noga, and Ms. Elizabeth Cantor-Graae.

schizophrenia, confirming the long-recognized fact that genes are more important in the etiology of bipolar disorder than they are in the etiology of schizophrenia. With the assistance of the National Alliance for the Mentally Ill, 8 pairs of identical twins discordant for bipolar disorder were recruited for the study.

Problems in Diagnosis

Most textbooks of psychiatry state that schizophrenia and bipolar disorder are separate diseases, following the dichotomy originally proposed by Emil Kraepelin. And, indeed, there are people with schizophrenia who have delusions and a thought disorder but no affective symptoms, just as there are people with bipolar disorder who have a mood disorder but no delusions or thought disorder.

Individuals with pure schizophrenia or pure bipolar disorder, however, are relatively unusual. The majority of those with schizophrenia have some depression or other affective symptoms, and the majority of those with bipolar disorder have some delusions or thought disorder. There is, in fact, a complete continuum of symptom complexes between the schizophrenia and bipolar ends of the clinical spectrum, with individuals in the center of the spectrum being labeled as having schizoaffective disorder. Michael Taylor of Chicago, in a recent review of studies that attempted to separate schizophrenia and bipolar disorder, concluded that data from family and twin studies "demonstrate that schizophrenia and affective disorder co-occur in some families.... All these data suggest that the Kraepelinian view of the psychoses may need to be modified" (Taylor, 1992). Timothy Crow of London, in another review of studies of schizophrenia and bipolar disorder, also reached "the inescapable conclusion that there is a continuum rather than two separate entities" (Crow, 1990).

In view of this continuum, it is not surprising that difficulties were encountered in diagnosing some of our twins with bipolar disorder. On the one hand, there were some pairs in the study in which the affected twin had a pure affective illness, with virtually no evidence of any thought disorder. For example, twin pair DB-7 included a 52-year-old woman with a history of three episodes of mania requiring hospitalization and one episode of depression; her co-twin has had no evidence of any mental illness. Similarly, pairs DB-3 and DB-5, ages 24 and 27, both met criteria for bipolar disorder because of recurrent episodes of mania and/or depression without any delusions, hallucinations, or thought disorder and their co-twins have remained completely well.

On the other hand, there were twins who met the DSM-III-R criteria for bipolar disorder but who also had various other psychotic features with their illnesses. Two affected twins, in particular, posed significant diagnostic dilemmas in deciding whether their illnesses should be categorized as bipolar disorder or as schizoaffective disorder. One of them (DB-1), a 30-year-old woman, had been hospitalized three times over a 6-year period with prominent affective and less prominent psychotic symptoms. She did not, however, meet the diagnostic criteria for schizoaffective disorder because she had never had "delusions or hallucinations for at least 2 weeks but no prominent mood symptoms." Another affected twin (DB-2), a 21-year-old woman, had had a 5-year history of major depressions accompanied by delusions, hallucinations, and self-mutilative behavior, as well as two brief episodes of mania. She did not meet diagnostic criteria for schizoaffective disorder because she had never had psychotic symptoms other than when she was severely depressed; she was therefore diagnosed with bipolar disorder with mood-congruent psychotic features. However, her bizarre delusions, self-mutilative behavior, and unremitting course all suggested schizophrenia more than bipolar disorder, despite her formal diagnosis. The clinical line that separates this affected twin from the four twins who were diagnosed with schizoaffective disorder and analyzed as part of our schizophrenia series is a thin line indeed.

Twins in Which One Has Schizophrenia and the Other Has Bipolar Disorder

If schizophrenia and bipolar disorder are really separate diseases as some researchers believe, and insofar as one or both of them have primarily genetic causes, then one would not expect to find both diseases occurring together in a single set of identical twins or triplets. For this reason, there has been considerable interest in three such cases described in recent years.

The first report (McGuffin et al., 1982) concerned a set of 28-year-old identical triplets in which two had been diagnosed with schizophrenia or schizoaffective disorder and the third had been diagnosed with bipolar disorder. The triplets' father was described as having had "a long-standing persecutory world-view," had been treated for depression, and was said to meet criteria for "borderline psychosis." The triplets, identical by blood tests, were secondborn to a 30-year-old woman and were delivered by Caesarian section. All three were premature, with triplet C being the largest; specific birth weights were not given. "All achieved normal milestones" and "showed academically average ability."

Triplet C was the first to become ill at age 14. He withdrew, became paranoid, and was hospitalized after violently attacking a stranger because of his delusional thinking. He was treated with electroconvulsive therapy and lithium, producing a good remission, and he then obtained a job. Over the subsequent 14 years he had three additional hospitalizations for symptoms of mania (e.g., pressure of speech, lavish overspending, sleeplessness, grandiose delusions), auditory hallucinations, or depression. Between such episodes he was maintained on lithium and worked steadily. When interviewed at age 28 (when he was taking lithium) "his mental state was normal."

Triplets A and B both became ill at age 16 with symptoms of schizophrenia. Triplet A had "four lengthy inpatient stays that were characterized by persecutory ideas, auditory hallucinations, and passivity feelings." He functioned poorly between hospital admissions, was unable to work, and had no friends. Triplet B began outpatient psychiatric treatment at age 16 and was subsequently hospitalized continuously for 4½ years. His predominant symptoms were delusions, auditory hallucinations, and "an irregular cycle of passive lethargy alternating with cheerful, restless activity." CT scans done on the triplets were reported as "normal in all three."

The second case (Dalby et al., 1986) described a set of 25-year-old identical twin brothers. An uncle was said to have been "hospitalized at the age of 30 for depression and delusions." The twins' early development was reported as having been unremarkable and within normal limits.

Twin A did well in school until grade 11, when he began using alcohol and marijuana, tried LSD twice, skipped classes, and then dropped out of school altogether. Three years of unstable employment and involvement with a "charismatic religious group" followed, and at age 20 he was hospitalized with delusions, feelings of passivity, and a flattened affect. On hospital admission he acknowledged auditory and visual hallucinations, occasional olefactory hallucinations, thought insertion, loosening of associations, and preoccupation with paranoid and religious themes. He was treated with antipsychotic medication, with modest improvement. Psychological testing and all psychiatric evaluations concluded that he had schizophrenia; no affective symptoms had been noted up to the time of publication of the case report. He subsequently developed tardive dyskinesia and depression, although it was unclear whether the depression was inherent in his illness, reactive to his illness, or reactive to his tardive dyskinesia.

Twin B was said to be "high-strung," have a "bad temper," and to have had "inconsistent and labile behavior" in high school, but he was able to graduate. His subsequent work history was unstable, he was hypersexual (claiming to masturbate up to 10 times a day), and had great energy ("often running 4 or 5 miles, four or five times per day"). He was first psychiatrically hospitalized following an assault charge at age 25 and was rehospitalized six more times in the following 2 years. His symptoms included pressured speech, flight of ideas, loosening of associations, sexual and religious preoccupation, and hypomanic affect. An MMPI profile was said to be "indicative of mania," and he was diagnosed with bipolar disease. He was treated with antipsychotic medication and lithium but quickly developed tardive dyskinesia, necessitating treatment with lithium alone; this was reasonably efficacious when he took it, but compliance was poor. Up to the time of the case report, no hallucinations had been noted, but on a subsequent hospital admission, it was said that "he heard voices in the past that were talking to one another." He was also noted to talk in "a rambling way" with "tangential answers" and to be "incoherent at times," symptoms that are more suggestive of schizophrenia.

The third reported case of identical twins or triplets in which one was diagnosed with schizophrenia and the other with bipolar disorder left some doubt regarding the correct diagnosis of the latter twin (Lohr & Bracha, 1992). One twin became sick at age 22, exhibiting paranoid and bizarre delusions, auditory and visual hallucinations, inappropriate affect, and a thought disorder. She was hospitalized multiple times over the next 5 years and was consistently diagnosed with schizophrenia. The other twin became sick at age 19 with severe depression and vague ideas of persecution. She subsequently developed grandiosity, "severe mood changes," and episodes of pressured speech and irritability, but she had no delusions, hallucinations, or thought disorder. She responded poorly to lithium but was able to hold a job using low doses of haloperidol for agitation or depression. She was variously diagnosed as having either bipolar disorder or schizoaffective disorder.

These three case reports suggest that schizophrenia and a mood disorder may coexist in identical twins and triplets. Significantly, however, in no case does the one with schizophrenia have symptoms of psychosis with no alterations in mood, and the one with bipolar disorder have a mood disorder with no symptoms of psychosis. In all three case reports, one or more of the affected individuals has some symptoms that make a final diagnosis somewhat ambiguous. To date, therefore, there still has not been described a pair of identical twins or triplets in which one has unequivocal schizophrenia and the other has unequivocal bipolar disorder. This may simply be because such a case has not yet come to light. Alternatively, it may be because cases of classic schizophrenia and bipolar disorder, which are examples of the extreme ends of the clinical continuum, are primarily genetic in origin and therefore cannot coexist with the other in genetically identical twins or triplets.

Comparing Twins with Bipolar Disorder to Those with Schizophrenia and to Each Other

The 8 twin pairs discordant for bipolar disorder who took part in the present study were demographically similar to the 27 twin pairs discordant for schizophrenia in terms of age at time of testing (mean ages of 34 and 31) and years discordant for their illness (mean years of 14.9 and 14.0). They were, however, skewed toward including more females (7/8 vs. 11/27). Comparisons between the two groups are given in Table 10.1.

As discussed in Chapter 4, the twins with bipolar disorder had a higher frequency of family history for schizophrenia, bipolar disorder, and other psychoses than did the twins with schizophrenia (4 out of 8 vs. 6 out of 25). This is consistent with other research that has suggested that genetic antecedents are more important in bipolar disorder than they are in schizophrenia. The relatives of twins with bipolar disorder included individuals diagnosed with schizophrenia, just as the relatives of twins with schizophrenia included individuals diagnosed with bipolar disorder; this is also consistent with previous research.

Twin pair DB-8, in which the affected twin has a recurrent psychosis that meets full criteria for bipolar disorder, had an uncle diagnosed with probable schizophrenia, as well as three first cousins (third-degree relatives) who were diagnosed with schizophrenia. One twin pair with bipolar disorder who did *not* have a family history of psychosis had a mother who had been seriously depressed; in another such pair, both the mother and aunt had been depressed; and in a third pair, a grandparent had committed suicide. Overall, therefore, the history of mental illness in the families of twins with bipolar disorder was impressive.

Clinically, the major difference between the affected twins with bipolar disorder and the affected twins with schizophrenia is that the former are less symptomatic. The affected twins with bipolar disorder had significantly fewer negative symptoms ($p = .02$, Wilcoxon rank sum test) and a higher level of overall function at the time of testing ($p = .03$, Wilcoxon rank sum test for axis V scores). There was, however, almost no difference in the total mean years of psychiatric hospitalization between the two groups. Affected twins with bipolar disorder had taken significantly less antipsychotic medication ($p = .05$, Wilcoxon rank sum test), which is to be expected since lithium was not included in the list of antipsychotic medications. The affected twins with bipolar disorder and those with schizophrenia had almost identical mean scores for neurological abnormalities.

A comparison of neuropsychological test results between the affected

TABLE 10.1
*Comparison of Twins Discordant for Bipolar Disorder
with those Discordant for Schizophrenia*

	Discordant for Bipolar Disorder $n = 8$ Means	Discordant for Schizophrenia $n = 27$ Means	Statistical Significance
Age at time of testing (range)	34 (21–52)	31 (17–44)	n.s.
Years discordant for illness (as of 3/93)	14.9 (5–30)	14.0 (5–30)	n.s.
Family history of psychosis	50% (4/8)	27% (7/26)	n.s.
Age of first referral	23.6	21.1	n.s.
Negative symptom score (SANS)	18.6	41.5	$p = .02$, Wilcoxon rank sum test
Neurological abnormalities	5.0	5.2	n.s.
Total years psychiatrically hospitalized	1.0	1.1	n.s.
Lifetime antipsychotic medication intake (fluphenazine equivalents)	5,900	29,650	$p = .008$, Wilcoxon rank sum test
Level of function (axis V)	55.6	40.0	$p = .03$, Wilcoxon rank sum test
Minor physical anomalies			n.s.
scores	4.5	5.6	
affected twin has intrapair score > 2 points higher than well twin	13% (1/8)	23% (6/26)	

TABLE 10.1 (continued)
Comparison of Twins Discordant for Bipolar Disorder
with those Discordant for Schizophrenia

	Discordant for Bipolar Disorder n = 8 Means	Discordant for Schizophrenia n = 27 Means	Statistical Significance
Total finger ridge count (TFRC)			n.s.
TFRC count	144	129	
intrapair difference > 12%	43% (3/7)	33% (9/27)	
Birth weight			n.s.
wt. of affected twin	2,172 g	2,484 g	
wt. of well twin	2,249 g	2,567 g	
intrapair difference > 20%	13% (1/8)	15% (4/26)	
Affected twin first born	75% (6/8)	56% (15/27)	n.s.
Winter-spring births (Dec. to May)	50% (4/8)	67% (18/27)	n.s.
Obstetrical complications			n.s.
mean score for affected twin	7.6	4.7	
affected twin has intrapair difference > 5 points	25% (2/8)	31% (8/26)	
One or both twins non-right-handed	38% (3/8)	22% (6/27)	n.s.
Intrapair behavioral/ neurological divergence by age 5	25% (2/8)	26% (7/27)	n.s.

twins with bipolar disorder and those with schizophrenia also demonstrated the higher level of function in the former group. Three of the affected twins with bipolar disorder (DB-3, DB-5, and DB-7) had virtually no cognitive impairment, even outperforming their well co-twins on many of the tests. As previously noted, these are the affected twins who clinically had the purest examples of a mood disorder with no thought disorder, delusions, or hallucinations. Conversely, the affected twins in pairs DB-1 and DB-2 were the most neuropsychologically impaired compared with their co-twins, and these are the same two affected twins who clinically presented the most difficult diagnostic problems in deciding whether they should be included under schizoaffective disorder or under bipolar disorder.

When the twins with bipolar disorder and those with schizophrenia were compared on factors that may be related to perinatal liability, there were no significant differences on minor physical anomalies or total finger ridge counts. The birth weights of the twins with bipolar disorder were lower than those with schizophrenia, but the difference did not achieve statistical significance ($p = .07$ for the affected twins in each group). The mean score for obstetrical complications for affected twins with bipolar disorder was not significantly higher than for affected twins with schizophrenia, but this difference was markedly influenced by one twin with bipolar disorder (DB-6) whose obstetrical complication score was twice as high as any other twin in the study. Overall, then, on factors relating to possible perinatal liability, the affected twins with bipolar disorder were remarkably similar to those with schizophrenia.

In addition to comparing the twins with bipolar disorder to those with schizophrenia, the 8 twin pairs discordant for bipolar disorder were also examined for within-pair differences. No significant differences between the affected and well twins were found for minor physical anomalies, total finger ridge counts, birth weight, or obstetrical complications by paired t tests. When the pairs were examined individually, however, there were found to be two pairs with multiple indicators of perinatal liability, and the affected twins in these pairs were behaviorally and/or neurologically different from their co-twins by the age of 5 (see Chapter 5, age of divergence). A description of these two pairs follows:

> DB-3: There was a family history of bipolar disorder. The pregnancy was complicated by probable toxemia and a complicated birth for the affected twin, who was the first born and "started to come breech but they pushed her back and turned her around." The affected twin also weighed 20% less at birth, presumptive evidence of a twin

transfusion syndrome. From infancy, the twin who later developed bipolar disorder was more clumsy than her co-twin; family members described her as always "tripping over her own shoelaces" and she described herself as a "klutz." The affected twin had enuresis until age 6, which was more than 3 years longer than her co-twin. At age 16 she began having mood swings and at 18 was evaluated psychiatrically and diagnosed with bipolar disorder.

DB-6: There was a family history of bipolar disorder. The pregnancy was complicated by toxemia. The affected twin was born second, following a hemorrhage by the mother. He was rushed to intensive care because of problems breathing, was said to have "remained blue-black for two or three days," and was not expected to live. He weighed 19% less than his co-twin. His score for minor physical anomalies was 5 points higher than that of his co-twin. Developmentally, he was more withdrawn and less socially mature than his co-twin. He began having severe behavioral problems at age 12 and was diagnosed with bipolar disorder at age 19.

Thus the perinatal findings among the individual pairs with bipolar disorder are similar to the findings among individual pairs with schizophrenia.

Except for the two pairs just described, however, there were no significant childhood differences between the twins who would later develop bipolar disorder and the twins who would remain well. Nonfebrile seizures were experienced by 2 affected and 1 well twin; febrile seizures by 1 affected and 3 well twins; and a mononucleosis-like syndrome by 2 affected and 1 well twin. There was no history of head trauma with unconsciousness among these twins. One major illness that was noted in one of the well twins at 10 months of age was cerebral palsy, but there was no evidence of this in the twin who later developed bipolar disorder. Regarding leadership among these twins in childhood, the *affected* twin was the leader of the two in 6 pairs, the well twin in 1 pair, and they were equal in the remaining pair.

Finally, MRI scans were assessed for cerebral structural changes in the pairs discordant for bipolar disorder, and the results were compared to the pairs discordant for schizophrenia. Previous CT and MRI studies of non-twin individuals with bipolar disorder have yielded conflicting results regarding enlargement of the cerebral ventricles, decreased volume of the temporal lobes, or other changes (Jeste et al., 1988; Nasrallah et al., 1987; Goodwin & Jamison, 1990). No other MRI study of identical twins with bipolar disorder has been carried out.

The results are shown in Figures 10.1 and 10.2. The outlier for the right ventricular dilatation is pair DB-4, with a well co-twin with no known reason for having an enlarged right ventricle. The outlier for left ventricular and third ventricular dilatation is pair DB-6, with a well co-twin who had a history of chronic alcohol abuse. Comparing Figures 10.1 and 10.2 with Figures 6.2 and 6.3 from Chapter 6 suggests that there is a trend toward ventricular dilatation in the affected twins with bipolar disorder being similar to that found in the affected twins with schizophrenia. Any trend for a diminution of the hippocampus-amygdala among the bipolar affected twins is less clear, however. In fact, the mean diminution of the right hippocampus-amygdala for the affected twins with bipolar disorder is –2.5% compared to –10.1% for the affected twins with schizophrenia (p = .10, Wilcoxon rank sum test). Comparable figures for the left hippocampus-amygdala is –2.1% for bipolar disorder and –7.2% for schizophrenia (p = .44, Wilcoxon rank sum test). To date, therefore, the within-pair difference of the hippocampus-amygdala differentiated the twins with bipolar disorder from those with schizophre-

FIGURE 10.1

Cerebral ventricular size in identical twins discordant for bipolar disorder; percentage difference of affected twin minus well twin.

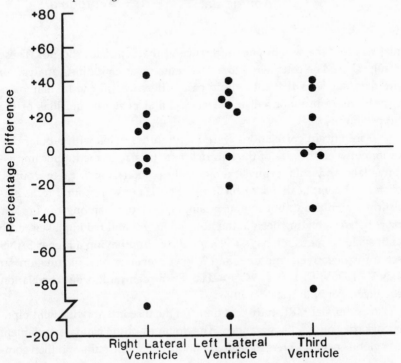

FIGURE 10.2

Hippocampus-amygdala size in identical twins discordant for bipolar disorder;
percentage difference of affected twin minus well twin.

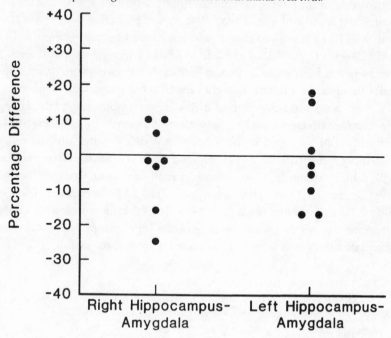

nia, whereas the within-pair difference of the ventricles did not. These results should be considered to be preliminary, as continuing analysis of the data suggests that the within-pair differences in the bipolar pairs may be more pronounced in the middle and posterior portions of the hippocampus.

No significant correlations were found in the twins with bipolar disorder between the size of the ventricles or the size of the hippocampus-amygdala and minor physical anomalies, total finger ridge counts, obstetrical complications, or birth weights. There were found to be statistically significant, but not surprising, correlations among the bipolar pairs between having been in the hospital longer and having taken more antipsychotic medications ($r = .96$, $p = .0005$) and having a higher SANS score for negative symptoms and a lower level of overall function on axis V of DSM-III-R ($r = .94$, $p = .005$, Spearman rank order correlation coefficient for both tests).

An additional MRI study was done on the discordant twins with bipolar disorder on the basal ganglia. The volumes of the caudate, putamen, and globus pallidus were measured blindly in 7 of the pairs and then compared. No significant within-pair differences were found, suggesting that the basal ganglia is not structurally impaired in bipolar disorder (Noga et al., 1993).

In summary, identical twins with bipolar disorder have more family history of psychosis, are less impaired clinically and neuropsychologically, and may have less structural pathology on the hippocampus-amygdala than identical twins with schizophrenia. On measures of perinatal liability, however, the twins with bipolar disorder and those with schizophrenia appear similar. In both diagnostic groups, approximately 25% of the affected twins have indicators of perinatal complications and premorbid behavioral and/or neurological problems in childhood.

It should again be cautioned, however, that these perinatal indicators of liability are not good predictors for any given case. There were individual twins among those discordant for bipolar disorder who had an outcome exactly the opposite of what would have been predicted using perinatal indicators alone, as was the case with the twins discordant for schizophrenia. In pair DB-8, for example, the second-born twin had a higher obstetrical complications score, a higher minor physical anomalies score, was less coordinated in childhood, and had a nonfebrile seizure at age 12. It was the firstborn twin, however, who was diagnosed with bipolar disorder at age 24, while the second-born twin continues to be well 10 years later.

CHAPTER 11

Triplets and Beyond

ULTIPLE HUMAN births beyond twins evokes an ambivalent fascination in many people, and the use of fertility drugs in recent years has increased interest in such births. Prior to the use of these drugs, the record number of children born at one time was said to have been seven children born in 1600; all were said to have died within two weeks. In this century the Dionne quintuplets, born in 1934, survived and became well known. They were thought to have all come from a single ovum and therefore to be identical.

The frequency of multiple births beyond twins varies, like twins, with the age of the mother and by ethnic group. In the United States the frequency of triplet births was formerly said to be 1 per 9,828 births for whites and 1 per 5,631 births for blacks (Eastman, 1956, p. 654), although it is said to have increased substantially in the past 30 years (Allen, 1988). The rate for triplets, as for twins, is lower in countries such as Japan and higher in countries such as Nigeria.

Triplet births come about by one of three mechanisms. All three may come from the same ovum and be identical. Or they may come from two separate ova, with one ovum splitting; in this case two will be identical and the other fraternal. Or they may arise from three separate ova and all be fraternal. There is controversy regarding the relative frequencies of

Contributing to research for this chapter were Drs. Kenneth C. Rickler, Katalin Vladar, Daniel R. Weinberger, Terry E. Goldberg, and Llewellyn B. Bigelow. The original clinical data for triplets 3 and 4 (case numbers 5 and 8, respectively) were collected by Drs. William Pollin, Loren R. Mosher, James R. Stabenau, and Joseph Tupin, and Ms. Barbara Spillman.

these three types of triplets, but a composite of studies from the United States and Australia suggests that the ratio of the three is approximately 1:2:1 (MacGillivray et al., 1988, p. 63). Further confusing the issue, some triplets are thought to be the product of quadruplets, in which one of the four fetuses did not survive the early course of development. It is also known that a substantial number of triplets conceived are not born as such. One prospective study of 51 triplet conceptions reported that in 8 sets, one did not survive early development (so they were born as twins), and in 1 set, two died (so the surviving triplet was born as a singleton) (MacGillivray et al., 1988, p. 42). In such cases, the mother and obstetrician are usually unaware of the existence of the other fetuses.

It is remarkable that there has not heretofore been published a single case study of schizophrenia in American triplets. Two case studies have been published on triplets in England (to be discussed), but not a single one from the United States has appeared. Most attention of American researchers interested in schizophrenia in multiple births other than twins has focused on the Genain quadruplets.

The Genain Quadruplets

The pseudonymous Genain quadruplets were extensively studied at the National Institute of Mental Health (NIMH) for 3 years in the mid-1950s by David Rosenthal and his colleagues. *The Genain Quadruplets*, a book edited by Dr. Rosenthal, was published in 1963. The quadruplets were restudied in 1981, with the results being published in the professional journal *Psychiatry Research* in 1984 (DeLisi et al., Mirsky et al., and Buchsbaum et al.). The quadruplets are known to many American students of abnormal psychology and genetics because their picture graces several standard textbooks. Blood studies have shown them to be identical.

The quadruplets were firstborn children to a 31-year-old woman. There was a history of mental illness on the father's side of the family. The mother's pregnancy was marked by vomiting and a 23-pound weight loss in the early months, then by extreme discomfort and excessive weight gain in the latter months. Delivery was without complications (except for the use of ether anesthesia), with the birth order and birth weights being as follows: Nora (2,041 g), Iris (1,490 g), Myra (1,928 g), and Hester (1,350 g). The pseudonymous first names of the quadruplets were selected by Dr. Rosenthal and his colleagues to correspond with the initials of NIMH.

From the beginning, Hester (the last born and lightest) lagged behind her sisters in developmental milestones. She did not sit up by herself until more than a month after the others, and she was not toilet trained until two months later than the others. In school her grades were the lowest, although all four girls averaged between B and C. They were tightly restricted in their social activities by their strict parents and grew up playing mostly with each other.

Hester was also the first to show behavioral signs of later illness. As a young girl, she was noted by her parents to masturbate frequently, a habit that Iris adopted to a lesser degree. After seeking help from a child guidance clinic and despairing of failed remedies, Mr. and Ms. Genain arranged for a surgical circumcision (clitorectomy) for both Hester and Iris when they were young adolescents.

Nora, at age 22, was the first to be hospitalized for overt psychosis, although she had started having phobias and compulsions 3 years earlier. She believed people were talking about her, developed somatic delusions, and exhibited bizarre behavior (e.g., "stands on her elbows and knees till her elbows bleed") (Rosenthal, 1963, p. 525). Nora was hospitalized four more times during the next 4 years with delusions and hallucinations, and following her stay at NIMH, she remained in a state psychiatric hospital for 18 months. Since that time, she has lived in the community on antipsychotic medication except for two hospitalizations, and she was able to hold clerical jobs for as long as 3 years at a time.

Iris was first admitted to a psychiatric hospital 7 months after Nora. She had become withdrawn and paranoid and was experiencing auditory hallucinations and multiple somatic complaints. Following her stay at NIMH, she was hospitalized in a state psychiatric hospital for more than 10 years. Since that time, she has lived in a foster home, taking antipsychotic medication and attending a day care center, and she has had two brief rehospitalizations.

Although not the first to be hospitalized, Hester has been regarded as clinically the most severely ill of the quadruplets. Following her initial hospitalization at NIMH at age 24, she was transferred to a state psychiatric hospital, where she remained for the next 12 years with classical symptoms of schizophrenia. Since that time, she has lived in the community and is taking antipsychotic medication.

Myra has been the least sick of the quadruplets and, had they not participated in the NIMH study, she would probably never have been hospitalized until age 46. During the NIMH years, she exhibited "psychomotor retardation, hysteroid symptomatology, multiple somatic complaints, and periods of depression and anxiety" (DeLisi et al., 1984) as well as some paranoid ideation, but she had no overt psychotic symptoms. She worked steadily in clerical jobs and at age 26 she married. She subsequently raised two children and functioned normally until age 46 when, under stress, "she became paranoid and delusional" (ibid.), was hospitalized for two months, and treated with antipsychotic medication. Three years later she had a similar episode with depression, necessitating a 3-week hospitalization.

Clinically, the most striking feature about the Genain quadruplets is how different their clinical courses have been. Nora, Iris, and Hester all have easily met criteria for a diagnosis of chronic schizophrenia (variously subtyped as undifferentiated, hebephrenic, or catatonic), with the latter two having been hospitalized for a total of more than 15 years. Myra, on the other hand, was able to marry, raise children, and work regularly until her late 40s, when she had two brief psychotic episodes; since these occurred after the age of 45 and lasted less than 6 months, Myra does not meet the technical criteria for a DSM-III-R diagnosis of schizophrenia, although there is no doubt that she has had a lesser degree of the same illness as her sisters have had. When the quadruplets were taken off medication during their 1981 retesting at NIMH, Nora and Hester "deteriorated substantially," Iris "maintained herself reasonably well while off active drugs," and Myra "actually appeared better compensated off neuroleptics than on them, and consequently was kept off drugs upon discharge from NIMH" (Mirsky et al., 1984).

The results of various tests done on the quadruplets revealed few correlations with their clinical status. Nora and Hester had the most neurological soft-sign abnormalities (6.0 and 5.5, respectively) compared with Iris (2.5) and Myra (2.0). On the Luria battery for brain function, Iris and Hester showed temporal and parietal lobe dysfunction, while Nora and Myra showed the fewest signs of organicity. All four had CT scans in 1981, which were within normal limits and very similar. On PET scans, Myra and Iris showed the greatest degree of abnormality (hypofrontality). EEGs both in 1955 and again in 1981 were very similar for all four women and showed a nonspecific slowing of alpha waves in the occipital region; the father of the quadruplets showed a similar pattern when tested. The results of testing their blood and cerebrospinal fluid in 1981 showed that all four quadruplets had some unusual chemical results in dopamine metabolites, but the interpretation of this finding was unclear.

Researchers who have studied the Genain quadruplets have had difficulty in constructing a framework to explain their illnesses. The women all began life with the same genes and experienced a similarly strict and repressive household environment, yet the clinical range of illnesses from Hester's to Myra's is very broad. Extensive attempts were made during their initial stay at NIMH to discover psychosocial and intrafamilial reasons to explain their variable illnesses applying diathesis-stress and life-experience theories, but these attempts failed. For example, Iris and Hester—but not Nora—underwent circumcision as adolescents, surely a traumatic experience for a young woman by any psychosocial standard, yet Nora had a chronic course of illness almost as severe as her sisters.

Hester was the one with the most clearly abnormal premorbid personality while Nora was the leader of the quadruplets in early childhood, yet it is Hester and Nora who showed the most neurological soft-sign abnormalities. On the other hand, Myra and Iris showed more abnormalities on PET scans, while all four quadruplets had CT scans that were essentially equal and within normal limits. Other than Hester, who was both the lightest at birth and premorbidly and morbidly the most disabled, it is not possible to fit the illnesses of the Genain quadruplets into any recognizable pattern of causation. It appears that the tests being used to assess brain function were, at least at the time of testing, insufficiently sensitive to provide an understanding of why four individuals with the same genes should have so variable an illness.

Triplets with Schizophrenia

Turning to triplets with schizophrenia, two sets from England have been described in the *British Journal of Psychiatry*; two sets were included in the 1966 Pollin et al. twin study, but the case material was not published; two sets were included in the present twin study; and an additional set was identified by us, but the triplets were unable to take part in our study. A summary of these seven sets of triplets follows.

1. *McGuffin et al. (1982)*, British Journal of Psychiatry 140:1–6

This triplet set is described in Chapter 10.

2. *Anonymous (1991), Letter in* British Journal of Psychiatry 159:734–735

This brief case report of identical male triplets stated that they were born following an uncomplicated full-term pregnancy. Their birth weights were 1,910 g, 1,770 g, and 1,770 g. Their mother had "a history of intermittent depressive disorder and two episodes of major depression"; it is not noted whether she had any psychotic symptoms with her depression.

At age 32 triplet B "developed a major depression" followed by "delusions, hallucinations and passivity experiences." He was diagnosed with schizoaffective disorder, hospitalized, and treated with antipsychotic medication and electroconvulsive therapy. MRI scans, done on all three triplets apparently for research purposes, were normal for triplet B, showed an enlarged right temporal horn for triplet A, and "possibly also in the last born" (triplet C).

Three years after the onset of his illness, triplet B continued to take antipsychotic medication and lithium and remained unable to work. Triplets A and C were said to "remain well, apart from intermittent episodes of depression not severe enough to interfere with work." Given the late age of onset of psychosis in triplet B and the relatively short (3-year) follow-up period at the time the report was written, it is too early to say whether the other triplets will also get sick.

3. Pollin et al. (1966) twin study, case number 5

Two members of this set (triplet A as a control and triplet C as the affected member) were included as twins in the Pollin et al. twin study. There was a history of psychosis (probably schizophrenia) in the mother's brother. The triplets were firstborn children to a mother in her late 20s. The pregnancy was marked by a 60-pound weight gain and edema, necessitating hospitalization of the mother in the last month of pregnancy. Despite excessive weight gain and a history of twinning in the mother's family, the obstetrician assured the mother that there was only one fetus, right up to the time of delivery.

The delivery was difficult, necessitating the use of forceps for all three births, and all the infants were said to have had misshapen heads. Triplet A was born breech and the other two were vertex. The weights of the triplets were 2,380 g, 1,885 g, and 1,590 g. At birth triplet C was said to be "in very bad shape," "quite blue," and in need of resuscitation. It is not clear how long the delay was between the delivery of triplets B and C, but it was apparently a substantial period; C's birth was completely unexpected, even after the delivery of the first two. The parents were told initially that triplet C might not live.

At age 1 month triplet C was hospitalized with pneumonia; again the parents were told that he might not live. At age 4 years triplet C had an infection that was suspected of possibly being meningitis, but he was not hospitalized.

Triplet C lagged behind his brothers in virtually all developmental landmarks and was perceived by the family as being the weakest and most vulnerable of the three. In primary school he was both lighter and shorter; triplets A and B got average grades, but triplet C's grades were below average. The triplets all became Boy Scouts and participated in school activities but were not leaders among their peers. Among the triplets, A was clearly the leader of the three.

Following graduation from high school, all three attended college and graduated. Triplets A and C began dating, but B did not. All began working after college but C decided to get advanced training and returned to graduate school. It was during this period, at age 24, that triplet C developed paranoid ideation and anxiety and sought psychiatric help. The treating psychiatrist diagnosed him with a neurosis, although retrospectively the psychiatrist said he suspected a psychosis. Less than 2 years later, triplet C was voluntarily hospitalized with acute paranoid schizophrenia with delusions, a belief that the radio was broadcasting his thoughts, loose associations, concrete thinking, and flat affect. While participating in the Pollin et al. twin study, he was evaluated neurologically and found to have more abnormalities than triplet A. All three triplets received EEGs during this study, which were said to be "slightly irregular"; the abnormalities for triplets A and B were focused in the temporal lobe, but for triplet C the abnormalities were "more generalized."

Triplet C continued to have recurrent psychiatric symptoms for the remainder of his life. He lived alternatively with triplet B and with his mother, but medication compliance was poor, necessitating periodic brief rehospitalizations. He also developed increasingly severe medical problems, for which he was unable and/or unwilling to follow the prescribed regimens. At age 52 he died from complications of his medical condition.

Triplet B had the onset of epilepsy (grand mal and psychomotor) at age 22 and thereafter took antiepileptic medication, with good seizure control. Because of his bad temper, he was asked to leave several jobs. He retu ned to graduate school but failed and dropped out. He then took a job as a career government employee, which he held for more than 20 years. He never married and lived alone during those periods when triplet C was not living with him. He became the primary caregiver of triplet C. Triplet B was killed in an accident at age 56. During his participation in the Pollin et al. twin study, no evidence of psychosis or prepsychotic thinking was found, and he was apparently never treated psychiatrically in subsequent years.

Triplet A married shortly after leaving college and raised a family. He held a single professional job for 30 years until he retired, at which point he became involved in community activities. At age 57 he continues to be pleasant and cooperative, and in a telephone interview, there was no evidence of any thought disorder.

In summary, these identical triplets include one who developed chronic paranoid schizophrenia, one who developed epilepsy and had a schizoid lifestyle although no apparent psychosis, and one who has remained completely well for more than 31 years, when his brother first became ill.

4. Pollin et al. twin study, case number 8

This set of triplets consists of two identical males and a female; the males were included as a twin pair in the Pollin et al. twin study (triplet A as a control and triplet B as the affected member). There was no known family history of psychosis in first- or second-degree relatives. The triplets were born to a mother in her 20s who had had one previous child. Both the pregnancy, which lasted 7½ months, and the delivery, which lasted 6 hours, were said to have been uncomplicated. Triplets A and B, the males, weighed 1,950 g and 1,640 g, respectively, and triplet C weighed 1,660 g. All three infants were discharged from the hospital at 5 weeks, at which time triplet B had a persistent scalp abscess, which slowly resolved.

Developmentally, the girl progressed faster than the boys, whose development was said to be equal. From the earliest years, the girl was more outgoing and self-confident, while both boys tended to be more quiet and shy. All the triplets had repeated ear infections, which produced modest hearing loss for them in the first grade; triplet B's grades lagged behind those of triplet A during the early grades, but it is unclear whether this was due to his hearing loss.

All the triplets were said to have developed normally, but as they became older, the girl was increasingly noted to be more social and the boys more studious (neither dated during high school). During their high school years, the boys did equally well academically.

Following high school, the triplets went to college, and it was during these years that triplet B's problems began. During his senior year, at age 20, his grades fell markedly and he became "nervous," withdrawn, hostile, and depressed. He was referred for psychiatric care and was initially diagnosed with a neurosis. He managed to complete his course requirements but had increasing problems after graduation. Approximately 1 year following the onset of his initial symptoms, he was hospitalized psychiatrically. He was said to be "almost catatonic," withdrawn, had a marked thought disorder, and was depressed; this time he was diagnosed with chronic undifferentiated schizophrenia. His first hospitalization lasted 11 weeks, and a second hospitalization followed 5 months later. At that time he was transferred to NIMH to participate in the Pollin et al. twin study, where he was diagnosed with "chronic undifferentiated schizophrenia with paranoid and obsessive-compulsive features." EEGs done on triplets A and B were both normal. Neurologically, triplet A was found to have slightly more neurological abnormalities than triplet B; this was contrary to the findings for most twin pairs in that study in which the affected twin had, in most cases, more neurological abnormalities.

Pollin et al. examined triplets A and C in depth as part of their twin study. Triplet A was said to be "rigid" and "emotionally constricted" but otherwise completely normal. Triplet C was said to be engaging, outgoing, and impressively devoid of any psychopathology.

Since 1964 triplet B has required intermittent hospitalization and has remained severely affected. When not hospitalized, he has lived in group homes but has required considerable supervision. His response to antipsychotic medication has been poor. Triplet A, by contrast, completed an advanced degree, has had a successful professional career, married, and raised a family. In recent years he has sought counseling for interpersonal problems, but he continues to show no symptoms of mental illness 32 years after the onset of illness in his brother. Triplet C also married and raised a family. When her children were grown, she returned to school and obtained an advanced degree. She has also shown no symptoms of mental illness.

5. Present study, concordant pair CS-9

Triplets A and B of this identical set of concordant triplets were used as a concordant twin pair; triplet C could not be used because the severity of her illness made it impossible for her to complete some parts of the testing.

The triplets were third-born children to a 31-year-old mother. Except for the mother's depression, which did not require hospitalization, there was no family history of mental illness. The pregnancy and delivery were uncomplicated except for thrombosis in the mother's leg, which resolved with conservative treatment. The triplets were said to have been healthy and weighed 2,052 g, 2,421 g, and 2,363 g. They had no significant childhood illnesses except for "the flu," which they all got at age 3 months and which lasted 2 weeks. Their early development was similar and considered to be completely normal.

They began first grade without having gone to kindergarten and were found to be immature. They therefore repeated the grade, but their behavior became progressively worse, so they were referred to a special education class. Performance IQ at that time was slightly below average for all three triplets. By age 8 their problematic behavior had evolved into frank psychotic symptoms, with delusions, auditory hallucinations, and bizarre behavior. From the beginning, triplet C was the most severely affected and was also inclined toward self-mutilation. The severity of their psychotic symptoms increased, and at age 12 all three were started on antipsychotic medication. This provided only modest improvement, and at age 14, following a suicide attempt by triplet B, all three were simultaneously committed to a state psychiatric hospital.

Now age 38, triplets A and B have spent approximately half of the intervening years hospitalized, while triplet C has been hospitalized almost continuously. Triplet A, who has functioned at the highest level, has exhibited predominantly paranoid and somatic delusions, auditory and probably tactile hallucinations, and loose associations. Triplet B has complained of bizarre delusions (e.g., she believes that animals can read her mind) and thought insertion and has also had continuous loose associations; auditory hallucinations have been present but not prominent. Triplet C, by contrast, has had severe auditory hallucinations, delusions, loose associations, self-mutilative behavior, and marked withdrawal. All three have been diagnosed with chronic schizophrenia (undifferentiated, disorganized, and undifferentiated, respectively) and none has been able to return to school or work.

On neurological examination triplet A had almost no abnormalities, while triplet B had multiple hard and soft neurological signs. On neuropsychological testing triplets A and B were also very dissimilar. Triplet C was not testable either neurologically or neuropsychologically because of the severity of her symptoms. On MRI scans triplet A had the smallest right lateral, left lateral, and third ventricles. Triplet B's ventricles were larger than A's by 60, 19, and 18%, respectively, and triplet C's ventricles were larger than A's by 45, 10, and 72%, respectively. Their right hippocampus-amygdala were of equal size; for the left, triplet A's was the largest, with B's and C's being 15 and 9% smaller, respectively. Recently, all three triplets were started on clozapine, and triplet C has shown an especially good response.

6. Present study, discordant pair DS-25

Triplets A (affected) and C (control) were used as a discordant twin pair in our study; the diagnostic status of triplet B was not clear at the time of testing.

These identical triplets were second-born children to a 20-year-old mother. There was no family history of psychosis in first- or second-degree relatives. The pregnancy was marked by episodic bleeding in the second and third trimesters caused by placenta previa, so delivery was by Caesarean section. The triplets were said to be healthy at birth and weighed, 2,534 g, 2,502 g, and 2,277 g. Development was approximately equal and within normal limits for all three. Triplet A (but not his brothers) had "hepatitis" at age 4; the following year in kindergarten he was said to have been "more nervous," "more anxious," and to have more difficulty sitting still. Triplet A was considered to be the leader of the triplets throughout primary school.

Triplet A began showing signs of illness at age 15 immediately following a "viral illness," which included a rash. He became depressed, withdrawn, felt that "everything seemed interrelated," and began having auditory hallucinations. He was treated psychiatrically as an outpatient, with some improvement. A year later his symptoms recurred and included depression, emotional lability, pressure of speech, compulsive behavior, delusions, auditory hallucinations, and loose associations. He had a good response to antipsychotic medication and was able to continue in school without being hospitalized. He was diagnosed with schizoaffective disorder.

Triplet B also experienced some psychiatric problems at age 16, including insomnia, difficulty concentrating, ideas that the sounds and actions of people and objects in his environment referred to him, compulsive behavior, and possible auditory hallucinations. The following year he participated in our twin study and was formally diagnosed with schizotypal personality disorder. Because of his young age, it was considered likely that he would subsequently develop schizophrenia. Triplet C at age 17 showed no psychiatric symptoms at all and was considered to be within normal limits.

Neurologically, all three triplets had a moderate number of neurological abnormalities and the same overall score. On neuropsychological testing triplet A showed minor deficits on tests of attention but outperformed triplets B and C on tests of memory. On MRI scans no consistent pattern was seen. Triplet A, who had become sick first, had the largest left lateral ventricle but the smallest right lateral ventricle among the three. In measurements of the hippocampus-amygdala triplet C, the well triplet, had the smallest volume, the opposite of what would be predicted by their clinical status.

In the four years since participating in the study, triplet A successfully completed 3 years of college while on no medication. During that time he is said to have been shy and to have periods of anxiety but showed no symptoms of severe mental illness. As this book was being completed, triplet A experienced a manic episode and was diagnosed with bipolar disorder. Triplet B, by contrast, has had four episodes of psychosis requiring hospitalization since participation in the study. He has been variously diagnosed with schizoaffective disorder and bipolar disorder, and does well on lithium alone when he takes it regularly. Triplet C has successfully pursued a career following high school and has shown no signs of mental illness. In view of the course of triplet A's illness and the bipolar diagnosis for triplet B, it seems increasingly likely that these triplets have bipolar disorder rather than schizophrenia.

7. Present study, identified discordant triplets

These triplets were identified in the process of recruiting for the twin study, but because of their work schedules, they were unable to participate in the study.

There is a family history of mental retardation and depression. When they were born, the mother was told by the doctor that they were identical. Triplets A and C look alike but triplet B does not, so these triplets probably consist of an identical twin pair plus a fraternal triplet. During the third trimester of pregnancy, the mother had "a bad head cold [which she] could not shake" and immediately following delivery she developed measles and pneumonia. The triplets weighed 2,609 g, 2,439 g, and 2,353 g and were said to be healthy babies.

At age 23 triplet C developed symptoms of psychosis, which has been diagnosed as both bipolar disorder and schizophrenia, predominantly the latter. He has been on intramuscular fluphenazine, and after 8 years he is in good remission and is able to hold a full-time, responsible job. Triplet A has had some mood swings but has otherwise been well, and triplet B has remained well. Both are also employed full-time.

What Can Be Learned?

This collection of triplets in which one or more of each set has been diagnosed with schizophrenia (summarized in Table 11.1) is not representative of triplets with schizophrenia in general, since both the Pollin et al. study and the present study were specifically seeking identical subjects. Thus there are no triplets included who were formed from three separate ova (trizygotic). An adequate study of a representative triplet population would require a national registry of multiple births such as exists in Scandinavian nations but not in the United States.

What can be learned from these cases? First, it is clear that true discordance for schizophrenia can exist in identical triplets just as it can in identical twins. In the two cases studied by Pollin et al., one of the identical triplets has continued to show no symptoms of illness 31 and 32 years after the onset of illness in his brothers.

TABLE 11.1
Identical Triplets with Schizophrenia

	Family History of Mental Illness	Pregnancy and Birth Problems	Diagnosis and Birth Weight (g)		
			A (firstborn)	B (second-born)	C (third-born)
McGuffin et al.	"Borderline psychosis" (father)	No data	Schizophrenia wt. not given	Schizoaffective wt. not given	bipolar "largest"
Anonymous	Depression (mother)	None	Well 1,910	Schizoaffective 1,770	Well 1,770
Pollin et al. case no. 5	Psychosis (uncle)	Severe problems; resuscitation of triplet C	Well 2,380	Schiz., undiff. 1,885	Schiz., paranoid 1,590
Pollin et al. case no. 8	None	None	Well 1,950	Schiz., undiff. 1,640	Well (fraternal) 1,660
Present study CS-9	Depression (mother)	None	Schiz., undiff. 2,052	Schiz., disorg. 2,421	Schiz., undiff. 2,363
Present study DS-25	None	Placenta previa with Caesarean section	Probably bipolar 2,534	Schizoaffective/ bipolar 2,502	Well 2,277
Present study (identified but not studied)	Depression (aunt)	Mother had cold in last trimester and measles immediately postpartum	Well 2,609	Well (fraternal) 2,439	Schizophrenia 2,353

It is also evident that even when all three identical triplets are affected by psychosis, the clinical expression of the disease may be variable. The case study by McGuffin et al. illustrates this point dramatically, as does case CS-9 in our study. This is consistent with the variable clinical expression of schizophrenia seen in identical twins concordant for the disease (see Chapter 9) as well as in the identical Genain quadruplets described earlier. This variable clinical expression could theoretically be explained by a variety of mechanisms, including variable expression of the gene, variable effects of a biological insult on different parts of the brain, or variable effects of a biological insult at different stages of fetal development (e.g., one triplet may be smaller and have more vulnerable cerebral hemispheres at the time of the insult). The Pollin et al. case number 5, in which the affected triplet was both smaller at birth and had more perinatal anoxia, fits such a theoretical chain of events.

As was found for our identical twins discordant and concordant for schizophrenia, the correlations between the clinical status of the triplets and the measures of brain function or structure were not impressive. In the Pollin et al. case number 8, triplet A, who has remained completely well, had more neurological abnormalities than triplet B, who had had severe schizophrenia. On MRI scans, in the case reported by Anonymous, triplet B, who is sick, had the *smallest* ventricles (lateral horn) of the three. In the two sets of triplets for which MRI data were available in the present study, neither ventricular size nor hippocampus-amygdala size were good predictors of clinical status.

CHAPTER 12

What Do Twin Studies Tell Us About the Causes of Schizophrenia?

I N ORDER to interpret and evaluate the findings from the present study, we have assembled three fictional authorities. "Dr. Mendel M. Malgene" represents the genetic viewpoint, "Dr. Dena S. Daverus" takes the virological position, and "Dr. A. Dominic D'Velupmoni" speaks from a developmental perspective. Each was asked to summarize the important findings from the study and then to critique each other's summaries.

Geneticist's Viewpoint: Dr. Malgene

I have the dubious honor of leading off the discussion today and exposing my genetic bias before I have had the opportunity to hear from my colleagues. I think it is important to note at the outset that this research project was not planned to answer genetic questions. On the contrary, it explicitly focused its primary attention on monozygotic twins in which one is affected with schizophrenia or bipolar disorder and the other is well. As such, this project selectively focused on individuals who are *least* likely to have genetic variants of these diseases. Many identical twins in which only one is affected may represent phenocopies of the true disease; that is, they have the outward manifestations and symptoms but not the underlying genetic substrate. We accept that some cases of schizophrenia and bipolar disorder are not genetic in origin, and this project focused on that group.

Regarding the paucity of family history for schizophrenia or other serious mental diseases among the twins discordant (and especially those concordant) for schizophrenia, one likely reason for this is that the researchers did not look hard enough. Recall that in the earliest stages of the project they collected personality questionnaires (MMPIs) on first-degree relatives (mother, father, brothers, and sisters) of their subjects, but then the researchers abandoned this procedure because they found it to be too intrusive. That was a mistake, for if they had continued with the MMPIs, they almost certainly would have found more members of the families, especially the families of the concordant pairs, to have schizoid personality disorder and other diagnoses considered to be part of the schizophrenia spectrum. For example, in reviewing older twin studies, Cadoret found among the families of the twins "a high proportion of individuals with significant character abnormalities or neurotic symptoms" (Cadoret, 1973). Kringlen also found more family history of serious mental diseases in his twin study than were found in the present study. The researchers should have personally interviewed all first-degree relatives, and in this way they could have truly ascertained the prevalence of serious mental illnesses among the relatives.

In this regard, I would like to bring to my colleagues' attention the important findings of Gottesman and Bertelsen, who found an increased incidence of schizophrenia among the children of the *well* twins in Fischer's Danish study of identical twins discordant for schizophrenia (Gottesman & Bertelsen, 1989). This would appear to be strong evidence suggesting that the well twins in the present study may also be carrying a schizophrenia gene that, for one reason or another, is not being expressed. We know also that genes may be pleiotropic, by which I mean that the same gene may be expressed in a variety of ways in different individuals. For example, the gene known to cause von Recklinghausen's disease may express itself as tan spots on the skin, areas of skin depigmentation, abnormalities of the bones, or as tumors of the nerves. If a single gene can express itself in so many different ways, then why should we be surprised if the gene or genes implicated in schizophrenia also manifest themselves in a variety of ways in different individuals?

Within the present study there is some evidence that the well co-twins in the discordant pairs may have some genetic loading for the disease. Note that the discordant twins with a family history of serious mental diseases have higher scores for minor physical anomalies; a logical explanation for this association is that one or more genes are responsible for both phenomena. There is also a trend for the affected twins with a family history of serious mental diseases to have an earlier age of divergence, which also suggests a genetic subgroup.

Several additional findings support my belief that at least some of the co-twins in this project are carriers of the disease. The concordant twins have significantly fewer obstetrical complications than the discordant twins, which would be consistent with the concordant twins having a more genetic form of the disease. Also note that the well co-twins in the discordant pairs had scores for neurological abnormalities that fell midway between the scores of the twins with schizophrenia and the normal controls. The well co-twins in the discordant pairs also had more abnormalities on neuropsychological tests than did the normal controls.

I would caution my colleagues about interpreting the genetic aspects of schizophrenia too narrowly. We are just beginning to learn how complex genetic makeup can be. Not only do we have proposed single-gene and polygenic models for schizophrenia, but the genes involved may also be scattered at different sites on the same chromosome or on different chromosomes. Some researchers have postulated that there are both major genes and minor genes involved. The genes may also have varying levels of penetrance, by which I mean that they may be expressed more overtly in one individual but more covertly in another.

Furthermore, the gene or genes involved in schizophrenia may do so in one of many ways. The schizophrenia gene(s) may be like the gene that causes phenylketonuria, a metabolic disease that begins in childhood, in which the gene causes a defect in the enzyme that normally breaks down phenylalanine; the symptoms of the disease come from the accumulation of phenylalanine in the brain. The child does not get phenylketonuria unless phenylalanine is ingested in the diet. This is an example of a genetic disease that only becomes manifest if certain environmental conditions are present.

Alternatively, the schizophrenia gene(s) may act by altering the metabolism of dopamine and its metabolites. In one sense, the dopamine theory of schizophrenia can be considered a subtype of the genetic theory. Recently there has been speculation that multiple sclerosis may be caused by genetically transmitted defects in myelin basic protein (Tienari et al., 1992), and schizophrenia may be caused in a similar fashion. Since genes govern the embryological developmental processes of the brain and its susceptibility to decreased oxygen or other environmental insults, developmental theories may also be considered as a kind of genetic theory. Furthermore, genes are known to play an important role in determining susceptibility of the body to various infectious agents, and it is well known that the body's response to specific bacteria and viruses is partly determined by genetics. In that sense, the viral theory of schizophrenia is also a type of genetic theory.

Finally, I would add that recent research on adoptees and on identical twins raised apart has strongly supported the importance of genetics in determining normal personality traits. Since genes play such a prominent role in normal personality traits, it is certainly reasonable to expect that they also play a prominent role in determining the abnormal personality traits we categorize as schizophrenia.

Virologist's Viewpoint: Dr. Daverus

In reviewing the findings from this ambitious study, I was impressed by how well the findings fit a viral hypothesis of schizophrenia. Of course, the report of finding antibodies to pestiviruses in the plasma and cerebrospinal fluid of some affected twins is exciting, but that is only a preliminary report and needs to be replicated. Additional findings of interest include the increased number of spontaneous abortions among the mothers of the discordant twins, and the trend toward a winter-spring birth seasonality in the discordant twins who have more perinatal indicators of risk. Both of these could be explained by prenatal viral infections.

What I am most impressed with is the evidence that the schizophrenia disease process goes back to the period prior to birth in some cases, and perhaps to the first few weeks after birth in others. The cumulative evidence from minor physical anomalies, total finger ridge counts, and obstetrical complications is impressive in confirming that something begins to go wrong in the early developmental stages of life in some cases of schizophrenia, even though the individual does not develop the actual symptoms of the disease until many years later.

Recent studies have shown how frequently viruses may be transmitted from mother to fetus across the placenta or during the birth process. For example, hepatitis C virus, which is in the same Flavivirus family as pestiviruses, is commonly transmitted from infected mothers to fetuses and then initiates a silent disease process or chronic carrier state (Thaler et al., 1991). Recent studies have also shown that the HIV virus is commonly transmitted from infected mothers to their children late in pregnancy or at the time of delivery (Ehrnst et al., 1991). Similarly, one-third of babies born to women who have a primary herpes simplex virus genital infection will become infected during the birth process (Brown et al., 1991). We know now that many different viruses are capable of getting into the brain and remaining latent there for many years before causing symptomatic infection. And we know that viruses may infect only one twin *in utero* in an identical twin pair (reviewed in Chapter 2).

Even following birth, we know that both twins in an identical pair may be infected with a virus and yet have very different reactions to that virus. In one case reported, identical twins both had measles at age 4; 10 years later one of them developed subacute sclerosing panencephalitis, a severe and ultimately fatal complication of measles infection, but the other twin did not (Whitaker et al., 1972). In another case, both twins were infected with the hepatitis B virus; one of them developed active disease, but the other only developed a chronic carrier state (Peters et al., 1977).

The consistent finding of smaller hippocampus-amygdala complexes in the affected twins is also intriguing. Something has either impaired the development of that part of the brain or has caused cell death to reduce its size. There are a limited number of agents that could reduce the size of the hippocampus-amygdala, and a viral infection is one of them. We now know that you would not necessarily find neuropathological changes if a viral infection were responsible for the brain changes. Early in development the fetus's immune system is not sufficiently developed to mount an immune response to the infection. And later in development it has been shown that viruses can sometimes disrupt cell function—for example, alter the production of dopamine or another neurotransmitter—without producing any cellular pathology visible under a microscope (Oldstone et al., 1982).

I also agree with Dr. Malgene's comments regarding the importance of genetic predisposition to viral diseases. We know there is a genetic factor that plays a role in determining whether any given virus will infect the brain, and this genetic factor has been shown to affect viruses that are in the same family as the pestivirus (Roos, 1985). Recall also that for the polio virus, a virus that has been carefully studied in the central nervous system, the pairwise concordance rate for infection in identical twins is 36% and in fraternal twins 6%; these concordance rates are virtually identical to those for schizophrenia (28% in identical twins, 6% in fraternal twins) as was discussed in Chapter 1.

Finally, I would like to remind my colleagues that viral infections that might cause schizophrenia may also begin after the perinatal period. I was especially impressed by the history of discordant pair DS-19, in which neurological ("a strange gait") and behavioral problems began at age 5, with no preexisting indicators of risk or illness. Discordant pair DS-25, in which the schizophrenia began immediately following a viral illness and rash, and pair DS-3, in which symptoms began shortly after a severe flu-like syndrome, are also noteworthy.

Developmentalist's Viewpoint: Dr. D'Velupmoni

I have the pleasure of going last, which is appropriate because my explanation for the causes of schizophrenia both builds upon and incorporates the explanations of my colleagues. It seems to me that this twin study provides strong evidence for a developmental theory of the disease, one substantially more complex than a genetic or viral explanation alone. I am reminded of a quotation by Dr. R. S. Nowakowski who, in a review of brain development, said: "The human central nervous system is, without a doubt, the single most complicated organ in the body, and the processes involved in its development are commensurately complex" (Nowakowski, 1987).

Perhaps the most striking finding from this exhaustive study is that no single etiological factor is prominent. There are indications that *something* is going on in the developing brain of some of the people who later develop schizophrenia, but no one factor appears to be clearly associated. The pathology observed on the MRIs includes some dilatation of the cerebral ventricles, as well as some loss of volume of the hippocampus-amygdala complex. Both of these changes are nonspecific and, at least the latter, most likely take place during early stages of brain development.

The combination of nonspecific indicators of developmental problems and nonspecific cerebral pathology suggests a nonspecific or multietiological developmental explanation. The developmental theory postulates that any one of a number of etiological agents could initiate the causative cascade leading to schizophrenia *if* that agent affected the brain at a crucial stage of development. The etiological agents could include, in the words of Dr. Daniel R. Weinberger, "a hereditary encephalopathy or predilection to environmental injury, an infection or postinfectious state, damage from an immunologic disorder, perinatal trauma or encephalopathy, toxin exposure early in development, a primary metabolic disease, or other early developmental events" (Weinberger, 1987).

Once the original insult takes place at a critical stage of brain development, the damage is done. In most cases, however, its effects are not immediately noticeable, except perhaps for nonspecific signs such as lack of coordination or behavioral problems in childhood. In the majority of cases, the effects of the early brain damage must await the maturation of the brain, at which point the developmental damage becomes noticeable as the signs and symptoms of schizophrenia. There are now rat models that show you can cause lesions in the hippocampus of a rat's brain during early development, but the effects of the lesions will not show up behaviorally until the rat matures (Lipska et al., 1993). Some people believe that this developmental model also explains many cases of epilepsy as well as schizophrenia.

There is one other finding from this study that is important from a developmental point of view. The affected twins who scored the highest on indicators of perinatal liability, such as minor physical anomalies, total finger ridge counts, obstetrical complications, and lower birth weight, tended to do *better* clinically than the affected twins with fewer indicators of perinatal liability. Most theories of schizophrenia would postulate that these affected twins should do *worse* than the others because the brain damage occurred at an earlier stage or was more extensive. The developmental theory, however, might explain this by postulating that the earlier damage allowed for the formation of alternative pathways of neural development, thus partially compensating for the injury.

In deference to Dr. Malgene, I should add that the developmental theory does not ignore genetics. Brain development is largely under genetic control, and it would be reasonable to expect that some individuals would have a higher degree of genetic predisposition to brain insults. The genes might operate directly to cause abnormal migration of cells or abnormal innervation of a particular area of the brain, or the genes might operate indirectly by making the hippocampus more susceptible to decreased oxygen or other insults.

Discussion

The participants were encouraged to critique each other's presentation, restricting their remarks to the twin study as much as possible.

DR. DAVERUS: Let me begin by raising questions about Dr. Malgene's presentation. I would first note that most of his presentation focused on theoretical genetic models of disease rather than on this twin study per se. The reason he did this, I believe, is that the present twin study produced very little support for genetic theories. The concordant twins compared to the discordant twins did not have a higher frequency of family history of serious mental illness as one would expect in a genetically transmitted disease. This finding is in agreement with the study by Gottesman and Shields (1982) in which the concordant twins compared to the discordant twins also did not have a greater family history of serious mental diseases.

One would also expect the concordant twins, in whom genetic factors by definition are maximal, to differ from the affected discordant twins in whom genetic factors are presumed to be less important. When the two groups were compared, however, they were remarkably alike in clinical manifestations, including negative symptoms, neurological abnormalities, and neuropsychological functioning, as well as in indicators of perinatal liability such as minor physical anomalies, total finger ridge counts, and obstetrical complications.

Perhaps even more important is the fact that the twins who do have a family history of serious mental illnesses do not appear to be significantly different from the twins with no such history. On both clinical measures and etiological indicators, the two groups are alike. There were also no significant differences between the groups on brain structure as measured by MRIs. No single measure emerged as a possible genetic marker for schizophrenia. Even eye-tracking dysfunction, which has been widely considered to be a genetic marker for this disease, was not consistently found in the well co-twins in the discordant pairs, thereby casting doubt on its candidacy as a genetic marker.

DR. D'VELUPMONI: I would also like to question some of Dr. Malgene's statements. He said that evidence of psychopathology was not found in the well co-twins in the discordant pairs because the researchers did not look closely enough. We must be cautious in making such statements. One of the things we should have learned from the psychiatric misadventures with Freudian theory is that one can find psychopathology, loosely defined, in virtually everybody if one looks closely enough. The question is not whether there is any psychopathology in the well co-twins, but rather whether there is any *more* psychopathology in these co-twins than could be found in any group of identical twins randomly selected off the street.

Dr. Malgene also cited the Gottesman and Bertelsen (1989) study of mental illness in the offspring of the well co-twins in Fischer's Danish twin study. It should be pointed out that the methodology of that study has been criticized on a variety of grounds (Torrey, 1990). The 21 identical twins with schizophrenia who were included in the Gottesman and Bertelsen follow-up had had a total of 31 children, whereas their 21 well co-twins had had a total of only 11 children. In other words, the *sick* twins had almost *three times more* children than the well twins. Similarly, in the Kringlen and Cramer (1989) follow-up of the offspring of identical twins in Norway, the 22 twins with schizophrenia in that study had had a total of 28 children, and their 22 well co-twins had a total of 45 children. These are extraordinarily high fertility rates for individuals with schizophrenia, especially since these births occurred during years when most people with even moderately severe schizophrenia were kept in psychiatric hospitals for many years. For comparison purposes, the 27 affected twins in the present study have had only 3 children compared to 28 children among the well co-twins; the average age of these twins is now 34. And this low fertility among the affected twins is at a time when most individuals with schizophrenia are not kept in hospitals for long periods. It makes one wonder whether some of the affected twins in the Danish and Norwegian studies may have had bipolar disorder rather than schizophrenia, especially since some of the twins in the Danish study were never examined personally by any of the researchers.

Dr. Malgene does a nice job of reviewing genetic models for phenylketonuria, von Recklinghausen's disease, and other disorders. The important question, however, is not whether such models *can* theoretically account for the findings in schizophrenia, but rather how well such models actually fit the findings. I believe we all accept the fact that genes play *some* role in the etiology of schizophrenia, but postulating that schizophrenia is a genetic disease, like phenylketonuria or von Recklinghausen's disease, is quite different from saying there is a genetic predisposition to a developmental anomaly or to a viral infection. It is the difference between saying that the genetic factor is necessary for the etiology of a disease or saying that a genetic predisposition increases the chances of getting that disease, but that genes by themselves are not sufficient or necessary to cause it. Dr. Malgene seems to slide back and forth across this spectrum without making clear distinctions.

Finally, Dr. Malgene implies that just because genes are important in determining normal personality traits, they are also likely to be important in the etiology of schizophrenia. This is a specious argument because schizophrenia is a brain disease, not a collection of personality traits. Genes may or may not play an important role in causing schizophrenia, but this has nothing to do with their role in determining normal personality traits.

I will turn my attention next to Dr. Daverus's presentation. And much of what I just said in criticism of Dr. Malgene applies equally well to Dr. Daverus. She lays out for us a variety of models in which viruses might cause a chronic infection of the central nervous system and the symptoms of schizophrenia. However, it is not a question of whether viruses *can* do such things, but rather whether viruses *do* do such things. And if they do, how often? Dr. Daverus mentions the data on birth seasonality in schizophrenia, but as she is aware, the excess winter-spring birth seasonality associated with schizophrenia accounts for no more than 10% of all individuals with schizophrenia.

I would like to add that even if the pestiviruses or other viruses are identified in the serum or cerebrospinal fluid of people with schizophrenia, that does not necessarily mean that the viruses are associated with the disease process. They could be reactivated by an altered immune system in the disease and their presence would then be merely an epiphenomenon. So I would ask Dr. Daverus, How do you know whether the putative viruses are causal or merely casual?

DR. MALGENE: I certainly agree with Dr. D'Velupmoni's remarks and would like to raise a few additional questions for Dr. Daverus. If viruses are truly implicated in many cases of this disease, wouldn't you expect to see more explicit neuropathology on MRI scans and in neuropathological research? For example, shouldn't there be prominent gliosis of the hippocampus-amygdala and not merely a nonspecific reduction in size?

I am also puzzled by how Dr. Daverus can account for the evidence of widespread cerebral dysfunction in the twins. Both the neurological and the neuropsychological findings suggest a broad, scattered type of dysfunction rather than a focal type. Many neuroviruses primarily attack one specific area (e.g., rabies) or one specific cell type (e.g., polio), but in schizophrenia there is no evidence of such localization.

Finally, I would offer a brief comment on those cases of schizophrenia in this study that began immediately following an infection. If you take any illness, you can find such preceding infections because they are so ubiquitous. Although such individual cases are interesting, it is noteworthy that no single type of infection was found to occur in an unusual incidence in the twins prior to the onset of their schizophrenia.

DR. DAVERUS: I would like to offer a few comments on Dr. D'Velupmoni's theory of schizophrenia. It is a difficult theory to criticize because it has so many parts. It reminds me of the game we used to play at birthday parties when I was a child in which everybody won and therefore everybody got a prize. The developmental theory is like that—everybody will turn out to be right because almost everything can cause the putative brain lesion.

But let's think more clearly about this theory. It postulates the damage as taking place early in the course of brain development. And yet known causes of brain damage early in development, such as chromosomal abnormalities or metabolic diseases, usually cause mental retardation, not schizophrenia. And if the brain damage really takes place so early in development, wouldn't we expect developmental markers, such as minor physical anomalies and dermatoglyphic changes, to be much more prominent?

Another problem with the developmental theory is epidemiological. The areas of the world where there is the worst prenatal care and the highest occurrence of malnutrition of pregnant women, obstetrical complications, and postnatal infections are the developing nations. The developmental theory would predict that increased incidence of developmental insults should produce an increase of schizophrenia in such countries. Yet there is no evidence for this, and, in fact, what evidence exists points in the opposite direction: that schizophrenia has a *lower* incidence in developing nations.

DR. MALGENE: Along those same lines, I would like to focus on the nature of the insults. Many of the theoretical insults that can disrupt brain development and lead to late schizophrenia, such as decreased oxygen supply, are also thought to cause epilepsy and cerebral palsy. If, in fact, these insults are the original cause of schizophrenia, shouldn't epilepsy and cerebral palsy co-occur with schizophrenia more often than by chance? There is an example of one such case (cerebral palsy in one twin, schizoaffective disorder in the other) among the twins in this study, but I would expect a much higher incidence.

Where Do We Go From Here?

To close the fictional discussion, the three experts were asked to state briefly what they believed to be the most important next steps to be taken for a better understanding of the causes of schizophrenia.

DR. MALGENE: Well, I think that the most important steps have already been taken by the support of multicenter molecular genetics studies in Europe and in the United States. In Europe 18 centers, supported by the European Science Foundation, have been coordinating efforts for over 3 years to look for loci associated with schizophrenia and bipolar disorder by using 150 genetic markers spread across all chromosomes. A similar multicenter study is under way in the United States, supported by the National Institute of Mental Health. Such linkage studies assume that one or more major genes are important etiological factors.

Alternatively, there are those of us who favor a theory of polygenic inheritance of schizophrenia without the involvement of a major gene. We are counting on association strategies, in which different alleles of a genetic marker (i.e., occurring alternatively) are studied in individuals with schizophrenia and in normal controls, for the answers. The problem with this strategy, however, is that we still have not identified genetic markers that are essential for these strategies. I would therefore strongly support continued research on dopamine and other neurotransmitters in hopes that one or more of them will be found to be a genetic marker. Linkage and association strategies are the psychiatric wave of the future, and the research leaders of the next decade will be molecular geneticists.

DR. DAVERUS: Viruses as possible etiological agents for schizophrenia and bipolar disorder have been greatly underresearched. That is now starting to change, primarily with the fiscal support of the Theodore and Vada Stanley Foundation. The increasing realization that the HIV virus, which causes AIDS, also causes widespread pathology in the central nervous system has increased interest in this field. Studies that have linked exposure to influenza in the middle trimester of pregnancy to the development of schizophrenia in the offspring many years later have also helped bring neurovirology into psychiatry.

The future holds great promise. Answers are likely to come from studies of serum, lymphocytes, cerebrospinal fluid, and postmortem brain tissue from individuals with schizophrenia. Personally, I suspect that viruses are also involved in the etiology of most cases of bipolar disorder as well, although a genetic predisposition appears to be more prominent in bipolar disorder than it is in schizophrenia. Another important research area will be the study of mothers during pregnancy and of infants in their first months of life, for those may be the periods when the virus that causes schizophrenia is transmitted. Future psychiatric researchers, then, will be experts in both neurovirology and perinatology, and the future schizophrenia research team may be centered in the departments of infectious disease and/or pediatrics.

DR. D'VELUPMONI: I'm afraid that I cannot share the optimism of my colleagues that either molecular genetics or virology will give us the answers. Schizophrenia probably involves many different factors, any one of which can impair the development of the brain at crucial stages of growth and thereby lead to later dysfunction.

The answers to this disease, therefore, are going to come more slowly as we gain a better understanding of brain development. We need to support more basic research—neuroanatomical, neurochemical, and embryological—on how normal brains develop and function. This should also include more research on animal models of normal and abnormal brain development. Only when we have gone through the tedious but necessary steps of understanding this normal development will we be able to understand what goes wrong in the developmental process to produce schizophrenia. The future leadership of psychiatric research, therefore, will be in the hands of the neuroanatomists and other basic brain researchers.

Summary of Major Findings

- The research project included 66 pairs of identical twins studied over 6 years:

  27 pairs discordant for schizophrenia
  13 pairs concordant for schizophrenia
   8 pairs discordant for bipolar disorder
   8 pairs normal controls
   8 pairs mixed diagnoses
   2 pairs not testable

- A family history of serious mental disease was found less often among the concordant twins (15%) than among the discordant twins (26%). Having a family history for serious mental disease was not found to be associated with any clinical or etiological measures, with the exception of minor physical anomalies.

- Perinatal (pregnancy and birth) factors appeared to be important in the etiology of at least 30% of the twins with schizophrenia. Obstetrical complication scores and within-pair variability in total finger ridge counts were significantly increased in the twins with schizophrenia compared to normal controls. Obstetrical complication scores and total finger ridge counts were also significantly related to each other in the discordant affected twins. However, no significant group differences were found between affected and well twins for minor physical anomalies, birth weights, or non-right-handedness, contrary to some previous studies. Markers of perinatal liability for schizophrenia did not correlate with clinical aspects of the disease.

- Approximately 30% of the twins who developed schizophrenia had been different as children—behaviorally, cognitively, and/or neurologically. Many of these twins appeared to have widespread early central nervous system dysfunction similar to what Barbara Fish has called "pandysmaturation." These twins included many of the same twins in whom perinatal factors were also prominent. It is suggested that these individuals have pre-schizophrenia of childhood, and that this is an early *latent* form of schizophrenia, just as childhood onset schizophrenia is the *manifest* form.

- The question of whether head trauma and antecedent physical illnesses play a role in causing schizophrenia was not answered.

- Preliminary viral research suggested a link between pestiviruses and schizophrenia in the affected twins. Preliminary immunological studies found altered interleukin receptors. Additional studies are in progress.

- Changes in brain structure, as measured by magnetic resonance imaging (MRI), were prominent in the twins with schizophrenia. Among the twins discordant for schizophrenia, the affected twins had a smaller right hippocampus-amygdala 81% of the time and a smaller left hippocampus-amygdala 78% of the time, compared to the well co-twins. Ventricular dilatation was also found but was not as consistently associated with the disease. The changes in brain structure were on a continuum with almost all affected twins, not merely a subgroup, showing some changes; this suggests that changes in brain structure are an integral part of the schizophrenia disease process.

- Changes in brain structure did not correlate with clinical aspects of schizophrenia. There were, however, suggestions that the changes in brain structure were associated with events that occurred earlier in life. Statistically significant correlations were found between dilatation of the left lateral ventricle and lower birth weight, dilatation of the third ventricle and an early age of divergence (as defined in Chapter 5), a smaller right hippocampus-amygdala and total finger ridge count, and a smaller left hippocampus-amygdala and a later age of first referral.

- Changes in brain function, as measured by cerebral blood flow, neuropsychological tests, neurological examination, and eye tracking were also prominent in the twins with schizophrenia. Cerebral blood flow studies showed reduced flow to the frontal lobes (hypofrontality) on all 10 affected twins with schizophrenia tested compared to their well co-twins. Data suggested that this is not a medication effect. Cerebral blood flow to the frontal lobes correlated directly with reduced size of the anterior hippocampus.

- Some degree of cognitive dysfunction was found on neuropsychological tests in most twins with schizophrenia, not merely in a subgroup. Moderate or severe cognitive impairment was present in 14 of the 27 affected twins in the discordant pairs.

- Both the discordant and concordant twins with schizophrenia had significantly more neurological impairment than the normal controls. Overall, 29 of the 53 twins with schizophrenia were neurologically impaired. This did not appear to be an effect of medication. The well co-twins in the discordant pairs also showed more neurological impairment than normal controls, consistent with the suggestion of either genetic factors or a cerebral insult sustained by both twins.

- Significant eye-tracking dysfunction was found in the majority of affected twins with schizophrenia. However, since the well twins in the discordant pairs showed no eye-tracking dysfunction when compared with normal controls, no support was found for using eye-tracking dysfunction as a genetic marker for schizophrenia.

- Cognitive and neurological dysfunction scores in the twins with schizophrenia each significantly correlated with higher negative symptoms scores (SANS) and with lower overall function (axis V on DSM-III-R). They did not, however, correlate with other clinical or etiological measures, so cognitive and neurological dysfunction appear to be nonspecific measures of disease severity and impaired function in general rather than representative of any clinical or etiological subgroup.

- Although the symptoms of schizophrenia may add new elements to a person's personality, such as a paranoid trait or depression, comparison of the affected and well twins in the discordant pairs suggested that the disease does not change a person's underlying personality.

- In most identical twins concordant for schizophrenia, there are substantial within-pair differences on clinical and etiological measures. When the twins concordant for schizophrenia were compared with the twins with schizophrenia in discordant pairs, no significant clinical or etiological differences were found.

- When identical twins discordant for bipolar disorder were compared with the identical twins discordant for schizophrenia, the affected bipolar twins had more frequent family history of serious mental disease and were less impaired clinically and neuropsychologically. However, 25% (2 of 8) of the bipolar affected twins had evidence of perinatal liability and childhood indicators of disease, similar to the findings for the twins with schizophrenia. On MRI scans, the affected twins with bipolar disorder had ventricular dilatation similar to the affected twins with schizophrenia, but less prominent diminution of the hippocampus-amygdala.

- Two sets of identical triplets were included in the present study, and data for another 5 sets was summarized. True discordance was documented. When more than one triplet becomes affected, the clinical manifestations of the disease may be quite variable.

- Despite the knowledge of multiple measures of brain structural pathology and brain dysfunction in schizophrenia, it is not yet possible to use these measures diagnostically to say whether any given individual is or will become affected.

Appendix A: Final Diagnostic Groups

I.

Discordant for Schizophrenia
16 males, 11 females; mean age at time of testing, 31 years (17–44)

Discordant Twin Pair	Affected Twin	Well Twin	Age at Time of Testing	Years Discordant (from age of first referral to 3/93)
DS-1	chronic paranoid schizophrenia	normal	38	14
DS-2	chronic undifferentiated schizophrenia	normal	38	30
DS-3	chronic paranoid schizophrenia	normal	33	10
DS-4	chronic paranoid schizophrenia	normal	35	19
DS-5	chronic undifferentiated schizophrenia	normal	31	12
DS-6	chronic undifferentiated schizophrenia	normal	25	11
DS-7	chronic residual schizophrenia	normal	28	14
DS-8	chronic disorganized schizophrenia	normal	28	12
DS-9	chronic undifferentiated schizophrenia	normal	44	18
DS-10	chronic undifferentiated schizophrenia and antisocial personality disorder	antisocial personality disorder	28	9
DS-11	schizoaffective disorder	normal	30	11
DS-12	chronic undifferentiated schizophrenia	past single episode of major depression (reactive); simple phobia	27	15
DS-13	chronic undifferentiated schizophrenia; past developmental disorder not otherwise specified.	normal except past developmental disorder not otherwise specified.	35	21

Discordant for Schizophrenia
16 males, 11 females; mean age at time of testing, 31 years (17–44)

Discordant Twin Pair	Affected Twin	Well Twin	Age at Time of Testing	Years Discordant (from age of first referral to 3/93)
DS-14	chronic undifferentiated schizophrenia	normal	36	20
DS-15	chronic disorganized schizophrenia	normal	26	11
DS-16	schizoaffective disorder	normal	27	12
DS-17	chronic paranoid schizophrenia	normal	24	5
DS-18	chronic undifferentiated schizophrenia	normal	34	23
DS-19	chronic paranoid schizophrenia	normal	34	26
DS-20	chronic paranoid schizophrenia	normal	28	12
DS-21	chronic paranoid schizophrenia	normal	40	18
DS-22	chronic undifferentiated schizophrenia	normal	39	20
DS-23	chronic paranoid schizophrenia	normal	31	6
DS-24	chronic undifferentiated schizophrenia	normal	24	6
DS-25	schizoaffective disorder	normal	17	6
DS-26	schizoaffective disorder	normal	25	8
DS-27	chronic disorganized schizophrenia	normal	25	10

II.

Discordant for Bipolar Disorder and Related Disorders
1 male, 7 females; mean age 34 (21–52)

Discordant Twin Pair	Affected Twin	Well Twin	Age at Time of Testing	Years Discordant (as of 3/93)
DB-1	bipolar disorder, mixed with mood incongruent psychotic features	normal	30	11
DB-2	bipolar disorder, depressed, with mood congruent psychotic features	normal	21	6
DB-3	bipolar disorder, in partial remission	normal	24	8
DB-4	major depression, recurrent, with mood congruent psychotic features	normal	42	28
DB-5	bipolar disorder, not otherwise specified	normal	27	5
DB-6	bipolar disorder, mixed, with mood congruent psychotic features	personality disorder, not otherwise specified	41	30
DB-7	bipolar disorder, manic	normal	52	21
DB-8	bipolar disorder, mixed in partial remission	avoidant personality disorder	33	10

III.

Normal Controls
3 males, 5 females; mean age 31 (19–44)

Normal Twin Pair	Firstborn	Second-born	Age at Time of Testing	Years Discordant (as of 3/93)
N-1	normal	normal	31	—
N-2	normal	normal	26	—
N-3	normal	normal	26	—
N-4	normal	normal	19	—
N-5	normal	normal	32	—
N-6	normal	normal	44	—
N-7	normal	normal	36	—
N-8	normal	normal	31	—

IV.
Concordant for Schizophrenia
10 males, 3 females; mean age 30 (22–41)

Concordant Twin Pair	Firstborn	Second-born	Age at Time of Testing	Years Discordant (as of 3/93)
CS-1	schizoaffective disorder	chronic undifferentiated schizophrenia	31	—
CS-2	chronic residual schizophrenia	chronic undifferentiated schizophrenia	38	—
CS-3	schizoaffective disorder	chronic undifferentiated schizophrenia	25	—
CS-4	chronic disorganized schizophrenia	chronic undifferentiated schizophrenia	41	—
CS-5	chronic undifferentiated schizophrenia	chronic undifferentiated schizophrenia	31	—
CS-6	chronic paranoid schizophrenia	chronic paranoid schizophrenia	27	—
CS-7	chronic undifferentiated schizophrenia	chronic undifferentiated schizophrenia	26	—
CS-8	chronic undifferentiated schizophrenia	chronic undifferentiated schizophrenia	22	—
CS-9	chronic undifferentiated schizophrenia (childhood onset)	chronic disorganized schizophrenia (childhood onset)	35	—
CS-10	schizoaffective disorder (discordant when initially tested, then became concordant)	chronic undifferentiated schizophrenia	32	—
CS-11	chronic undifferentiated schizophrenia	schizotypal personality disorder*	24	—
CS-12	chronic undifferentiated schizophrenia	schizotypal personality disorder*	28	—
CS-13	schizotypal personality disorder*	chronic undifferentiated schizophrenia	29	—

V.

Other Twins Studied

6 males, 2 females; mean age 33 (19–50)

Other Twin Pair	Firstborn	Second-born	Age at Time of Testing	Years Discordant (as of 3/93)
O-1	delusional disorder	normal	44	9
O-2	chronic undifferentiated schizophrenia	personality disorder, not otherwise specified	29	15
O-3	chronic residual schizophrenia	schizoid personality disorder	19	6
O-4	chronic undifferentiated schizophrenia	schizotypal personality disorder	31	—
O-5	psychosis, not otherwise specified	schizoid personality disorder	21	9
O-6	depressive disorder, not otherwise specified	major depression, recurrent and schizoid personality disorder	40	—
O-7	chronic undifferentiated schizophrenia	major depression, recurrent, with paranoid delusions	50	—
O-8	psychosis, not otherwise specified	dysthymia	30	14

*Technically did not meet full criteria for DSM-III-R diagnosis of schizophrenia at the time of testing, but overall picture suggests that they would have met such criteria if additional information had been available; see Chap. 3.

Note: Additional diagnoses were suggested for 6 well co-twins by Dr. Gottesman on the basis of their MMPI and his review of videotaped SCID interviews: paranoid personality disorder, antisocial personality disorder (2), dysthymic disorder and obsessive-compulsive personality disorder, schizotypal personality disorder, and dysthymic disorder. Drs. Torrey and Bigelow did not concur with these diagnoses.

Appendix B: Neuropsychological Examination

The following neuropsychological tests were included in the test battery for almost all twins. Additional tests were used on subgroups of the twins.

Wechsler Adult Intelligence Scale, Revised: This is a standard measure of intelligence. A validated short form (which includes four parts) was administered: Picture Arrangement, Vocabulary, Block Design, and Arithmetic. It provides both verbal and performance IQ measures and also is a good indicator of gross organic impairment.

Wechsler Memory Scale: This is a six-part test measuring a wide range of verbal and visual memory functions. Both an immediate and a delayed version of the test were administered to evaluate both long-term memory and the rate of forgetting.

Trail Making Test: This test is composed of two parts: in part A the subject connects sequential numbers, and in part B both numbers and letters are used. This provides information on psychomotor speed and cognitive flexibility.

Stroop Color-Word Interference Test: This is composed of three pages, each of which the subject is asked to read aloud as rapidly as possible. The first page is colored Xs, the second page has names of colors, and the third page has names of colors printed in different colors. The number of words read in 45 seconds is the dependent measure that provides information on the subject's access to verbal responses in the face of interference.

Continuous Performance Test: This is a test of sustained attention that requires subjects to attend to a sequence of flashing letters and to respond selectively to a specified sequence (e.g., "Press the button when you see an *A* followed by an *X*").

Road Map Test: This is a test of directional sense in which the subject must tell the experimenter which way to turn (left or right) as the experimenter traces a route through a simulated map of city streets. This test is sensitive to visual-spatial impairment.

Controlled Word Association Test: This test of verbal fluency requires subjects to generate words according to an initial letter (e.g., words that start with the letter *F*), and measures their ability to develop strategies for word production. This test has also been shown to be sensitive to frontal lobe lesions.

Go/No Go Test: This test asks the subject to make a response (e.g., "Raise your hand") for one cue and to inhibit a response for a second cue. It therefore measures discrimination of response cues and approach/non-approach responses. The test appears to be sensitive to frontal lobe impairment.

Tower of Hanoi Type Puzzles: This is a "brain teaser" task in which subjects must move a stack of different-sized disks (with smallest on top and largest on bottom) from one peg through a second peg to a third peg, where they must end in the same order. Only one disk can be moved at a time and a larger disk cannot go on top of a smaller disk. The goal of the test is to do it in as few moves as possible. Both a 3-disk and a 4-disk version of the test were administered. The 3-disk version appears to be sensitive to frontal lobe function, and the 4-disk version to basal ganglia function.

Wisconsin Card Sorting Test: This test was administered along with tests of cerebral metabolism (rCBF, SPECT, or PET). It requires subjects to sort a deck of 128 response cards to different stimulus cards. Cards can be sorted on the basis of color, number, or form, and the subject must decide on the correct sorting principle based on the experimenter's response (i.e., "Right" or "Wrong") to each sort. This test requires the development of problem-solving strategies and mental flexibility and reveals deficits specific to lesions in the dorsolateral area of the frontal lobes.

Pursuit Rotor: This test requires that the subject try to keep a stylus in contact with a target on a rotating disk. It measures motor-skill learning, which may be mediated by the basal ganglia.

Dichotic Listening Test: This test presents words simultaneously to each ear and asks the subject to choose the word he or she heard from four alternatives (the two words presented and two distractors). The words are presented so that they fuse into a single auditory image, and the word chosen indicates which hemisphere of the subject's brain is specialized for speech. The test provides a good measure of hemispheric laterality.

Wide Range Achievement Test, Reading Subtest: This requires subjects to read a list of words and to try to pronounce them correctly (e.g., "schism"). This word-reading ability has been shown to be a good measure of premorbid intelligence, and it thus gives information on the subject's intellectual level before he or she became mentally ill.

Judgment of Line Orientation: This test is composed of a booklet with two stimulus lines at different angles on top, and a response-choice display composed of an array of lines drawn at 18-degree intervals. The subject is asked to look at the two stimulus lines and decide which two lines in the response-choice display are in the same position and point in the same direction. This test is thought to measure basic perceptual skills that are localized in the right parietal area of the brain.

Facial Recognition: In this test the subject is shown a single stimulus photo of a person's face and asked to find another picture of the same face in a display of six photos of faces. Next, a series of stimuli are shown and the subject is asked to find three photos of the stimulus face. In this part of the test, display photos differ in lighting and facial angle. The test provides a measure of visual facial-feature recognition that is believed to be mediated by the inferior parietal-occipital area.

Appendix C: Neurological Examination

The following is an outline of the neurological examination used in the study.

General: The subject's general body build and any abnormalities of head, neck, spine, or extremities were described. The pulse was recorded and the carotid pulses were also palpated. The examiner also listened over the head and neck for possible sounds made by abnormal blood flow.

Speech: The rhythm, rate, prosody (inflection used for emphasis), and clarity were assessed.

Cranial nerves: The field of vision, eye movements, pupillary reactions to light, and the retina and optic nerve heads were assessed. Facial movements, tongue movements, palatal movements, and hearing were also examined. The capacity to move eyes synchronously to command and to keep gaze fixed in a direction for 30 to 45 seconds was also assessed (gaze persistence and impersistence).

Motor: The motor examination included an assessment of muscle tone at rest and during passive movements of the limbs while the subject was instructed to relax. Muscle strength and bulk (the size of muscle mass) were noted. Complex motor movements such as walking (gait), hopping on each leg five times in a row, and skipping across the room were observed. The subject was also observed for any involuntary movements of body, face, or extremities.

Coordination: These tests included finger-to-nose movements, in which the subject moved his finger rapidly between his nose and the examiner's finger; rapid alternating movements, in which the subject turned his hand palm down and then palm up in rapid succession (pronation and supination); tandem gait, during which the subject walked heel-to-toe on an imaginary straight line; rapid foot tapping; and rapid movement of each index finger against the thumb, first one side at a time and then both together.

Primary sensory function: These tests involved touching each limb distally with fingertips gently (light touch), with a pin (pinprick), and also moving the fingers and toes very slightly up or down with the subject's eyes closed (position sense). The subject was also asked to stand with feet together and eyes closed, and postural stability was assessed (Romberg's sign). Finally, the subject was instructed to extend both arms and was observed for any abnormal movements of fingers or downward drift of arms suggesting a subtle weakness.

Reflexes: Deep tendon reflexes at the elbows, wrists, knees, and ankles were elicited and scaled for symmetry. The plantar response was checked by scraping the lateral underside of the foot with an object such as a key or a pointed reflex hammer in order to determine whether the great toe goes down (normal) or up (abnormal) (Babinski's sign). Frontal lobe reflex release was checked by tapping the forehead and observing for sustained synchronous blinking (glabellar reflex), and also by gently sliding the examiner's hand across the subject's palm and observing for involuntary closure of the subject's hand (grasp reflex). Oral frontal lobe release reflexes were tested by tapping the lips and observing for a pursing movement (snout reflex), and by stroking the lips with a tongue blade and observing for sucking movements (suck reflex), or for turning of the head to follow the blade and continuation of the sucking motion (rooting response).

Clonus: The foot or hand was moved rapidly upward and then subsequent movements were observed.

Higher cortical sensory function: These tests included assessment of perception by using double simultaneous stimulation (touching the subject's face and opposite hand at the same time); graphesthesia, in which a number was written on the palm; and stereognosis, in which coins or other objects (pen/pencil) were placed in the subject's palm, and with eyes closed, the subject was asked to identify the objects.

Constructional praxis: This was tested as part of the mini-mental state examination by having the subject copy a diagram of two intersecting pentagons.

Motor praxis: The subject was asked to perform various motor tasks involving mouth, face, limb, and whole body to command (ideomotor apraxia), as well as certain sequences, such as placing a candle in a holder and lighting it with a match (ideational apraxia).

Right-left orientation: This was assessed by giving the subject commands to touch a specific hand on the examiner using a specific hand when one or both of them had crossed hands.

Finger agnosia: The subject was asked to identify fingers on his hand and on the examiner's hand.

Visual agnosia: This was tested by having the subject name and identify the use of common objects.

Appendix D: Personality Inventory for Children

One of the sources of information used in the study to assess development and personality differences in the twins as children was the Personality Inventory for Children (PIC). This is a 600-item observation scale in which the informant scores each item as either true (the stated behavior applies) or false (the stated behavior has not been observed). The parent was instructed to rate the twins' behaviors prior to the onset of mental illness or prior to their 18th birthday, whichever came first. They were told to mark an item as true if (1) it was known by the parent that the identified behavior occurred, (2) another family member who had significant access to the twins observed the behavior, or (3) the parent did not recall specifics about the behavior but remembered being concerned or worried about the category of behavior represented by that item.

It should be noted that the PIC was not designed as a retrospective measurement instrument but is a scale routinely used by clinicians and completed by care providers currently observing children and adolescents within their natural environments. Our instructional alterations requiring each informant to recall rather than observe behaviors raises questions about the instrument's reliability and validity. We nonetheless selected the PIC for investigating the twins' personality formation because it (1) provided a comprehensive list of developmental, diagnostic, and behavioral questions; (2) ensured that the same questions would be collected for each twin; and (3) is known to be sensitive for identifying problems in children who have brain impairments (Rourke et al., 1983). The PIC is similar to, and was modeled after, the Minnesota Multiphasic Personality Inventory (MMPI). It surveys the individual's global functioning on a variety of scales: adjustment, achievement, anxiety, intellectual skills, development, depression, delinquency, family relations, hyperactivity, psychosis, somatic symptoms, social skills, and withdrawal behaviors.

All twins with schizophrenia, as well as those with bipolar disorder, were scored by the parents on developmental problems for any of the PIC personality or behavioral constructs. The group means of both affected and well twins were clustered around the expected t score range for normal personality development. Within the group discordant for schizophrenia, the affected twins had more difficulty with overall adjustment ($t = .09$) and significantly more psychotic-oriented behaviors ($t = .04$). However, the mean scores for the affected twins for both behavioral categories indicated normal development, and are only different in relationship to the well twins' adjustment and psychosis score. In almost all other categories, the affected and well twins scored similarly, with the former always having had slightly more difficulty than the twin who remained well. It is impossible to determine if the psychosis score represents an actual developmental difference or simply the informant knowing (and being biased by) which twin became ill.

The PIC scores, along with family interviews, helped clarify the twins' development, personality traits, and interpersonal relationships prior to the onset of illness. They also illustrate that standard personality traits alone are poor indicators for screening children at risk for severe and persistent mental illness.

Glossary

The following terms, which may be unfamiliar to some readers, are used frequently in this book:

anoxia: decreased oxygen supply

axis I: in the official diagnostic scheme of the American Psychiatric Association (DSM-III-R), axis I includes all clinical syndromes such as schizophrenia and bipolar disorder

axis II: in DSM-III-R, axis II includes personality disorders and developmental disorders

axis V: a scale that measures a person's overall psychological, social, and occupational function; technically, it is called the Global Assessment of Functioning Scale and is included in DSM-III-R

basal ganglia: an area of the brain located adjacent to the medial temporal area, known to be involved in diseases such as Parkinson's and also being studied in its relationship to schizophrenia and bipolar disorder

bipolar disorder: same as manic-depressive psychosis; a disorder of mood (depression or mania) frequently accompanied by delusions and/or hallucinations

concordant: when referring to diseases in twins, it means that both members of the twin pair are affected

congenital: being born with, meaning that it either originated genetically or during development *in utero* prior to birth

CT scans: computerized tomography scans (also known as computerized axial tomography or CAT scans) which use X-rays to visualize brain structures

discordant: when referring to diseases in twins, it means that only one member of the twin pair is affected

dizygotic twins (DZ) (fraternal): from two eggs fertilized by two sperm

etiology: concerning the cause

hippocampus-amygdala: contiguous structures in the limbic system in the center of the brain; thought to be impaired in schizophrenia and bipolar disorder

interpair: comparisons in which one pair of twins is compared to another pair of twins

intrapair: comparisons between the two twins who constitute a twin pair; same as within-pair

in utero: in the uterus, referring to the fetus before it is born

MMPI: Minnesota Multiphasic Personality Inventory, a widely used test of personality traits

monozygotic twins (MZ) (identical): from one egg fertilized by one sperm, which then splits into two

MPQ: Multidimensional Personality Questionnaire, a personality test

MRI: magnetic resonance imaging scans, which produce pictures of the body (including the brain) using magnetic fields and radio waves

neurotropic: having an affinity for nerve tissue, such as neurotropic viruses, which selectively attack the brain

perinatal: pregnancy, delivery, and the period immediately after delivery

PET: positron emission tomography, a means of measuring brain metabolism

phenocopy: a nongenetic clinical imitation of a disease thought to be genetically caused; thus the phenocopy has the outward manifestations and symptoms of the disease without having the genes thought to be associated with it

PIC: Personality Inventory for Children, a questionnaire measuring children's personality traits

premorbid: the period before the sickness became manifest

prenatal: the period from the beginning of pregnancy until birth

SANS: Scales for the Assessment of Negative Symptoms, which measures such traits as withdrawal, flat affect, and the loss of self-care skills

SCID: Structured Clinical Interview for DSM-III-R, a structured interview that assists the examiner in making a DSM-III-R diagnosis in accordance with the official diagnostic nomenclature of the American Psychiatric Association *schizoid:* a psychiatric term for personality traits of emotional aloofness, indifference to praise or criticism, and social isolation

schizotypal: a psychiatric term for personality traits of social isolation, magical thinking, odd speech, suspiciousness, hypersensitivity, and inappropriate emotions; thought by many researchers to be a partial form of schizophrenia

total finger ridge count (TFRC): the number of ridges between the core of a fingerprint to the triradial point, as counted for all 10 fingers

ventricles (cerebral): fluid-filled spaces in the brain, which are often enlarged in individuals with serious mental illnesses and also in other brain diseases

within-pair: comparisons between the two twins who constitute a twin pair; same as intrapair

zygote: the cell formed when an egg and sperm fuse

Bibliography

An asterisk (*) indicates a publication utilzing data from the present study.

Abraham, J. M. Intrauterine Feto-Fetal Transfusion Syndrome. *Clinical Pediatrics* 6:405–410, 1967.

Achs, R., Harper, R. G., and Siegel, M. Unusual Dermatoglyphic Findings Associated with Rubella Embryopathy. *New England Journal of Medicine* 274:148–150, 1966.

Aldous, P. The Promise and Pitfalls of Molecular Genetics. *Science* 257:164–165, 1992.

Allen, G. Frequency of Triplets and Triplet Zygosity Types among U.S. Births. *Acta Geneticae Medicae et Gemellologiae* 37:299–306, 1988.

Alter, M., and Schulenberg, R. Dermatoglyphics in the Rubella Syndrome. *Journal of the American Medical Association* 197:93–96, 1966.

Ambelas, A. Preschizophrenics: Adding to the Evidence, Sharpening the Focus. *British Journal of Psychiatry* 160:401–404, 1992.

American Psychiatric Association. *Diagnostic and Statistical Manual of Mental Disorders, DSM-III-R* (3rd ed., rev.). Washington, D.C.: 1987.

Andreasen, N. C. *Scales for the Assessment of Negative Symptoms (SANS).* Iowa City: University of Iowa Press, 1981.

Andreasen, N. C., Rezai, K., Alliger, R., Swayze, U. W., Flaum, M., Kirchner, P., Cohen, G., and O'Leary, D. S. Hypofrontality in Neuroleptic-Naive Patients and in Patients with Chronic Schizophrenia. *Archives of General Psychiatry* 49:943–958, 1992.

Anonymous. Monozygotic Male Triplets Discordant for Psychosis. Letter, *British Journal of Psychiatry* 159:734–735, 1991.

Babson, S. G., Kangas, J., Young, N., and Bramhall, J. L. Growth and Development of Twins of Dissimilar Size at Birth. *Pediatrics* 33:327–333, 1964.

Bacic, G., and Mahnik, M. MRI Diagnosis Anatomical Abnormalities of Brain in Schizophrenia. Abstract, *Biological Psychiatry* 29:569-S, 1991.

Bailar, J. D., and Gurian, J. Congenital Malformations and Season of Birth: A Brief Review. *Eugenics Quarterly* 12:146–153, 1965.

Barr, C. E., Mednick, S. A., and Munk-Jorgensen, P. Exposure to Influenza Epidemics during Gestation and Adult Schizophrenia. *Archives of General Psychiatry* 47:869–874, 1990.

Barry, H. Abnormally Large Birth Weights of Psychiatric Patients. *Archives of Neurology and Psychiatry* 57:98–101, 1947.

*Bartley, A. J., Jones, D. W., Torrey, E. F., Zigun, J. R., and Weinberger, D. R. Sylvian Fissure Asymmetries in Monozygotic Twins: A Test of Laterality in Schizophrenia. Submitted for publication, 1993.

Beckman, L., and Norring, A. Finger and Palm Prints in Schizophrenia. *Acta Genetica* (Basel) 13:170–177, 1963.

Beitchman, J. H. Childhood Schizophrenia: A Review and Comparison with Adult Onset Schizophrenia. *Psychiatric Clinics of North America* 8:793–814, 1985.

Belmaker, R., Pollin, W., Wyatt, R. J., and Cohen, S. A Follow-up of Monozygotic Twins Discordant for Schizophrenia. *Archives of General Psychiatry* 30:219–222, 1974.

Bender, L. The Life Course of Children with Schizophrenia. *American Journal of Psychiatry* 130:783–786, 1973.

Benirschke, K., and Kim, C. K. Multiple Pregnancy, II. *New England Journal of Medicine* 288:1329–1336, 1973.

Berker, E., Goldstein, G., Lorber, J., Priestley, B., and Smith, A. Reciprocal Neurological Developments of Twins Discordant for Hydrocephalus. *Developmental Medicine and Child Neurology* 34:623–632, 1992.

Berman, K. F., Daniel, D. G., and Weinberger, D. R. Schizophrenia: Brain Structure and Function. In H. I. Kaplan and B. J. Sadock (Eds.), *Comprehensive Textbook of Psychiatry*, 6th ed. Baltimore: Williams and Wilkins, in press, 1994.

*Berman, K. F., Torrey, E. F., Daniel, D. G., and Weinberger, D. R. Regional Cerebral Blood Flow in Monozygotic Twins Discordant and Concordant for Schizophrenia. *Archives of General Psychiatry* 49:927–934, 1992.

Berman, K. F., Weinberger, D. R., Shelton, R. C., and Zec, R. F. A Relationship between Anatomical and Physiological Brain Pathology in Schizophrenia: Lateral Cerebral Ventricular Size Predicts Cortical Blood Flow. *American Journal of Psychiatry* 144:1277–1282, 1987.

Bertelsen, A., Harvald, B., and Hauge, M. A Danish Twin Study of Manic-Depressive Disorders. *British Journal of Psychiatry* 130:330–351, 1977.

Biale, R. Counseling Families of Disabled Twins. *Social Work* 34:531–535, 1989.

Bloom, M. New Theory on the Phenomenon of Identical Twins. *Washington Post Health*, August 11, 1992, p. 7.

Boklage, C. E. Schizophrenia, Brain Asymmetry Development and Twinning: Cellular Relationship with Etiological and Possibly Prognostic Implications. *Biological Psychiatry* 12:19–35, 1977.

Bolton, P., Pickles, A., Harrington, R., Macdonald, H., and Rutter, M. Season of Birth: Issues, Approaches and Findings for Autism. *Journal of Child Psychology and Psychiatry* 33:509–530, 1992.

Bouchard, T. J., Lykken, D. T., McGue, M., Segan, N. L., and Tellegen, A. Sources of Human Psychological Differences: The Minnesota Study of Twins Reared Apart. *Science* 250:223–228, 1990.

Boyd, J. H., Pulver, A. E., and Stewart, W. Season of Birth: Schizophrenia and Bipolar Disorder. *Schizophrenia Bulletin* 12:173–186, 1986.

Bracha, H. S. Etiology of Structural Asymmetry in Schizophrenia: An Alternative Hypothesis. Letter, *Schizophrenia Bulletin* 17:551–552, 1991.

*Bracha, H. S., Gottesman, I. I., Torrey, E. F., Pezybyla, B. D., Bigelow, L. B., and Mayfield, J. Fifth Month Fetal Size Markers in Schizophrenia: A Discordant MZ Twin Study. Abstract, 8th International Congress of Human Genetics, Washington, D.C., October 6–11, 1991.

*Bracha, H. S., Torrey, E. F., and Bigelow, L. B. Prenatal Maldevelopment of the Palm/Thumb in Schizophrenia: A Monozygotic Twins Study. Abstract, *Schizophrenia Research* 4:274, 1991.

*Bracha, H. S., Torrey, E. F., Bigelow, L. B., Lohr, J. B., and Linington, B. B. Subtle Signs of Prenatal Maldevelopment of the Hand Ectoderm in Schizophrenia. *Biological Psychiatry* 30:719–725, 1991.

*Bracha, H. S., Torrey, E. F., Gottesman, I. I., Bigelow, L. B., and Cunniff, C. Second-Trimester Markers of Fetal Size in Schizophrenia: A Study of Monozygotic Twins. *American Journal of Psychiatry* 149:1355–1361, 1992.

*Bracha, H. S., Torrey, E. F., Karson, C. N., and Bigelow, L. B. A Twin Study of Prenatal Injury Markers in Psychosis: Timing the Insult. Abstract, *Schizophrenia Research* 4:250, 1991.

Bradbury, T. N., and Miller, G. A. Season of Birth in Schizophrenia: A Review of Evidence, Methodology and Etiology. *Psychological Bulletin* 98:569–594, 1985.

Breggin, P. Recorded remarks at Conference for National Association for

Rights, Protection and Advocacy, Portland, Oregon, October 26–29, 1988.

Brown, Z. A., Benedetti, J., Ashley, R., Burchett, S., Selke, S., Berry, S., Vontuer, L. A., and Corey, L. Neonatal Herpes Simplex Virus Infection in Relation to Asymptomatic Maternal Infection at the Time of Labor. *New England Journal of Medicine* 324:1247–1252, 1991.

Bryan, E. M. *The Nature and Nurture of Twins.* London: Bailliere Tindall, 1983.

Bryan, E., and Slavin, B. Serum IgG Levels in Feto-Fetal Transfusion Syndrome. *Archives of Disease in Childhood* 49:908–910, 1974.

Buchanan, R. W., Breier, A., Kirkpatrick, B., Elkashef, A., Munson, R. C., Gellad, F., and Carpenter, W. T. Structural Abnormalities in Deficit and Nondeficit Schizophrenia. *American Journal of Psychiatry* 150:59–65, 1993.

Buchsbaum, M. S., Mirsky, A. F., DeLisi, L. E., Morihisa, J., Karson, C. N., Mendelson, W. B., King, A. C., Johnson, J., and Kessler, R. The Genain Quadruplets: Electrophysiological, Positron Emission, and X-ray Tomographic Studies. *Psychiatry Research* 13:95–108, 1984.

Buckley, P., O'Callaghan, E., Larkin, C., and Waddington, J. L. Schizophrenia Research: The Problem of Controls. *Biological Psychiatry* 32:215–217, 1992.

Burn, J., and Corney, G. Zygosity Determination and the Types of Twinning. In MacGillivray et al. (Eds.), *Twinning and Twins* (pp. 7–25). New York: John Wiley, 1988.

Cadoret, R. J. Toward a Definition of the Schizoid State: Evidence from Studies of Twins and Their Families. *British Journal of Psychiatry* 122:679–685, 1973.

Caldwell, C. B., and Gottesman, I. I. Schizophrenia—A High-Risk Factor for Suicide: Clues to Risk Reduction. *Suicide and Life-Threatening Behavior* 22:479–493, 1992.

Cameron, A. H., Edwards, J. H., Derom, R., Thiery, M., and Boelaert, R. The Value of Twin Surveys in the Study of Malformations. *European Journal of Obstetrics, Gynecology and Reproductive Biology* 14:347–356, 1983. ·

Campbell, M., Geller, B., Small, A. M., Petti, J. A., and Ferris, S. H. Minor Physical Anomalies in Young Psychotic Children. *American Journal of Psychiatry* 135:573–575, 1978.

Cannon, M., Byrne, M., Cassidy, B., Sheppard, N., Larkin, C., and O'Callaghan, E. Dermatoglyphic Fluctuating Asymmetry and Handedness in Schizophrenia. Presented at the International Congress on Schizophrenia Research, Colorado Springs, Colorado, April 17–21, 1993.

*Carosella, N. W., Casanova, M. F., Torrey, E. F., and Weinberger, D. R. Quantitation of Iron in the Globus Pallidus of Monozygotic Twins Discordant for Schizophrenia. Presented at the annual meeting of the Society for Biological Psychiatry, May 11–13, 1989.

*Casanova, M. F., Sanders, R. D., Goldberg, T. E., Bigelow, L. B., Christison, G., Torrey, E. F., and Weinberger, D. R. Morphometry of the Corpus Callosum in Monozygotic Twins Discordant for Schizophrenia: A Magnetic Resonance Imaging Study. *Journal of Neurology, Neurosurgery and Psychiatry* 53:416–421, 1990.

*Casanova, M. F., Weinberger, D. R., Torrey, E. F., Xu, B., Sobus, J., and Pourdeyhimi, B. Focal Temporal Lobe Abnormalities in Schizophrenia. Presented at the annual meeting of the American Psychiatric Association, Washington, D.C., May 3–8, 1992.

*Casanova, M. F., Zito, M., Goldberg, T., Abi-Dargham, A., Sanders, R., Bigelow, L. B., Torrey, E. F., and Weinberger, D. R. Shape Distortion of the Corpus Callosum of Monozygotic Twins Discordant for Schizophrenia. Letter, *Schizophrenia Research.* 3:155–156, 1990.

*Casanova, M. F., Zito, M., Goldberg, T. E., Suddath, R. L., Torrey, E. F., Bigelow, L. B., Sanders, R. D., and Weinberger, D. R. Corpus Callosum Curvature in Schizophrenic Twins. Letter, *Biological Psychiatry* 27:83–84, 1990.

Cederlof, R., Friberg, L., Jonsson, E., and Kaij, L. Studies on Similarity Diagnosis in Twins with the Aid of Mailed Questionnaires. *Acta Genetica et Statistica Medica* 11:338–362, 1961.

Chasnoff, I. J. Fetal Alcohol Syndrome in Twin Pregnancy. *Acta Geneticae Medicae et Gemelloligicae* 34:229–232, 1985.

Corney, G., Robson, E. B., and Strong, S. J. The Effect of Zygosity on the Birth Weight of Twins. *Annals of Human Genetics* (London) 36:45–58, 1972.

Costa, P. T., and McCrae, R. R. On the Need for Longitudinal Evidence and Multiple Measures in Behavioral-Genetic Studies of Adult Personality. *Behavioral and Brain Sciences* 10:22–23, 1987.

Craig, T. J., Richardson, M. A., Pass, R., and Haugland, G. Impairment of the Gag Reflex in Schizophrenic Inpatients. *Comprehensive Psychiatry* 24:514–520, 1983.

Crow, T. J. The Continuum of Psychosis and Its Genetic Origins: The Sixty-fifth Maudsley Lecture. *British Journal of Psychiatry* 156:788–797, 1990.

Crow, T. J., Done, D. J., Frith, C. D., Golding, J., Johnstone, E. C., and Shepherd, P. M. Complications of Pregnancy and Delivery in Relation to Psychosis in Adult Life: A Study Using the Perinatal Mortality Survey. *Schizophrenia Research* 4:253, 1991.

Crow, T. J., Done, D. J., Johnstone, E. C., and Sacker, A. Childhood Antecedents of Schizophrenia and Affective Disorder—A Prospective Study. *Biological Psychiatry* 31:191A, 1992.

Cummings, C., Flynn, D., and Preus, M. Increased Morphological Variants in Children with Learning Disabilities. *Journal of Autism and Developmental Disorders* 12:373–383, 1982.

Czeizel, A. E., and Dudas, I. Prevention of the First Occurrence of Neural-Tube Defects by Periconceptional Vitamin Supplementation. *New England Journal of Medicine* 327:1832–1835, 1992.

Dalby, J. T., Morgan, D., and Lee, M. L. Schizophrenia and Mania in Identical Twin Brothers. *Journal of Nervous and Mental Disease* 174:304–308, 1986.

Daniel, D. G., Goldberg, T. E., Gibbons, R. D., and Weinberger, D. R. Lack of a Bimodal Distribution of Ventricular Size in Schizophrenia: A Gaussian Mixture Analysis of 1056 Cases and Controls. *Biological Psychiatry* 30:887–903, 1991.

Davison, K., and Bagley, C. R. Schizophrenia-like Psychoses Associated with Organic Disorders of the Central Nervous System: A Review of the Literature. *British Journal of Psychiatry* 4 (Suppl.):113–184, 1969.

Daw, E., and Walker, J. Biological Aspects of Twin Pregnancy in Dundee. *British Journal of Obstetrics and Gynecology* 82:29–34, 1975.

Degreef, G., Wellington, G., Alvir, J., Woerner, M., Ashtari, M., Loebel, A., and Lieberman, J. Relationship of Obstetric Complications to Brain Pathomorphology as Seen on MR Scans in Schizophrenia. Presented at the International Conference on Schizophrenia Research, Tucson, Arizona, April 21–25, 1991.

DeLisi, L. E., Boccio, A. M., Riordan, H., Hoff, A. L., Dorfman, A., McClelland, J., Kushner, M., Van Eyl, O. V., and Oden, N. Familial Thyroid Disease and Delayed Language Development in First Admission Patients with Schizophrenia. *Psychiatry Research* 38:39–50, 1991.

DeLisi, L. E., Dauphinais, I. D., and Gershon, E. S. Perinatal Complications and Reduced Size of Brain Limbic Structures in Familial Schizophrenia. *Schizophrenia Bulletin* 14:185–191, 1988.

DeLisi, L. E., Goldin, L. R., Maxwell, E., Kazuba, D. M., and Gershon, E. S. Clinical Features of Illness in Siblings with Schizophrenia or Schizoaffective Disorder. *Archives of General Psychiatry* 44:891–896, 1987.

DeLisi, L. E., Mirsky, A. F., Buchsbaum, M. S., van Kammen, D. P., Berman, K. F., Caton, C., Kafka, M. S., Ninan, P. T., Phelps, B. H., Karoum, F., Ko, G. N., Korpi, E. R., Linnoila, M., Sheinan, M., and Wyatt, R. J. The Genain Quadruplets 25 Years Later: A Diagnostic and Biochemical Followup. *Psychiatry Research* 13:59–76, 1984.

Der, G., Gupta, S., and Murray, R. M. Is Schizophrenia Disappearing? *Lancet* 335:513–516, 1990.

*DiLalla, D. L., and Gottesman, I. I. Personality Characteristics in MZ Twins Discordant for Schizophrenia. Submitted for publication, 1993.

Done, D. J., Crow, T. J., Johnstone, E. C., and Sacker, A. Antecedents of Schizophrenia and Affective Disorders—Social Behaviour at 7 and 11 Years of Age Recorded in the National Child Development Study. Abstract, *Schizophrenia Research* 9:131, 1993.

Done, D. J., Johnstone, E. C., Frith, C. D., Goldring, J., Shepherd, P. M., and Crow, T. J. Complications of Pregnancy and Delivery in Relation to Psychosis in Adult Life: Data from the British Perinatal Mortality Survey Sample. *British Medical Journal* 302:1576–1580, 1991.

Dworkin, R. H., and Lenzenweger, M. F. Symptoms and the Genetics of Schizophrenia: Implications for Diagnosis. *American Journal of Psychiatry* 141:1541–1546, 1984.

Eagles, J. M. Is Schizophrenia Disappearing? *British Journal of Psychiatry* 158:834–835, 1991.

Eagles, J. M., Gibson, I., Bremner, M. H., Clunie, F., Ebmeier, K. P., and Smith, N. C. Obstetric Complications in DSM-III Schizophrenics and Their Siblings. *Lancet* 335:1139–1141, 1990.

Eastman, N. J. *Williams Obstetrics.* New York: Appleton-Century-Crofts, 1956.

Eaves, L. J., Eysenck, H. J., and Martin, N. *Genes, Culture and Personality: An Empirical Approach.* San Diego: Academic Press, 1989.

Eberhard, G. Psychosis in Twins: A Longitudinal Study. *Clinical Genetics* 19:372–379, 1981.

Eberhard, G., Ross, S., Saaf, J., Wahlund, B., and Wetterberg, L. Psychoses in Twins: A 10-year Clinical and Biochemical Follow-up Study. *Schizophrenia Research* 2:367–374, 1989.

Edwards, J. H. The Syndrome of Sex-Linked Hydrocephalus. *Archives of Disease in Childhood* 36:486–493, 1961.

Edwards, J. H., Dent, T., and Kahn, J. Monozygotic Twins of Different Sex. *Journal of Medical Genetics* 3:117–123, 1966.

Eggers, C. Course and Prognosis of Childhood Schizophrenia. *Journal of Autism and Childhood Schizophrenia* 8:21–36, 1978.

Ehrnst, A., Lindgren, S., Dictor, M., Johansson, B., Sonnerborg, A., Czajkowski, J., Sundin, G., and Bohlin, A. B. HIV in Pregnant Women and Their Offspring: Evidence for Late Transmission. *Lancet* 338:203–207, 1991.

Essen-Moller, E. Twenty-one Psychiatric Cases and Their MZ Cotwins. *Acta Geneticae Medicae et Gemellologiae* 19:315–317, 1970.

Farber, S. L. *Identical Twins Reared Apart.* New York: Basic Books, 1981.

Farmer, A. E., McGuffin, P., and Gottesman, I. I. Twin Concordance for DSM-III Schizophrenia: Scrutinizing the Validity of the Definition. *Archives of General Psychiatry* 44:634–641, 1987.

Farmer, A., McGuffin, P., and Gottesman, I. I. Problems and Pitfalls of the Family History Positive and Negative Dichotomy: Response to Dalen. *Schizophrenia Bulletin* 16:367–370, 1990.

Fennell, E. B. Handedness in Neuropsychological Research. In H. J. Hannay (Ed.), *Experimental Techniques in Neuropsychology* (pp. 15–44). New York: Oxford University Press, 1986.

Fernandez, A., Hewicker, M., Trautwein, G., Pohlenz, J., and Liess, B. Viral Antigen Distribution in the Central Nervous System of Cattle Persistently Infected with Bovine Viral Diarrhea Virus. *Veterinary Pathology* 26:26–32, 1989.

Fischer, M. Genetic and Environmental Factors in Schizophrenia. *Acta Psychiatrica Scandinavica,* Supplementum 238:1–153, 1973.

Fish, B., Marcus, J., Hans, S. L., Auerbach, J. G., and Perdue, S. Infants at Risk for Schizophrenia: Sequelae of a Genetic Neurointegrative Defect. *Archives of General Psychiatry* 49:221–235, 1992.

Foerster, A., Lewis, S., Owen, M., and Murray, R. Pre-morbid Adjustment and Personality in Psychosis: Effects of Sex and Diagnosis. *British Journal of Psychiatry* 158:171–176, 1991.

Fogel, B. J., Nitowsky, H. M., and Gruenwald, P. Discordant Abnormalities in Monozygotic Twins. *Journal of Pediatrics* 66:64–72, 1965.

Forrester, R. M., Lees, V. T., and Watson, G. H. Rubella Syndrome: Escape of a Twin. *British Medical Journal* 1:1403, 1966.

Friston, K. J., Liddle, P. F., Frith, C. D., Hirsch, S. R., and Frackowiak, R. S. J. The Left Medial Temporal Region and Schizophrenia. *Brain* 115:367–382, 1992.

Galea, P., Scott, J. M., and Goel, K. M. Feto-Fetal Transfusion Syndrome. *Archives of Disease in Childhood* 57:781–794, 1982.

Galton, F. The History of Twins as a Criterion of the Relative Powers of Nature and Nurture. *Journal of the Anthropological Institute* 5:391–406, 1875.

Ganguli, R., and Rabin, B. S. Increased Serum Interleukin 2 Receptor Concentration in Schizophrenic and Brain-Damaged Subjects. Letter, *Archives of General Psychiatry* 46:292, 1989.

Gedda, L. *Twins in History and Science.* Springfield, Ill: Charles C Thomas, 1961.

Gerlach, J., and Casey, D. E. Tardive Dyskinesia. *Acta Psychiatrica Scandinavica* 77:369–378, 1988.

Gershon, E. S. Review of *Murderous Science: Elimination by Scientific Selection of Jews, Gypsies and Others, Germany 1933–1945* by B. Muller-Hill. *American Journal of Psychiatry* 146:265–267, 1989.

Gittelman-Klein, R., and Klein, D. F. Premorbid Asocial Adjustment and Prognosis in Schizophrenia. *Journal of Psychiatric Research* 7:35–53, 1969.

Goddard, K. E., Broder, G., and Wenar, C. Reliability of Pediatric Histories. *Pediatrics* 28:1011–1018, 1961.

Goedert, J. J., Duliege, A. M., Amos, C. I., Felton, S., and Biggar, R. J. High-Risk of HIV-1 Infection for First-Born Twins. *Lancet* 338:1471–1475, 1991.

Goldberg, T. E., Gold, J. M., and Braff, D. L. Neuropsychological Functioning and Time-Linked Information Processing in Schizophrenia. In A. Tasman and S. Goldfinger (Eds.), *Review of Psychiatry*, Vol. 10 (pp. 60–78). Washington, D.C.: American Psychiatric Press, 1991.

Goldberg, T. E., Hyde, T. M., Kleinman, J. E., and Weinberger, D. R. The Course of Schizophrenia: Neuropsychological Evidence for a Static Encephalopathy. *Schizophrenia Bulletin*, in press.

*Goldberg, T. E., Ragland, J. D., Torrey, E. F., Gold, J. M., Bigelow, L. B., and Weinberger, D. R. Neuropsychological Assessment of Monozygotic Twins Discordant for Schizophrenia. *Archives of General Psychiatry* 47:1066–1072, 1990.

*Goldberg, T. E., Torrey, E. F., Berman, K. F., and Weinberger, D. R. Relations between Neuropsychological Performance and Brain Morphological and Physiological Measures in Monozygotic Twins. Submitted for publication, 1993.

*Goldberg, T. E., Torrey, E. F., Gold, J. M., Ragland, J. D., Bigelow, L. B., and Weinberger, D. R. Memory Function in Monozygotic Twins Discordant for Schizophrenia. Abstract, *Schizophrenia Research* 4:384, 1991.

*Goldberg, T. E., Torrey, E. F., Gold, J. M., Ragland, J. D., Bigelow, L. B., and Weinberger, D. R. Learning and Memory in Monozygotic Twins Discordant for Schizophrenia. *Psychological Medicine* 23:71–85, 1993.

*Goldberg, T. E., Torrey, E. F., Gold, J. M., and Weinberger, D. R. Neuropsychological Impairment in Monozygotic Twins Discordant and Concordant for Schizophrenia. Abstract, *Society for Neuroscience Abstracts* 18:911, 1992.

*Goldberg, T. E., Torrey, E. F., and Weinberger, D. R. Neuropsychological Performance in the Unaffected Twin. Response to letter, *Archives of General Psychiatry* 49:247, 1992.

Goldfarb, W. Factors in the Development of Schizophrenic Children: An Approach to Subclassification. In J. Romano (Ed.), *The Origins of Schizophrenia* (pp. 70–83). Amsterdam: Excerpta Medica Foundation, 1967.

Goodman, R. Are Complications of Pregnancy and Birth Causes of Schizophrenia? *Developmental Medicine* 30:391–395, 1988.

Goodwin, F. K., and Jamison, K. R. *Manic-Depressive Illness.* New York: Oxford University Press, 1990.

Gottesman, I. I., and Bertelsen, A. Confirming Unexpressed Genotypes for Schizophrenia. *Archives of General Psychiatry* 46:867–872, 1989.

Gottesman, I. I., and Shields, J. *Schizophrenia and Genetics: A Twin Study Vantage Point.* New York: Academic Press, 1972.

Gottesman, I. I., and Shields, J. A Critical Review of Recent Adoption, Twin and Family Studies of Schizophrenia: Behavioral Genetics Prospective. *Schizophrenia Bulletin* 2:360–401, 1976.

Gottesman, I. I., and Shields, J. *Schizophrenia: The Epigenetic Puzzle.* Cambridge: Cambridge University Press, 1982.

Green, J., Bax, M., and Tsitsikas, H. Neonatal Behavior and Early Temperament: A Longitudinal Study of the First Six Months of Life. *American Journal of Orthopsychiatry* 59:82–93, 1989.

Green, M. F., Satz, P., Gaier, D. J., Ganzell, S., and Kharabi, F. Minor Physical Anomalies in Schizophrenia. *Schizophrenia Bulletin* 15:91–99, 1989.

Green, M. F., Satz, P., Smith, C., and Nelson, L. Is There Atypical Handedness in Schizophrenia? *Journal of Abnormal Psychology* 98:57–61, 1989.

Green, M. F., Satz, P., Soper, H. V., and Kharabi, F. Relationship between Physical Anomalies and Age of Onset of Schizophrenia. *American Journal of Psychiatry* 144:666–667, 1987.

Green, W. H., Campbell, M., Hardesty, A. S., Grega, D. M., Padron-Gayol, M., Shell, J., and Erlenmeyer-Kimling, L. A Comparison of Schizophrenic and Autistic Children. *Journal of the American Academy of Child Psychiatry* 23:399–409, 1984.

Green, W. H., Padron-Gayol, M., Hardesty, A. S., and Bassiri, M. Schizophrenia with Childhood Onset: A Phenomenological Study of 38 Cases. *Journal of the American Academy of Child and Adolescent Psychiatry* 31:968–976, 1992.

Greene, G., Wilson, A., and Shapira, E. Prune Belly Syndrome and Heart Defect in One of Monozygotic Twins following Exposure to Tigan and Bendectin. *Acta Geneticae Medicae et Gemellologiae* 34:101–104, 1985.

Gualtieri, C. T., Adams, A., Shen, C. D., and Loiselle, D. Minor Physical Anomalies in Alcoholic and Schizophrenic Adults and Hyperactive and Autistic Children. *American Journal of Psychiatry* 139:640–643, 1982.

Gur, R. Motoric Laterality Imbalance in Schizophrenia. *Archives of General Psychiatry* 34:33–37, 1977.

Guy, J. D., Majorski, L. V., Wallace, C. J., and Guy, M. P. The Incidence of

Minor Physical Anomalies in Adult Male Schizophrenics. *Schizophrenia Bulletin* 9:571–582, 1983.

Haggard, E. A., Brekstad, A., and Skard, A. G. On the Reliability of the Anamnestic Interview. *Journal of Abnormal and Social Psychology* 61:311–318, 1960.

Halbreich, U., Bakhai, Y., Bacon, K. B., Goldstein, S., Asnis, G. M., Endicott, J., and Lesser, J. The Normalcy of Self-Proclaimed "Normal Volunteers." *American Journal of Psychiatry* 146:1052–1055, 1989.

Hanson, D. R., and Gottesman, I. I. The Genetics, If Any, of Infantile Autism and Childhood Schizophrenia. *Journal of Autism and Childhood Schizophrenia* 6:209–234, 1976.

Hanson, D. R., Gottesman, I. I., and Heston, L. L. Long-Range Schizophrenia Forecasting: Many a Slip Twixt Cup and Lip. In J. Rolf et al. (Eds.), *Risk and Protective Factors in the Development of Psychopathology* (pp. 424–444). New York: Cambridge University Press, 1990.

Hay, S., and Wehrung, D. A. Congenital Malformations in Twins. *American Journal of Human Genetics* 22:602–678, 1970.

Heinrichs, D. W., and Buchanan, R. W. Significance and Meaning of Neurological Signs of Schizophrenia. *American Journal of Psychiatry.* 145:11–18, 1988.

Hendren, R. L., Hodde-Vargas, J. E., Vargas, L. A., Orrison, W. W., and Dell, L. Magnetic Resonance Imaging of Severely Disturbed Children— A Preliminary Study. *Journal of the American Academy of Child and Adolescent Psychiatry* 30:466–470, 1991.

Hicks, R. A., Pellegrini, R. J., Evans, E. A., and Moore, J. D. Birth Risk and Left-Handedness Reconsidered. *Archives of Neurology* 36:119–120, 1979.

Hilbun, W. B. Dermatoglyphic Findings in a Group of Psychotic Children. *Journal of Nervous and Mental Disease* 151:352–358, 1970.

Holt, S. B. Quantitative Genetics of Finger-Print Patterns. *British Medical Bulletin* 17:247–250, 1961.

Holzman, P. S., Kringlen, E., Levy, D. L., and Haberman, S. J. Deviant Eye Tracking in Twins Discordant for Psychosis. *Archives of General Psychiatry* 37:627–631, 1980.

Holzman, P. S., Kringlen, E., Levy, D. L., Proctor, L. R., Haberman, S. J., and Yasillo, N. J. Abnormal-Pursuit Eye Movements in Schizophrenia. *Archives of General Psychiatry* 34:802–805, 1977.

Holzman, P. S., Kringlen, E., Matthysse, S., Flanagan, S. D., Lipton, R. B., Cramer, G., Levin, S., Lange, K., and Levy, D. L. A Single Dominant Gene Can Account for Eye-Tracking Dysfunctions and Schizophrenia in Offspring of Discordant Twins. *Archives of General Psychiatry* 45:641–646, 1988.

Holzman, P. S., Proctor, L. R., and Hughes, D. W. Eye-Tracking Patterns in Schizophrenia. *Science* 181:179–181, 1973.

Holzman, P. S., Solomon, C. M., Levin, S., and Waternaux, C. S. Pursuit Eye Movement Dysfunctions in Schizophrenia. *Archives of General Psychiatry* 41:136–139, 1984.

Honer, W. G., Smith, G. N., MacEwan, G. W., Smith, A., and Lang, M. Obstetric Complications in Severe Psychosis. Abstract, *Schizophrenia Research* 6:105, 1992.

Hrubec, Z., and Robinette, C. D. The Study of Human Twins in Medical Research. *New England Journal of Medicine* 310:435–441, 1984.

Hubner, C. V. K., Kohlmeyer, K., and Gattaz, W. F. Relationship between CT Findings, Pregnancy and Birth Complications and Premorbid Adjustment in Schizophrenia. Abstract, *Schizophrenia Research* 1:159, 1988.

Hyde, T. M., Casanova, M. F., Kleinman, J. E., and Weinberger, D. R. Neuroanatomical and Neurochemical Pathology in Schizophrenia. In A. Tasman and S. M. Goldfinger (Eds.), *Review of Psychiatry*, Vol. 10 (pp. 7–23). Washington, D.C.: American Psychiatric Association Press, 1991.

Iacono, W. G., and Clementz, B. A. A Strategy for Elucidating Genetic Influences on Complex Psychopathological Syndromes (With Special Reference to Ocular Motor Functioning and Schizophrenia). *Progress in Experimental Personality and Psychopathology Research* 16:11–65, 1993.

Iacono, W. G., and Lykken, D. T. Electro-Oculographic Recording and Scoring of Smooth Pursuit and Saccadic Eye Tracking: A Parametric Study Using Monozygotic Twins. *Psychophysiology* 16:94–107, 1979.

Inderbitzin, L. B., Lewine, R. R. J., Gloersen, B. A., Rosen, P. B., McDonald, S. C., and Vidanagama, B. P. Fluphenazine Decanoate: A Clinical Problem? *American Journal of Psychiatry* 146:88–92, 1989.

Inouye, E. Similarity and Dissimilarity of Schizophrenia in Twins. *Proceedings of the Third World Congress of Psychiatry*, Vol. 1 (pp. 524–530). Montreal: McGill University Press, 1961.

Inouye, E. Personality Deviation Seen in Monozygotic Co-Twins of the Index Cases with Classical Schizophrenia. *Acta Psychiatrica Scandinavica*, Supplementum 219, 46:90–96, 1970.

Jacobsen, B., and Kinney, D. K. Perinatal Complications in Adopted and Non-Adopted Schizophrenics and Their Controls. *Acta Psychiatrica Scandinavica*, Supplementum 285, 62:337–346, 1980.

Jeste, D. V., Lohr, J. B., and Goodwin, F. K. Neuroanatomical Studies of Major Affective Disorders: A Review and Suggestions for Further Research. *British Journal of Psychiatry* 153:444–459, 1988.

Kallmann, F. J. The Genetic Theory of Schizophrenia. *American Journal of Psychiatry* 103:309–322, 1946.

Kameyama, T., Niwa, S., Hiramatsu, K., and Saitoh, O. Hand Preference and Eye Dominance Patterns in Japanese Schizophrenics. In P. Flor-Henry and J. Gruzelier (Eds.), *Laterality and Psychopathology* (pp. 163–180). Amsterdam: Elsevier, 1983.

Kasanin, J., and Veo, L. A Study of the School Adjustments of Children Who Later in Life Became Psychotic. *American Journal of Orthopsychiatry* 2:212–227, 1932.

Katsanis, J., and Iacono, W. G. Association of Left-Handedness with Ventricular Size and Neuropsychological Performance in Schizophrenia. *American Journal of Psychiatry* 146:1056–1058, 1989.

Kemali, D. K., Polani, P. E., Polani, N., and Amati, A. Dermatoglyphics in a Small Sample of Italian Males, Mostly with Paranoid Schizophrenia. *Acta Neurologica* (Naples), 27:506–521, 1972.

Kendler, K. S. Overview: A Current Perspective on Twin Studies of Schizophrenia. *American Journal of Psychiatry* 140:1413–1425, 1983.

Kendler, K. S., and Robinette, C. D. Schizophrenia in the National Academy of Sciences-National Research Council Twin Registry: A 16-Year Update. *American Journal of Psychiatry* 140:1551–1563, 1983.

Kennard, M. A. Value of Equivocal Signs in Neurologic Diagnosis. *Neurology* 10:753–764, 1960.

Khot, V., and Wyatt, R. J. Not All That Moves Is Tardive Dyskinesia. *American Journal of Psychiatry* 148:661–666, 1991.

King, D. J., Wilson, A., Cooper, S. J., and Waddington, J. L. The Clinical Correlates of Neurological Soft Signs in Chronic Schizophrenia. *British Journal of Psychiatry* 158:770–775, 1991.

Kinney, D. K., Woods, B. T., and Yurgelun-Todd, D. Neurologic Abnormalities in Schizophrenic Patients and Their Families. *Archives of General Psychiatry* 43:665–668, 1986.

Kinney, D. K., Woods, B. T., Yurgelun-Todd, D. A., Medoff, D., and LaJonchere, C. Hard Neurologic Signs and Obstetric Complications: Evidence for Etiologic Roles in Schizophrenia. Presented at the International Congress on Schizophrenia Research, Tucson, Arizona, April 21–25, 1991.

Kinney, D. K., Yurgelun-Todd, D., and Woods, B. T. Hard Neurologic Signs and Psychopathology in Relatives of Schizophrenic Patients. *Psychiatry Research* 39:45–53, 1991.

Klonoff, H., Fibiger, C. H., and Hutton, G. H. Neuropsychological Patterns in Chronic Schizophrenia. *Journal of Nervous and Mental Disease* 150:291–300, 1970.

Kolakowska, T., Williams, A. O., Jambor, K., and Ardern, M. Schizophrenia with Good and Poor Outcome. *British Journal of Psychiatry* 146:348–357, 1985.

Kraepelin, E. *Dementia Praecox and Paraphrenia*. Huntington, N.Y.: Robert E. Krieger Publishing, 1971. Originally published in 1919.

Kringlen, E. *Heredity and Environment in the Functional Psychoses*, Vol. 1 (summary of study) and Vol. 2 (case studies). Oslo: Universitetsforlaget, 1967.

Kringlen, E., and Cramer, G. Offspring of Monozygotic Twins Discordant for Schizophrenia. *Archives of General Psychiatry* 46:873–877, 1989.

Kristen, K. J., Liddle, P. F., Frith, C. D., Hirsch, S. R., and Frackowiak, R. S. J. The Left Medial Temporal Region and Schizophrenia. *Brain* 115:367–382, 1992.

Kydd, R. R., and Werry, J. S. Schizophrenia in Children under 16 years. *Journal of Autism and Developmental Disorders* 12:343–357, 1982.

Lane, A., Cassidy, B., Sheppard, N., Kinsella, A., Waddington, J. L., Larkin, C., and O'Callaghan, E. Dysmorphogenesis in Schizophrenia and Its Quantitative Assessment. Presented at the International Congress on Schizophrenia Research, Colorado Springs, Colorado, April 17–21, 1993.

Lane, E. A., and Albee, G. W. Comparative Birth Weights of Schizophrenics and Their Siblings. *Journal of Psychology* 64:227–231, 1966.

Levi, S. Ultrasound Assessment of the High Rate of Human Multiple Pregnancy in the First Trimester. *Journal of Ultrasound* 4:3–5, 1976.

Levy, D. L., Bogerts, B., Degreef, G., Dorogusker, B., Waternaux, C., Ashtari, M., Jody, D., Geisler, S., and Lieberman, J. A. Normal Eye Tracking Is Associated with Abnormal Morphology of Medial Temporal Lobe Structures in Schizophrenia. *Schizophrenia Research* 8:1–10, 1992.

Lewis, S. W., Chitkara, B., and Reveley, A. M. Hand Preference in Psychotic Twins. *Biological Psychiatry* 25:215–221, 1989.

Lewis, S. W., Chitkara, B., Reveley, A. M., and Murray, R. M. Family History and Birthweight in Monozygotic Twins Concordant and Discordant for Psychosis. *Acta Geneticae Medicae et Gemellologiae* 36:267–273, 1987.

Lewis, S. W., Harvey, I., Ron, M., Murray, R., and Reveley, A. Can Brain Damage Protect Against Schizophrenia? A Case Report of Twins. *British Journal of Psychiatry* 157:600–603, 1990.

Lewis, S. W., Owen, M. J., and Murray, R. M. Obstetric Complications and Schizophrenia: Methodology and Mechanisms. In S. C. Schulz and C. A. Tamminga (Eds.), *Schizophrenia: Scientific Progress* (pp. 56–68). New York: Oxford University Press, 1989.

Lewis, S. W., Reveley, A. M., Reveley, M. A., Chitkara, B., and Murray, R. M. The Familial/Sporadic Distinction as a Strategy in Schizophrenia Research. *British Journal of Psychiatry* 151:306–313, 1987.

Lewontin, R. C., Rose, S., and Kamin, L. J. *Not in Our Genes: Biology, Ideology and Human Nature.* New York: Pantheon, 1984.

Licinio, J., Krystal, J. H., Seibel, J. P., Altemus, M., and Charney, D. S. Elevated Central Levels of Interleukin-2 in Drug-Free Schizophrenia. Abstract, *Schizophrenia Research* 4:372, 1991.

Liddle, P. F., Fristen, K. J., Frith, C. D., Hirsch, S. R., Jones, T., and Frackowiak, R. S. J. Patterns of Cerebral Blood Flow in Schizophrenia. *British Journal of Psychiatry* 160:179–186, 1992.

Lifton, R. J. *The Nazi Doctors.* New York: Basic Books, 1986.

Lipska, B. K., Jaskiw, G. E., Phillips, I., Chrapusta, S., Karoum, F., and Weinberger, D. R. Age-Dependent Effects of Ventral Hippocampal Lesions on Dopaminergic Behavior in Rats. *Biological Psychiatry* 31:198A, 1992.

Lipska, B. K., Jaskiw, G. E., and Weinberger, D. R. Postpubertal Emergence of Hyperresponsiveness to Stress and to Amphetamine after Neonatal Excitotoxic Hippocampal Damage: A Potential Animal Model of Schizophrenia. *Neuropsychopharmacology.,* 9:67–75, 1993

Little, J., and Thompson, B. Descriptive Epidemiology. In MacGillivray et al. (Eds.), *Twinning and Twins* (pp. 37–66). New York: John Wiley, 1988.

Loehlin, J., and Nichols, R. *Heredity, Environment and Personality: A Study of 850 Sets of Twins.* Austin: University of Texas Press, 1976.

Lohr, J. B. Transient Grasp Reflexes in Schizophrenia. *Biological Psychiatry* 20:172–175, 1985.

Lohr, J. B., and Bracha, H. S. A Monozygotic Mirror-Image Twin Pair with Discordant Psychiatric Illnesses: A Neuropsychiatric and Neurodevelopmental Evaluation. *American Journal of Psychiatry* 149:1091–1095, 1992.

Loughnan, P. M., Gold, H., and Vance, J. C. Phenytoin Teratogenicity in Man. *Lancet* 1:70–72, 1973.

Luchins, D., Pollin, W., and Wyatt, R. J. Laterality in Monozygotic Schizophrenic Twins: An Alternative Hypothesis. *Biological Psychiatry* 15:87–93, 1980.

Lykken, D. T. The Diagnosis of Zygosity in Twins. *Behavior Genetics* 8:437–473, 1978.

Lyster, W. R. Three Patterns of Seasonality in American Births. *American Journal of Obstetrics and Gynecology* 110:1025–1028, 1971.

MacGillivray, I., Campbell, D. M., and Thompson, B. (Eds.). *Twinning and Twins.* New York: John Wiley, 1988.

MacSweeney, D. A. A Report on a Pair of Male Monozygotic Twins Discordant for Schizophrenia. *British Journal of Psychiatry* 116:315–322, 1970.

MacSweeney, D., Timms, P., and Johnson, A. Thyro-Endocrine Pathology, Obstetric Morbidity and Schizophrenia: Survey of a Hundred Families with a Schizophrenic Proband. *Psychological Medicine* 8:151–155, 1978.

Malama, I. M., Papaioannou, D. J., Kaklamani, E. P., Katsouyanni, K. M., Koumantaki, I. G., and Trichopoulos, D. V. Birth Order, Sibship Size and Socio-Economic Factors in Risk of Schizophrenia in Greece. *British Journal of Psychiatry* 152:482–486, 1988.

Manschreck, T. C., and Ames, D. Neurologic Features and Psychopathology in Schizophrenic Disorders. *Biological Psychiatry* 19:703–719, 1984.

Manschreck, T. C., Maher, B. A., Rucklos, M. E., and Vereen, D. R. Disturbed Voluntary Motor Activity in Schizophrenic Disorder. *Psychological Medicine* 12:73–84, 1982.

Markow, T. A. Genetics and Developmental Stability: An Integrative Conjecture on Aetiology and Neurobiology of Schizophrenia. *Psychological Medicine* 22:295–305, 1992.

Markow, T. A., and Gottesman, I. I. Fluctuating Dermatoglyphic Asymmetry in Psychotic Twins. *Psychiatry Research* 29:37–43, 1989.

Markow, T. A., and Wandler, K. Fluctuating Dermatoglyphic Asymmetry and the Genetics of Liability to Schizophrenia. *Psychiatry Research* 19:323–328, 1986.

Marshall, E. J., Coid, B., Lewis, S. W., Macdonald, A., and Reveley, A. M. The New Maudsley Twin Study: DSM-III Evaluation of 280 Psychotic Probands and Their Co-Twins. Presented at the International Congress on Schizophrenia Research, Colorado Springs, Colorado, April 17–21, 1993, and as abstract, *Schizophrenia Research* 9:121, 1993.

Matthysse, S., and Holzman, P. S. Genetic Latent Structure Models: Implications for Research on Schizophrenia. *Psychological Medicine* 17:271–274, 1987.

Maugham, W. S. *The Summing Up.* New York: Literary Guild of America, 1938.

McCreadie, R. G., Hall, D. J., Berry, I. J., Robertson, L. J., Ewing, J. I., and Geals, M. F. The Nithsdale Schizophrenia Surveys X: Obstetric Complications, Family History and Abnormal Movements. *British Journal of Psychiatry* 161:799–805, 1992.

McGue, M. When Assessing Twin Concordance, Use the Probandwise Not the Pairwise Rate. *Schizophrenia Bulletin* 18:171–176, 1992.

McGuffin, P., Reveley, A., and Holland, A. Identical Triplets: Non-Identical Psychosis? *British Journal of Psychiatry* 140:1–6, 1982.

McKeown, T., and Record, R. G. Seasonal Incidence of Congenital Malformations of the Central Nervous System. *Lancet* 1:192–196, 1951.

McNeil, T. F. Obstetric Factors and Perinatal Injuries. In M. T. Tsuang and

J. C. Simpson (Eds.), *Handbook of Schizophrenia*, Vol. 3 (pp. 319–344). New York: Elsevier, 1988.

McNeil, T. F., and Kaij, L. Obstetric Factors in the Development of Schizophrenia. In L. C. Wynne et al. (Eds.), *The Nature of Schizophrenia* (pp. 401–429). New York: John Wiley, 1978.

McNeil, T. F., Raff, C. S., and Cromwell, R. L. A Technique for Comparing the Relative Importance of Season of Conception and Season of Birth: Application to Emotionally Disturbed Children. *British Journal of Psychiatry* 118:329–335, 1971.

Medalia, A., Gold, J. M., and Meriam, A. The Effects of Neuroleptics on Neuropsychological Test Results of Schizophrenics. *Archives of Clinical Neuropsychology* 3:249–271, 1988.

Mednick, S. A. Breakdown in Individuals at High Risk for Schizophrenia: Possible Predispositional Perinatal Factors. *Mental Hygiene* 54:50–63, 1970.

Mednick, S. A., Machon, R. A., Huttenen, M. O., and Bonett, D. Adult Schizophrenia Following Prenatal Exposure to an Influenza Epidemic. *Archives of General Psychiatry* 45:189–192, 1988.

Mednick, S. A., Mura, E., Schulsinger, F., and Mednick, B. Perinatal Conditions and Infant Development in Children with Schizophrenic Parents. *Social Biology* 18:S103–S113, 1971.

Mellin, G. W., and Katzenstein, M. The Saga of Thalidomide. *New England Journal of Medicine* 267:1184–1190, 1962.

Mellor, C. S. Dermatoglyphics in Schizophrenia. *British Journal of Psychiatry* 114:1387–1397, 1968.

Mellor, C. S. Dermatoglyphic Evidence of Fluctuating Asymmetry in Schizophrenia. *British Journal of Psychiatry* 160:467–472, 1992.

Menez-Bautista, R., Fikrig, S. M., Pahwa, S., Sarangadharan, M. G., and Stoneburner, R. L. Monozygotic Twins Discordant for the Acquired Immunodeficiency Syndrome. *American Journal of Diseases of Children* 140:678–679, 1986.

Menninger, K. A. Reversible Schizophrenia. *American Journal of Psychiatry* 1:573–588, 1922.

Michel, G. F. Maternal Influences on Infant Handedness during Play with Toys. *Behavior Genetics* 22:163–175, 1992.

Mirsky, A. F., DeLisi, L. E., Buchsbaum, M. S., Quinn, O. W., Schwerdt, P., Siever, L. J., Mann, L., Weingartner, H., Zec, R., Sostek, A., Alterman, I., Revere, V., Dawson, S. D., and Zahn, T. P. The Genain Quadruplets: Psychological Studies. *Psychiatry Research* 13:77–93, 1984.

Moore, S. J., and Munger, B. L. The Early Ontogeny of the Afferent Nerves and Papillary Ridges in Human Digital Glabrous Skin. *Developmental Brain Research* 48:119–141, 1989.

Morrison, J. E. Congenital Malformations in One of Monozygotic Twins. *Archives of Disease in Childhood* 24:214–218, 1949.

Mosher, L. R., Pollin, W., and Stabenau, J. R. Identical Twins Discordant for Schizophrenia: Neurological Findings. *Archives of General Psychiatry* 24:422–430, 1971.

Mulvihill, J. J., and Smith, D. W. The Genesis of Dermatoglyphics. *Journal of Pediatrics* 75:579–589, 1969.

Munk-Jorgensen, P. Why Has the Incidence of Schizophrenia in Danish Psychiatric Institutions Decreased since 1970? *Acta Psychiatrica Scandinavica* 75:62–68, 1987.

Munsinger, H. The Identical-Twin Transfusion Syndrome: A Source of Error in Estimating IQ Resemblance and Heritability. *Annals of Human Genetics* 40:307–321, 1977.

Murthy, R. S., and Wig, N. N. Dermatoglyphics in Schizophrenia: The Relevance of Positive Family History. *British Journal of Psychiatry* 130:56–58, 1977.

Myrianthopoulos, N. C. Congenital Malformations in Twins: Epidemiologic Survey. *Birth Defects*, Original Series, 9:1–28, 1975.

*Myslobodsky, M. S., Coppola, R., Torrey, E. F., and Weinberger, D. R. Regional Variation of Neuroanatomical Brain Abnormalities in Schizophrenia. Presented at the annual meeting of the Society for Neuroscience, St. Louis, Missouri, Oct. 28–Nov. 2, 1990.

Nasrallah, H. A., Coffman, J. A., and Olson, S. C. CT and MRI Findings in Affective Disorders: Clinical and Research Implications. In C. L. Cazzullo et al. (Eds.), *Plasticity and Morphology of the Central Nervous System* (pp. 53–62). Lancaster, Pa: MTP Press, 1987.

Nasrallah, H. A., Olsen, S. C., Coffman, J. A., Schwarzkopf, S. B., McLaughlin, J. A., Brandt, J. B., and Lynn, M. B. Magnetic Resonance Brain Imaging, Perinatal Injury and Negative Symptoms in Schizophrenia. Abstract, *Schizophrenia Research* 1:171–172, 1988.

Nelson, K. B., and Ellenberg, J. H. Antecedents of Cerebral Palsy: Multivariate Analysis of Risk. *New England Journal of Medicine* 315:81–86, 1986.

Newman, H. H. Studies of Human Twins: Asymmetry Reversal of Mirror Imaging in Identical Twins. *Biological Bulletin* 55:298–315, 1928.

Newman, H. H., Freeman, F. N., and Holzinger, K. J. *Twins: A Study of Heredity and Environment.* Chicago: University of Chicago Press, 1937.

Nielsen, J. Inheritance in Monozygotic Twins. *Lancet* 2:717–718, 1967.

Nimgaonkar, V. L., Wesseley, S., and Murray, R. M. Prevalence of Familiarity, Obstetric Complications, and Structural Brain Damage in Schizophrenic Patients. *British Journal of Psychiatry* 153:191–197, 1988.

*Noga, J. T., Vladar, K., Torrey, E. F., and Weinberger, D. R. Basal Ganglia Volumes on MRI of MZ Twins Discordant for Bipolar Disorder. Presented at the annual meeting of the Society of Biological Psychiatry, San Francisco, May 19–23, 1993.

Nowakowski, R. S. Basic Concepts of CNS Development. *Child Development* 58:568–595, 1987.

Nylander, P. P. S. Fingerprints and the Determination of Zygosity in Twins. *American Journal of Physical Anthropology* 35:101–108, 1971.

O'Callaghan, E., Gibson, T., Colohan, H. A., Buckley, P., Walshe, D. G., Larkin, C., and Waddington, J. L. Risk of Schizophrenia in Adults Born after Obstetric Complications and Their Association with Early Onset of Illness: A Controlled Study. *British Medical Journal* 305:1256–1259, 1992.

O'Callaghan, E., Larkin, C., Kinsella, A., and Waddington, J. L. Obstetric Complications, the Putative Familial-Sporadic Distinction, and Tardive Dyskinesia in Schizophrenia. *British Journal of Psychiatry* 157:578–584, 1990.

O'Callaghan, E., Larkin, C., Kinsella, A., and Waddington, J. L. Familial, Obstetric, and Other Clinical Correlates of Minor Physical Anomalies in Schizophrenia. *American Journal of Psychiatry* 148:479–483, 1991.

O'Callaghan, E., Larkin, C., and Waddington, J. L. Obstetric Complications in Schizophrenia and the Validity of Maternal Recall. *Psychological Medicine* 20:89–94, 1990.

O'Callaghan, E., Sham, P., Takei, N., Glover, G., and Murray, R. M. Schizophrenia after Prenatal Exposure to 1957 A-2 Influenza Epidemic. *Lancet* 337:1248–1250, 1991.

Offord, D. R., and Cross, L. A. Behavioral Antecedents of Adult Schizophrenia. *Archives of General Psychiatry* 21:267–283, 1969.

Oldfield, R. C. The Assessment and Analysis of Handedness: The Edinburgh Inventory. *Neuropsychologia* 9:97–113, 1971.

Oldstone, M. B. A., Sinha, Y. N., Blount, P., Tishon, A., Rodriguez, M., von Wedel, R., and Lampert, P. W. Virus-Induced Alterations in Homeostasis: Alterations in Differentiated Functions of Infected Cells In Vivo. *Science* 218:1125–1127, 1982.

Olson, S. C., Coffman, J. A., Schwarzkopf, S. C., Bornstein, R., and Nasrallah, H. A. Characteristics of "Normal" Controls Who Volunteer for Schizophrenia Research. *Schizophrenia Research* 3:92, 1990.

O'Neal, P., and Robins, L. N. Childhood Patterns Predictive of Adult Schizophrenia: A 30-year Follow-up Study. *American Journal of Psychiatry* 115:385–391, 1958.

Onstad, S., Skre, I., Edvardsen, J., Torgensen, S., and Kringlen, E. Mental

Disorders in First-Degree Relatives of Schizophrenics. *Acta Psychiatrica Scandinavica* 83:463–467, 1991.

Onstad, S., Skre, I., Torgensen, S., and Kringlen, E. Subtypes of Schizophrenia—Evidence from a Twin-Family Study. *Acta Psychiatrica Scandinavica* 84:203–206, 1991a.

Onstad, S., Skre, I., Torgensen, S., and Kringlen, E. Twin Concordance for DSM-III-R Schizophrenia. *Acta Psychiatrica Scandinavica* 83:395–401, 1991b.

Onstad, S., Skre, I., Torgensen, S., and Kringlen, E. Birthweight and Obstetric Complications in Schizophrenic Twins. *Acta Psychiatrica Scandinavica* 85:70–73, 1992.

Owen, M. J., Lewis, S. W., and Murray, R. M. Obstetric Complications and Schizophrenia: A Computed Tomographic Study. *Psychological Medicine* 18:331–339, 1988.

Paneth, N. Birth and the Origins of Cerebral Palsy. Editorial, *New England Journal of Medicine* 315:124–126, 1986.

Parnas, J., Mednick, S. A., and Moffitt, T. E. Perinatal Complications and Adult Schizophrenia. *Trends in Neuroscience* 4:262–264, 1981.

Parnas, J., Schulsinger, F., Neasdale, T. W., Schulsinger, H., Feldman, P. M., and Mednick, S. A. Perinatal Complications and Clinical Outcome within the Schizophrenia Spectrum. *British Journal of Psychiatry* 140:416–420, 1982.

Pearlson, G. D., Kim, W. S., Kubos, K. L., Moberg, P. J., Jayaram, G., Bascom, M. J., Chase, G. A., Goldfinger, A. D., and Tune, L. E. Ventricle-Brain Ratio, Computed Tomographic Density, and Brain Area in 50 Schizophrenics. *Archives of General Psychiatry* 46:690–697, 1989.

Pedersen, I. K., Philip, J., Sele, V., and Starup, J. Monozygotic Twins with Dissimilar Phenotypes and Chromosome Complements. *Acta Obstetricia et Gynecologia Scandinavica* 59:459–462, 1980.

Penrose, L. S. Congenital Syphilis in a Monovular Twin. *Lancet* 1:322, 1937.

Penrose, L. S. Dermatoglyphics. *Scientific American* 221 (Dec.):73–84, 1969.

Persson, S., and Dalen, P. Obstetric Complications in Familial and Sporadic Schizophrenia. Presented at the International Congress on Schizophrenia, Vancouver, July 19–22, 1992.

Peters, C. J., Reeves, W. C., and Purcell, R. H. Disparate Response of Monozygotic Twins to Hepatitis B Virus Infection. *Journal of Pediatrics* 91:265–266, 1977.

Pincus, J. H., and Tucker, G. J. *Behavioral Neurology*. New York: Oxford University Press, 1974.

Plato, C. C., Fox, K. M., and Garruto, R. M. Measures of Lateral Functional Dominance: Foot Preference, Eye Preference, Digital Interlocking, Arm Folding and Foot Overlapping. *Human Biology* 57:327–334, 1985.

Plato, C. C., and Garruto, R. M. Historical Notes on Dermatoglyphics: From Purkinje to Cummins. In N. M. Durham and C. C. Plato (Eds.), *Trends in Dermatoglyphic Research* (pp. 2–9). Amsterdam: Klumer Academic Publishers, 1990.

Plato, C. C., Schwartz, J. T., and Wertelecki, W. Dermatoglyphic Investigations in Twins and Siblings. *Acta Geneticae Medicae et Gemellologiae* 25:167–173, 1976.

Polednak, A. P. Dermatoglyphics of Negro Schizophrenic Males. *British Journal of Psychiatry* 120:397–398, 1972.

Pollack, M., and Woerner, M. G. Pre- and Perinatal Complications and "Childhood Schizophrenia": A Comparison of Five Controlled Studies. *Journal of Child Psychology and Psychiatry* 7:235–242, 1966.

Pollack, M., Woerner, M. G., Goodman, W., and Greenberg, I. M. Childhood Development Patterns of Hospitalized Adult Schizophrenic and Nonschizophrenic Patients and Their Siblings. *American Journal of Orthopsychiatry* 36:510–517, 1966.

Pollin, W., and Stabenau, J. R. Biological, Psychological and Historical Differences in a Series of Monozygotic Twins Discordant for Schizophrenia. In D. Rosenthal and S. Kety (Eds.), *The Transmission of Schizophrenia* (pp. 317–332). New York: Pergamon, 1968.

Pollin, W., Stabenau, J. R., Mosher, L., and Tupin, J. Life History Differences in Identical Twins Discordant for Schizophrenia. *American Journal of Orthopsychiatry* 36:492–509, 1966.

*Polymeropoulos, M. H., Xiao, H., Torrey, E. F., DeLisi, L., Crow, T., and Merril, C. R. Search for a Genetic Event in Monozygotic Twins Discordant for Schizophrenia.*Psychiatry Research* 48:27–36, 1993.

Price, B. Primary Biases in Twin Studies. *American Journal of Human Genetics* 2:293–352, 1950.

Price, B. Bibliography on Prenatal and Natal Influences in Twins. *Acta Genetica et Medicae Gemollologiae* 27:97–113, 1978.

Proctor, R. *Racial Hygiene: Medicine under the Nazis.* Cambridge: Harvard University Press, 1988.

Purvis-Smith, S. G., Hayes, K., and Menser, M. A. Dermatoglyphics in Children with Prenatal Cytomegalovirus Infection. *Lancet* 2:976–977, 1972.

Purvis-Smith, S. G., Howard, P. R., and Menser, M. A. Dermatoglyphic Defects and Rubella Teratogenesis. *Journal of the American Medical Association* 209:1865–1869, 1969.

Purvis-Smith, S. G., and Menser, M. A. Genetic and Environmental Influences on Digital Dermatoglyphics in Congenital Rubella. *Pediatric Research* 7:215–219, 1973.

Quinn, P. O., and Rapoport, J. L. Minor Physical Anomalies and Neurologic Status in Hyperactive Boys. *Pediatrics* 53:742–747, 1974.

Raese, J. D., Paulman, R. G., Steinberg, J. L., Devous, M. D., Judd, C. R., and Gregory, R. R. Wisconsin Card Sort Activated Blood Flow in Dorsolateral Frontal Cortex in Never Medicated and Previously Medicated Schizophrenics and Normal Controls. *Biological Psychiatry* 25:100A, 1989.

*Ragland, J. D., Goldberg, T. E., Wexler, B. E., Gold, J. M., Torrey, E. F., and Weinberger, D. R. Dichotic Listening in Monozygotic Twins Discordant and Concordant for Schizophrenia. *Schizophrenia Research* 7:177–183, 1992.

Rapaport, M. H., and McAllister, C. G. Neuroimmunologic Factors in Schizophrenia. In J. M. Gorman and R. M. Kertzner (Eds.), *Psychoimmunology Update* (pp. 31–47). Washington, D.C.: American Psychiatric Press, 1991.

*Rapaport, M. H., Torrey, E. F., McAllister, C. G., Nelson, D. L., Pickar, D., and Paul, S. M. Increased Serum Soluble Interleukin-2 Receptors in Schizophrenic Monozygotic Twins. *European Archives of Psychiatry and Clinical Neuroscience* 243: 7–10, 1993.

Raphael, T., and Raphael, L. G. Fingerprints in Schizophrenia. *Journal of the American Medical Association* 180:215–219, 1962.

Raskin, R. A. Congenital Syphilis in One of Apparently Identical Twins. *American Journal of Syphilis* 35:334–336, 1951.

Record, R. G., and McKeown, T. Congenital Malformations of the Central Nervous System. *Annals of Eugenics* 15:285–292, 1951.

Reddy, R., Mukherjee, S., Schnur, D. B., Chen, J., and Degreef, G. History of Obstetric Complications, Family History, and CT Scan Findings in Schizophrenic Patients. *Schizophrenia Research* 3:311–314, 1990.

*Resnick, S. M., Gur, R. E., Torrey, E. F., Mozley, P. D., Muehllehner, G., Gur, R. C., Gottesman, I. I., Reivich, M., and Alavi, A. PET-FDG Imaging in Identical Twins Discordant for Schizophrenia. Presented at the annual meeting of the Society of Nuclear Medicine, Washington, D.C., June 19–22, 1990.

Reveley, A. M., Reveley, M. A., Clifford, C. A., and Murray, R. M. Cerebral Ventricular Size in Twins Discordant for Schizophrenia. *Lancet* 1:540–541, 1982.

Reveley, A. M., Reveley, M. A., and Murray, R. M. Cerebral Ventricular Enlargement in Non-Genetic Schizophrenia: A Controlled Twin Study. *British Journal of Psychiatry* 144:89–93, 1984.

Reveley, M. A., Reveley, A. M., and Baldy, R. Left Cerebral Hypodensity in Discordant Schizophrenic Twins: A Controlled Study. *Archives of General Psychiatry* 44:625–632, 1987.

Rickler, J. P., Boring, R. H., Harris, A. E., and Markow, T. Fluctuating Dermatoglyphic Asymmetry and Its Association with Positive and Negative Symptoms in Schizophrenia. *Schizophrenia Research* 2:73, 1989.

Ricks, D. F., and Berry, J. C. Family and Symptom Patterns That Precede Schizophrenia. In M. Roff and D. F. Ricks (Eds.) *Life History Research in Psychopathology* (pp. 31–50). Minneapolis: University of Minnesota Press, 1970.

Ricks, D. F., and Nameche, G. Symbiosis, Sacrifice and Schizophrenia. *Mental Hygiene* 50:541–551, 1966.

Robbins, L. C. The Accuracy of Parental Recall of Aspects of Child Development and of Child Rearing Practices. *Journal of Abnormal and Social Psychology* 66:262–270, 1963.

Rogers, J. G., Voullaire, L., and Gold, H. Monozygotic Twins Discordant for Trisomy 21. *American Journal of Medical Genetics* 11:143–146, 1982.

Roos, R. P. Genetically Controlled Resistance to Virus Infections of the Central Nervous System. *Progress in Medical Genetics* 6:242–276, 1985.

Rosanoff, A. J., Handy, L. M., Plesset, I. R., and Brush, S. The Etiology of the So-Called Schizophrenic Psychoses. *American Journal of Psychiatry* 91:247–286, 1934.

Rosenthal, D. Some Factors Associated with Concordance and Discordance with Respect to Schizophrenia in Monozygotic Twins. *Journal of Nervous and Mental Disease* 129:1–10, 1959.

Rosenthal, D. Confusion of Identity and the Frequency of Schizophrenia in Twins. *Archives of General Psychiatry* 3:297–304, 1960.

Rosenthal, D. (Ed.). *The Genain Quadruplets.* New York: Basic Books, 1963.

Rosenthal, D., and Van Dyke, J. The Use of MZ Twins Discordant as to Schizophrenia in the Search for an Inherited Characterological Defect. *Acta Psychiatrica Scandinavica,* Supplementum 219:183–189, 1970.

Rosner, F., and Steinberg, F. S. Dermatoglyphic Patterns of Negro Men with Schizophrenia. *Diseases of the Nervous System* 29:739–743, 1968.

Rossi, A., DeCataldo, S., DiMichele, V., Ceccoli, S., Stratta, P., and Casacchia, M. Neurological Soft Signs in Schizophrenia. *British Journal of Psychiatry* 157:735–739, 1990.

Rothhammer, F., Pereira, G., Camousseight, A., and Benado, M. Dermatoglyphics in Schizophrenic Patients. *Human Heredity* 21:198–202, 1971.

Rourke, B. P., Fisk, J. L., and Strang, J. D. *Child Neuropsychology,* New York: Guilford Press, 1983.

Rubin, P., Holm, S., Friberg, L., Videbech, P., Andersen, H. S., Gendsen, V. B., Stromse, N., Larsen, J. K., Lassen, N. A., and Hemmingsen, R. Altered Modulation of Prefrontal and Subcortical Brain Activity in Novel Diagnosed Schizophrenia and Schizophreniform Disorder: A

Regional Cerebral Blood Flow Study. *Archives of General Psychiatry* 48:987–995, 1991.

Rushton, J. P., Fulker, D. W., Neale, M. C., Blizard, R. A., and Eysenck, H. J. Altruism and Genetics. *Acta Geneticae Medica et Gemellologiae* 33:265–271, 1984.

Russell, A. T., Bott, L., and Sammons, C. The Phenomenology of Schizophrenia Occurring in Childhood. *Journal of the American Academy of Child and Adolescent Psychiatry* 28:399–407, 1989.

*Sambunaris, A., Kulaga, H., Torrey, E. F., Glovinsky, D., Wyatt, R. J., and Kirch, D. G. Schizophrenia, MZ Twins, and Immunologic Variation. Presented at the annual meeting of the American Psychiatric Association, San Francisco, May 22–27, 1993.

Sank, D. Dermatoglyphics of Childhood Schizophrenia. *Acta Genetica* (Basel) 18:300–314, 1968.

Schlegel, L. Constitutional-Biological Observations on the Hands of Psychically Abnormal Personalities with Special Regard to Hand Furrows. *Schweizeriches Archiv Neurologie Psychiatrie* 62:305–351, 1948.

Schroder, J., Niethammer, R., Geider, F. J., Reitz, C., Binkert, M., Jauss, M., and Sauer, H. Neurological Soft Signs in Schizophrenia. *Schizophrenia Research* 6:25–30, 1992.

Schwarzkopf, S. B., Nasrallah, H. A., Olson, S. C., Coffman, J. A., and McLaughlin, J. A. Perinatal Complications and Genetic Loading in Schizophrenia: Preliminary Findings. *Psychiatry Research* 27:233–239, 1989.

Segal, N. L. Origins and Implications of Handedness and Relative Birth Weight for IQ in Monozygotic Pairs. *Neuropsychology* 27:549–561, 1989.

Seidman, L. J. Schizophrenia and Brain Dysfunction: An Integration of Recent Neurodiagnostic Findings. *Psychological Bulletin* 94:195–238, 1983.

Shapiro, T. Hand Morphology in Some Severely Impaired Schizophrenic Children. *American Journal of Psychiatry* 122:432–435, 1965.

Sharma, S., and Lal, R. Minor Physical Anomalies in Schizophrenia. *International Journal of Neuroscience* 31:138, 1986.

Shearer, W. T., Schreiner, R. L., Marshall, R. E., and Barton, L. L. Cytomegalovirus Infection in a Newborn Dizygous Twin. *Journal of Pediatrics* 81:1161–1165, 1972.

Shields, J. *Monozygotic Twins: Brought Up Apart and Brought Up Together.* London: Oxford University Press, 1962.

Shields, J., and Gottesman, I. I. Obstetric Complications and Twin Studies of Schizophrenia: Clarifications and Affirmations. *Schizophrenia Bulletin* 3:351–354, 1977.

Shields, J., Gottesman, I. I., and Slater, E. Kallman's 1946 Schizophrenic

Twin Study in the Light of New Information. *Acta Psychiatrica Scandinavica* 43:385–396, 1967.

Shtasel, D. L., Gur, R. E., Mozley, P. D., Richards, J., Taleff, M. M., Heimberg, C., Gallacher, F., and Gur, R. Volunteers for Biomedical Research. *Archives of General Psychiatry* 48:1022–1025, 1991.

Silverton, L., Finello, K. M., Schulsinger, F., and Mednick, S. A. Low Birth Weight and Ventricular Enlargement in a High-Risk Sample. *Journal of Abnormal Psychology* 94:405–409, 1985.

Singh, S. Dermatoglyphics in Schizophrenia. *Acta Genetica* (Basel) 17:348–356, 1967.

Slastenko, Y. V., Gladkova, T. D., and Shapiro, Y. L. On the Possibility of Using Dermatoglyphic Patterns for the Estimation of Genetic Hypotheses under Schizophrenia. *Genetica* 12:168–171, 1976.

Slater, E., and Shields, J. *Psychotic and Neurotic Illnesses in Twins.* London: Her Majesty's Stationery Office, 1953.

Small, N. E., Mohs, R. C., Halperin, R., Rosen, W. G., Masterson, C., Kendler, K. S., Horvath, T. B., and Davis, K. L. A Study of the Reliability of Reported Premorbid Adjustment in Schizophrenic Patients. *Biological Psychiatry* 19:203–211, 1984.

Smith, G. N., MacEwan, G. W., Dunn, H. D., and Ancill, R. J. Psychiatric Sequelae of Birth Problems: The Vancouver Study. Presented at the International Congress on Schizophrenia, Vancouver, July 19–22, 1992.

Specter, M. West Germany's Anguished Science. *Washington Post*, April 11, 1990, p. A–16.

Spellacy, W. N. Antepartum Complications in Twin Pregnancies. *Clinics in Perinatology* 15:79–86, 1988.

Spitzer, R. L., and Williams, J. B. W. *Structured Clinical Interview for DSM-III-R, Patient Version (SCID-P) and Non-Patient Version (SCID-NP).* New York: New York State Psychiatric Institute, 1986.

Spitzer, R. L., Williams, J. B. W., Gibbon, M., and First, M. B. *User's Guide for the Structured Clinical Interview for DSM-III-R.* Washington, D.C.: American Psychiatric Press, 1990.

Spitzer, R. L., Williams, J. B. W., Gibbon, M., and First, M. B. The Structured Clinical Interview for DSM-III-R (SCID), 1: History, Rationale and Description. *Archives of General Psychiatry* 49:624–629, 1992.

Stabenau, J. R., and Pollin, W. Early Characteristics of Monozygotic Twins Discordant for Schizophrenia. *Archives of General Psychiatry* 17:723–734, 1967.

Steg, J. P., and Rapoport, J. L. Minor Physical Anomalies in Normal, Neurotic, Learning-Disabled and Severely Disturbed Children. *Journal of Autism and Childhood Schizophrenia* 5:299–307, 1975.

Stern, C. *Principles of Human Genetics* (pp. 338–342). San Francisco: W. H. Freeman, 1960.

Stevens, J. R. Eye-Tracking Patterns in Schizophrenia. *Science* 184:1201–1202, 1974.

Stevenson, A. C., Johnston, H. A., Stewart, M. I. P., and Golding, D. R. Congenital Malformations. *Bulletin of the World Health Organization,* Supplement 34:1–127, 1966.

Still, G. F. Some Abnormal Conditions in Children. *Lancet* 1:1008–1012, 1077–1082, 1163–1168, 1902.

Stowens, D., Sammon, J. W., and Proctor, A. Dermatoglyphics in Female Schizophrenia. *Psychiatric Quarterly* 44:516–532, 1970.

Streissguth, A. P., and Dehaene, P. Twins of Alcoholic Mothers: Concordance and Discordance for FAS. *Teratology* 41:594, 1990.

*Suddath, R. L., Christison, G. W., Torrey, E. F., Casanova, M. F., and Weinberger, D. R. Anatomical Abnormalities in the Brains of Monozygotic Twins Discordant for Schizophrenia. *New England Journal of Medicine* 322:789–794, 1990.

Susser, E. S., and Lin, S. P. Schizophrenia after Prenatal Exposure to the Dutch Winter of 1944–1945. *Archives of General Psychiatry* 49:983–988, 1992.

Sydow, G. V., and Rinne, A. Very Unequal "Identical" Twins. *Acta Paediatrica* 47:163–171, 1958.

Tamminga, C. A., Thaker, G. K., Buchanan, R., Kirkpatrick, B., Alphs, L. D., Chase, T. N., and Carpenter, W. T. Limbic System Abnormalities Identified in Schizophrenia Using Positron Emission Tomography with Fluorodeoxyglucose and Neocortical Alterations with Deficit Syndrome. *Archives of General Psychiatry* 49:522–530, 1992.

Tan, K. L., Tan, R., Tan, S. H., and Tan, A. M. The Twin Transfusion Syndrome. *Clinical Pediatrics* 18:111–114, 1979.

Taylor, M. A. Are Schizophrenia and Affective Disorder Related? A Selective Literature Review. *American Journal of Psychiatry* 149:22–32, 1992.

Taylor, M. A., and Abrams, R. Cognitive Impairment in Schizophrenia. *American Journal of Psychiatry* 141:196–201, 1984.

Taylor, P. J. Hemispheric Lateralization and Schizophrenia. In H. Helmchen and F. A. Henn (Eds.), *Biological Perspectives of Schizophrenia* (pp. 213–236). New York: John Wiley, 1987.

Taylor, P. J., Dalton, R., and Fleminger, J. L. Handedness in Schizophrenia. *British Journal of Psychiatry* 136:375–383, 1980.

Tellegan, A. Manual for the Multidimensional Personality Questionnaire. Minneapolis: University of Minnesota Press, 1982.

Tellegan, A., Lykken, D. T., Bouchard, T. J., Wilcox, K. J., Segal, N. L., and

Rich, S. Personality Similarity in Twins Reared Apart and Together. *Journal of Personality and Social Psychology* 54:1031–1039, 1988.

Tellegen, A., and Waller, N. G. Exploring Personality through Test Construction: Development of the Multidimensional Personality Questionnaire. In S. R. Briggs and J. M. Cheek (Eds.), *Personality Measures: Development and Evaluation*, Vol. I. Greenwich, Conn.: JAI Press, in press.

Thaker, G. K., Moran, M., Lahti, A., Adami, H., and Tamminga, C. Psychiatric Morbidity in Research Volunteers. Letter, *Archives of General Psychiatry* 47:980, 1990.

Thaler, M. M., Park, C. K., Landers, D. V., Wara, D. W., Houghton, M., Veereman-Wauters, G., Sweet, R. L., and Han, J. H. Vertical Transmission of Hepatitis C Virus. *Lancet* 338:17–18, 1991.

Tienari, P. Psychiatric Illnesses in Identical Twins. *Acta Psychiatrica Scandinavica*, Supplementum 171, 39:10–195, 1963.

Tienari, P. Schizophrenia in Finnish Male Twins. In M. H. Lader (Ed.), *Studies of Schizophrenia. British Journal of Psychiatry Special Publication No. 10* (pp. 29–35), Ashford, Kent: Headley Brothers, 1975.

Tienari, P. J., Wikstrom, J., Sajantila, A., Palo, J., and Peltonen, L. Genetic Susceptibility to Multiple Sclerosis Linked to Myelin Basic Protein Gene. *Lancet* 340:987–991, 1992.

Tilley, B. C., Barnes, A. B., Bergstralh, E., Labarthe, D., Noller, K. L., Colton, T., and Adam, E. A Comparison of Pregnancy History Recall and Medical Records. *American Journal of Epidemiology* 121:269–281, 1985.

Torrey, E. F. Birth Weights, Perinatal Insults, and HLA Types: Return to "Original Din." *Schizophrenia Bulletin* 3:347–351, 1977.

Torrey, E. F. Neurological Abnormalities in Schizophrenic Patients. *Biological Psychiatry* 15:381–388, 1980a.

Torrey, E. F. *Schizophrenia and Civilization*. New York: Jason Aronson, 1980b.

Torrey, E. F. Functional Psychoses and Viral Encephalitis. *Integrative Psychiatry* 4:224–236, 1986.

Torrey, E. F. Prevalence Studies of Schizophrenia. *British Journal of Psychiatry* 150:598–608, 1987.

Torrey, E. F. *Surviving Schizophrenia: A Family Manual* (rev. ed.). New York: Harper and Row, 1988.

Torrey, E. F. Offspring of Twins with Schizophrenia. Letter, *Archives of General Psychiatry* 47:976–977, 1990.

Torrey, E. F. Are We Overestimating the Genetic Contribution to Schizophrenia? *Schizophrenia Bulletin* 18:159–170, 1992.

Torrey, E. F., and Bowler, A. Geographical Distribution of Insanity in

America: Evidence for an Urban Factor. *Schizophrenia Bulletin* 16:591–604, 1990.

Torrey, E. F., and Kaufmann, C. A. Schizophrenia and Neuroviruses. In H. A. Nasrallah and D. R. Weinberger (Eds.), *Handbook of Schizophrenia, Vol. 1: The Neurology of Schizophrenia* (pp. 361–376). New York: Elsevier, 1986.

*Torrey, E. F., Ragland, J. D., Gold, J. M., Goldberg, T. E., Bowler, A. E., Bigelow, L. B., and Gottesman, I. I. Handedness in Twins with Schizophrenia: Was Boklage Correct? *Schizophrenia Research* 9:83–85, 1993.

*Torrey, E. F., Rapaport, M. H., Ganguli, R., Honigman, A. M., Paul, S. M., McAllister, C. G., Rabin, B. S., Yolken, R. H., Nelson, D. L., Bigelow, L. B., and Gottesman, I. I. Immunological and Virological Aspects of Identical Twins with Schizophrenia. Abstract, *Biological Psychiatry* 29:375, 1991.

*Torrey, E. F., Rickler, K. C., Bowler, A. E., Bigelow, L. B., Taylor, E. H., Hyde, T. M., Goldberg, T. E., Weinberger, D. R., Litman, R., and Gottesman, I. I. Neurological Abnormalities in Identical Twins with Schizophrenia. Submitted for publication, 1993.

*Torrey, E. F., Taylor, E., Bowler, A., Bracha, S., Quinn, P. O., Bigelow, L., Rickler, K., Higgins, N., Wyatt, R. J., and Gottesman, I. I. Evidence of Early Brain Changes in Subgroup of Twins with Schizophrenia. Abstract, *Schizophrenia Research* 4:285, 1991.

*Torrey, E. F., Taylor, E. H., Bracha, H. S., Bowler, A. E., McNeil, T. F., Rawlings, R. R., Quinn, P. O,. Bigelow, L. B., Rickler, K., Sjostrom, K., Higgins, E. S., and Gottesman, I. I. Evidence for a Prenatal Origin of Schizophrenia in a Subgroup of Discordant Monozygotic Twins. *Schizophrenia Bulletin,* in press.

Tuckerman, E., Webb, T., and Bundey, S. E. Frequency and Replication Status of the Fragile X fra(X)(q27–28) in a Pair of Monozygotic Twins of Markedly Differing Intelligence. *Journal of Medical Genetics* 22:85–91, 1985.

Turek, S. Dermatoglyphics and Schizophrenia—Analysis of Quantitative Traits. *Collegium Antropologicum* 14:137–150, 1990.

Turner, T. Rich and Mad in Victorian England. *Psychological Medicine* 19:29–44, 1989.

Veliscu, C., Scripcaru, G. H., Pirozynski, T., and Alexandrescu, L. Dermatoglyphic Aspects of Schizophrenia. *Revista Medico-Chirurgicala, Iasi* 72:631–635, 1968.

*Vladar, K., Ljaljevic, Z. M., Zigun, J. R., Torrey, E. F., and Weinberger, D. R. An MRI Study of Septal Defects in Monozygotic Twins Discordant for Schizophrenia and in Normal Twins. *Biological Psychiatry* 31:124A, 1992.

*Vladar, K., Zigun, J. R., Jones, D. W., Torrey, E. F., and Weinberger, D. R. Basal Ganglia in Discordant Schizophrenic Monozygotic Twins. Presented at the annual meeting of the American Psychiatric Association, Washington, D.C., May 3–8, 1992.

Waddington, J. L. Ventricular Enlargement in Schizophrenia and the Historical Studies of John Haslam. Letter, *American Journal of Psychiatry* 141:1640, 1984.

Wahl, O. F. Monozygotic Twins Discordant for Schizophrenia: A Review. *Psychological Bulletin* 83:91–106, 1976.

Waldrop, M. F., Pederson, F. A., and Bell, R. Q. Minor Physical Anomalies and Behavior in Preschool Children. *Child Development* 39:391–400, 1968.

Walker, E., and Lewine, R. J. Prediction of Adult-Onset Schizophrenia from Childhood Home Movies of the Patients. *American Journal of Psychiatry* 147:1052–1056, 1990.

Walker, H. A. Incidence of Minor Physical Anomalies in Autism. *Journal of Autism and Childhood Schizophrenia* 7:165–176, 1977.

Watson, C. G., Thomas, R. W., Anderson, D., and Felling, J. Differentiation of Organics from Schizophrenics at Two Chronicity Levels by Use of the Reitan-Halstead Organic Test Battery. *Journal of Consulting and Clinical Psychology* 32:679–684, 1968.

Watt, N. F. Patterns of Childhood Social Development in Adult Schizophrenics. *Archives of General Psychiatry* 35:160–165, 1978.

Watt, N. F., and Lubensky, A. W. Childhood Roots of Schizophrenia. *Journal of Consulting and Clinical Psychology* 44:363–375, 1975.

Wehrung, D. A., and Hay, S. A Study of Seasonal Incidence of Congenital Malformations in the United States. *British Journal of Preventive and Social Medicine* 24:24–32, 1970.

Weinberger, D. R. Implications of Normal Brain Development for the Pathogenesis of Schizophrenia. *Archives of General Psychiatry* 44:660–669, 1987.

*Weinberger, D. R., Berman, K. F., Ostrem, J. L., and Torrey, E. F. rCBF Measured by 0–15 Water and PET during Four Cognitive Tasks in MZ Twins Discordant for Schizophrenia. *Journal of Cerebral Blood Flow and Metabolism* 13:5–511, 1993.

*Weinberger, D. R., Berman, K. F., Suddath, R., and Torrey, E. F. Evidence of Dysfunction of a Prefrontal-Limbic Network in Schizophrenia: A Magnetic Resonance Imaging and Regional Blood Flow Study of Discordant Monozygotic Twins. *American Journal of Psychiatry* 149:890–897, 1992.

*Weinberger, D. R., Berman, K. F., and Torrey, E. F. Correlations between Abnormal Hippocampal Morphology and Prefrontal Physiology in Schizophrenia. *Clinical Neuropharmacology* 15(Suppl. 1):393A–394A, 1992.

Weinberger, D. R., Cannon-Spoor, E., Potkin, S. G., and Wyatt, R. J. Poor Premorbid Adjustment and CT Scan Abnormalities in Chronic Schizophrenia. *American Journal of Psychiatry* 137:1410–1413, 1980.

Weinberger, D. R., and Wyatt, R. J. Cerebral Ventricular Size: A Biological Marker for Sub-Typing Chronic Schizophrenia. In E. Usdin and I. Handin (Eds.), *Biological Markers in Psychiatry and Neurology* (pp. 505–512). New York: Pergamon, 1982.

*Weinberger, D. R., Zigun, J. R., Bartley, A. J., Jones, D. W., and Torrey, E. F. Anatomical Abnormalities in the Brains of Monozygotic Twins Discordant and Concordant for Schizophrenia. *Clinical Neuropharmacology* 15(Suppl. 1):S-23–77, 1992.

Weller, M. P. I. Left Handedness in an Identical Twin Discordant to His Co-Twin for Handedness and Schizophrenia, with Neurological and Psychometric Evidence of Left Hemisphere Damage. *Postgraduate Medical Journal* 66:224–226, 1990.

Whitaker, J. N., Sever, J. L., and Engel, W. K. Subacute Sclerosing Panencephalitis in Only One of Identical Twins. *New England Journal of Medicine* 287:864–866, 1972.

Wilcox, J. A., and Nasrallah, H. A. Childhood Head Trauma and Psychosis. *Psychiatry Research* 21:303–306, 1987a.

Wilcox, J. A., and Nasrallah, H. A. Perinatal Distress and Prognosis of Psychotic Illness. *Neuropsychobiology* 17:173–175, 1987b.

Wirt, R. D., Seat, P. D., Broen, W. E., and Lachar, D. *Personality Inventory for Children, Revised Format*. Los Angeles: Western Psychological Services, 1981.

Woerner, M. G., Pollack, M., and Klein, D. F. Birth Weight and Length in Schizophrenics, Personality Disorders and Their Siblings. *British Journal of Psychiatry* 118:461–464, 1971.

Woerner, M. G., Pollack, M., and Klein, D. F. Pregnancy and Birth Complications in Psychiatric Patients: A Comparison of Schizophrenic and Personality Disorder Patients and Their Siblings. *Acta Psychiatrica Scandinavica* 49:712–721, 1973.

Wolkin, A., Sanfilipo, M., Wolf, A. P., Angrist, B., Brodie, J. D., and Rotrosen, J. Negative Symptoms and Hypofrontality in Chronic Schizophrenia. *Archives of General Psychiatry* 49:959–965, 1992.

Woody, R. C., Bolyard, K., Eisenhauer, G., and Altschuler, L. CT Scan and MRI Findings in a Child with Schizophrenia. *Journal of Child Neurology* 2:105–110, 1987.

Wright, H. T., Jr., Parker, C. E., and Mavalwala, J. Unusual Dermatoglyphic Findings Associated with Cytomegalic Inclusion Disease of Infancy: A First Report and Practical Review. *California Medicine*, 116:14–20, 1972.

Yassa, R., and Ananth, J. Familial Tardive Dyskinesia. *American Journal of Psychiatry* 138:1618–1619, 1981.

*Yolken, R. H., Collett, M., Petric, M., Yao, L., Sun, Y., and Torrey, E. F. Antibodies to Pestivirus in Identical Twins Discordant for Schizophrenia. Submitted for publication, 1993.

Zavala, C., and Nunez, C. Dermatoglyphics in Schizophrenia. *Journal de Genetique Humaine.* 18:407–420, 1970.

*Zigun, J. R., Carosella, N. W., Coppola, R., Torrey, E. F., and Weinberger, D. R. MRI Study of Monozygotic Twins Concordant for Schizophrenia. Abstract, *Biological Psychiatry* 31:64A, 1992.

Zigun, J. R., and Weinberger, D. R. In Vivo Studies of Brain Morphology in Schizophrenia. In J. P. Lindenmayer and S. R. Kay (Eds.), *New Biological Vistas on Schizophrenia* (pp. 57–81). New York: Brunner/Mazel, 1992.

Index

Abi-Dargham, A., 113
Abraham, J. M., 20
Abrams, R., 122, 123
Abstraction ability, 123
Achs, R., 54
Acuteness of onset: birth weight related to, 61; childhood differences and later schizophrenia and, 87; cognitive function and, 125; family history of psychosis and, 46; handedness and, 74; obstetrical complications and, 67; perinatal form of schizophrenia and, 76
Age of divergence: cognitive function and, 125; comparison of early and later, 87–89; later schizophrenia and, 86–89; metabolic function and, 120; neurological abnormalities and, 135; non-twin individuals with schizophrenia and, 92–95; in present study, 86–89
Age of first referral: birth weight and, 61; brain structure and, 112; concordant twin similarities and, 151; family history and, 46; neurological abnormalities and, 135; obstetrical complications and, 67; triplets and, 151
Age of onset of schizophrenia: brain structure and, 108, 114; childhood differences and later schizophrenia and, 89; concordant twin similarities and, 151–55, 163; minor physical anomalies and, 50; neurological abnormalities and, 135
Age of twin: cognitive function and, 125; handedness related to, 69

AIDS, 19
Albee, G. W., 59
Alcohol, and uterine development, 20, 21
Alcoholism, 4, 37–38, 42
Aldous, P., 5
Allen, G., 184
Alter, M., 54
Alzheimer's disease, 54, 103
Ambelas, A., 81
American Psychiatric Association, 10n, 26
Amnions, single, with birth of twins, 14, 22
Amygdala, 103, 108–11, 112, 114, 136, 164, 181–82, 202, 211
Ananth, J., 169
Andreason, N. C., 30, 87, 118
Anemia, and twin transfusion syndrome, 18
Anencephaly, 22, 24
Anoxia: brain structure changes and, 108, 138; genetic models and, 43; handedness related to, 72; minor physical anomalies related to, 50; perinatal form of schizophrenia and, 77, 78; twin transfusion syndrome and, 18–19; twins in present study with, 35
Antipsychotic medication: brain structure changes related to, 103–4, 141, 211–12; hyperfrontality and, 118, 119, 120; metabolic function and, 118; neurological abnormalities and, 128, 129–30, 134–35. See also Medication status; Response to medication
Antisocial personality disorder, 35, 36
Attention, 122, 124